Burning Bridges

Soon to Be a
Major Motion Picture

Australian filmmaker and producer Mark Morrissey of Mythmaker Media, winner of a Logie Award (Australian Emmy) and an AFI Award, and owner of Australia's most prestigious talent management company, talks about bringing the book to the silver screen.

What was it about this book that caught your attention?

Harry's untold story unfolded over the space of one weekend. I'm sent many projects and script synopses for projects to consider for developing. Peter's engaging and exciting book grabbed my attention immediately. (I read the book twice that weekend, attaching 117 sticky notes throughout the book.) Given it could have been conceived or considered as fairly dry material centered around a series of court cases spanning 20 years, it speaks volumes and attests to the author's writing skills and the extraordinary man that was HARRY BRIDGES. He never gave up. He never backed away. And he did this throughout two decades with an authentic Australian voice and candor. A man I would have dearly liked to have met and a man who represented many aspects of early Australian integrity.

Why do you feel like *now* is the right time for this story about Harry Bridges?

There are extraordinary theatrical moments in the book that highlight our current global political challenges, that highlight the need to question and hold government accountable, that enthuse the power of the civil common man. He inspired a generation of blue collar men and women when there was little around to celebrate. He quietly and respectfully responded to every challenge when the odds were against him. Now is the absolute time for this project. We crave statesmen we can believe in. We need intelligent orators who truly fight for the underdog and for what is right, who understand the people they represent and who are unbending when offered personal profit.

The story is set in the 1930s-1950s. How is this still relevant to us today?

The innocence of this period enables us to highlight what we no longer experience and what we miss. Everything was ahead for them. The future was to be sought out, to strive for, to make better. We will be able to truly and forensically explore Harry Bridges and those extraordinary people who surrounded and supported him.

What made you want to tell this story?

In all heroic journeys, the hero must go through adversity, must face every challenge, internal and external, and must learn from every experience. We will follow Harry's journey because the movie audience is Harry and yearns to be Harry. I was proud, and somewhat astounded, that an Australian has achieved so much and not been recognized or acknowledged in his and our country of origin. I plan to change that.

What are you hoping viewers would get out of it?

Like many who enjoy films of common man against adversaries, I adore to sit on the couch with my family and be swept away and enthused by the good within us all. Harry inspired me. I immediately started seeking more information about the time, about the conditions, and learning on a very basic level the import of what we all take for granted, the essence of good law. I hope they are truly invigorated and inspired in the human spirit as much as I was.

Harry Bridges' early life in Australia influenced a lot of his opinions/decisions later on. How do you plan to really capture that in the movie?

This will be special for me. Like Harry Bridges, my grandfather, father, and I were all born in Melbourne, Australia. This is and was a hard yet beautiful town to grow up in. Those were simple yet complex times in Australia. We felt a million miles from the world, governed and heavily influenced by the British, striving to find our own identity. I grew up with the simple lessons of being hard, yet fair. Don't be anyone's fool. That we were all equal and struggling—from my father. My grandfather actually looks like Harry, that lean, poised, resourceful nature. Never completely relaxing. Checking what was around the corner. I adore this time period and can't wait to replicate and celebrate Melbourne, Australia, during this time.

Which scenes/parts are you most looking forward to filming/ seeing?

Dramatically Bloody Thursday, the high court, the scenes with his legal counsel battling so bravely with the harsh judge, Harry finding that he was wire tapped and leading the agents on a wild goose chase, the scene in the town hall where the American Legion storm the stage yet it is Harry who finishes reciting the Pledge of Allegiance.

How does this story exemplify the Australian spirit?

I think it exemplifies the unifying spirit that exists in all of us. That laws are there to protect, and that good law should lead to justice. Australia started as a colony of convicts, sent from Ireland, England, etc., sentenced for the most minor of crimes. Australians may have a natural wariness of authority, but are driven toward what is "right"—what is "fair." Harry was wrongly accused and was able to overcome the odds, to overcome corruption and perjurers, to overcome adversity. He is to be admired and remembered. We all want and need to have a bit of Harry in us.

Tell us a little about you and your company. What other films have you worked on?

Most recently I won a 2017 Logie (Australian equivalent of Emmy) for Best Drama for Molly. *I Won an AFI Award for best short* The Last Time I Saw Richard *and produced in 2016* Boys in the Trees.

Other than Harry Bridges, which other character(s) are you really looking forward to casting?

I'm keen to explore the B-Men. I want to learn more and highlight the character of Secretary of Labor Frances Perkins and Harry's defense team, the spirited Carol King and the fighter Vince Hallinan.

When will the movie be released?

AS SOON AS POSSIBLE

> *"There will always be a place for us somewhere, somehow, as long as we see to it that working people fight for everything they have, everything they hope to get, for dignity, equality, democracy, to oppose war, and to bring to the world a better life."*
>
> —HARRY BRIDGES

Also by the Author

Show Trials

"POWERFUL...BEAUTIFUL PROSE...Peter's proposals for change provide a blueprint for essential reforms."
ERWIN CHEMERINSKY, nationally recognized as one of the "Top 20 legal thinkers in America"

SHOW TRIALS

HOW PROPERTY GETS MORE LEGAL PROTECTION THAN PEOPLE IN OUR FAILED IMMIGRATION SYSTEM

PETER AFRASIABI

BURNING BRIDGES

AMERICA'S 20-YEAR CRUSADE TO DEPORT LABOR LEADER HARRY BRIDGES

PETER AFRASIABI

With a Foreword by Erwin Chemerinsky, Famed Legal Scholar
and Supreme Court Advocate

Published by:
Thirlmere Books
104 Green St., #2
Brooklyn, NY 11222

ISBN: 978-0-9983471-0-3

Library of Congress Control Number: 2016919220

For my parents, Pauline and Faraj (Fred)

TABLE OF CONTENTS

FOREWORD

The story of Harry Bridges should be required reading for every law student in the country, but few ever have heard of him. The story of Harry Bridges should be required reading for every federal prosecutor, but few know anything about the abuses by federal law enforcement officials who investigated and prosecuted him. The story of Harry Bridges is a tale of the middle decades of the twentieth century and how those who wanted to stop a union leader used anti-communist hysteria to try and destroy a man's life.

Peter Afrasiabi has done a masterful job of telling the story of Harry Bridges, often relying on documents that never before have been made public. I have been teaching constitutional law for over 35 years and was familiar with the Supreme Court's decisions concerning Bridges, but most of what is in this book was new to me. The story of what the United States government did to Harry Bridges is deeply disturbing and a reminder of how the government can badly abuse its powers.

Harry Bridges was a brilliant, successful labor leader who was responsible for organizing longshoremen on the west coast. In retaliation, business leaders wanted to do anything they could to get rid of him, including discussing having him assassinated. Their primary effort was to have Bridges, an Australian, deported. In four separate proceedings, each of which Afrasiabi describes in compelling detail, the United States government tried to have Bridges removed from the country on the ground that he was a member of the Communist Party. Bridges ultimately prevailed in every one of these, including twice having the United States Supreme Court rule in his favor.

This is a story of a shocking abuse of government power. The United States government used illegal wiretapping, repeatedly relied on testimony that they knew to be perjured, and even engaged in using illegal means to influence a jury. The repeated claim was that Bridges was a member of the Communist Party, even though there never was any reliable evidence to support that charge. After Bridges prevailed in an immigration proceeding presided over by the then dean of the Harvard Law School, James Landis, the government brought another immigration proceeding to have Bridges deported. After the Supreme Court ruled in favor of Bridges, with justices chastising the government in strong language, the United States brought a criminal proceeding against Bridges to have him deported. After the Supreme Court again ruled in favor of Bridges, the government brought a civil proceeding against him. Bridges prevailed again. At one point, Congress even changed federal law with the goal of having Bridges removed. All of this went on for decades.

And all of it was because of Bridges' speech, his advocacy for the rights of workers, which was clearly protected by the First Amendment. There never was evidence, other than lies and fabricated documents, supporting the allegation that Bridges was a member of the Communist Party. But even if he had been, that, too, was speech and association protected by the First Amendment.

Yet none of this stopped the United States government from using all of the resources at its disposal, legal and illegal, to deport Harry Bridges. The government did so in a realm, immigration, where there is tremendous judicial deference to the executive branch of government and where it is so very difficult for any individual to prevail.

In one sense, this book is a story of the success of the legal system. Harry Bridges ultimately won. But in a much larger way, this book tells a cautionary tale of how the United States government can engage in persecution of a single person and abuse the legal system. It is about how the government can be captured by business to shut down labor protests and how the hysteria of the times can cause us to lose sight of our most basic constitutional values.

Peter Afrasiabi has written a terrific book that deserves a wide readership. The story of Harry Bridges and what the government did to him never should be forgotten.

Erwin Chemerinsky
Founding Dean and Distinguished Professor of Law
at the University of California, Irvine School of Law,
and Raymond Pryke Professor of First Amendment Law

INTRODUCTION

> *"To be ignorant of what occurred before you were born is to remain always a child. For what is the worth of human life, unless it is woven into the life of our ancestors by the records of history?"*
>
> CICERO (46 BCE)

"The record in this case will stand forever as a monument to man's intolerance of man. Seldom if ever in the history of this nation has there been such a concentrated and relentless crusade to deport an individual because he dared to exercise the freedom that belongs to him as a human being and that is guaranteed to him by the Constitution."

Justice Frank Murphy of the United States Supreme Court wrote those words in 1945, words aimed directly at the executive branch of the United States government for its relentless campaign to deport Australian-born Harry Bridges. By the time the Supreme Court heard the case in 1945, the campaign had already consumed the full prior decade. With those words from the highest court of the land, end of story, right? Not so quickly.

Those words, it turned out, were only the halftime commentary in what would ultimately be a twenty-year crusade to deport Bridges, the longest and most bitter deportation proceeding in

American history. When those words were penned, the case had been in an administrative civil court. But after those words, the government would amend the immigration laws specifically to retarget Bridges, and then move the deportation case to federal criminal court where it would seek not only to deport Bridges, but to send him to federal prison first.

How is it possible that the executive branch of the U.S. government, accused by the highest court of its judicial branch of such abuse and intolerance, could proceed to spend another ten years prosecuting a campaign to deport one man? What invoked such profound intolerance of this Harry Bridges? Surely, you ask, he must have been a spy, a terrorist, or some such similar public danger?

Yet Harry Bridges was none of these things: he was a labor leader. Having arrived in the United States as a teenage sailor from Australia in 1920, by the tumultuous 1930s he was working in San Francisco as a longshoreman. After living with the frustrations and indignities that all longshoremen of the time suffered, he began challenging the economic and political landscape within the weak longshoremen's union on the West Coast. Men followed him even though he lacked formal power within the union, and in 1934 Bridges managed to lead the largest West Coast strike ever seen to that day, a strike that paralyzed shipping on the West Coast for eighty-three days. During one of the protests, police attacked with tear gas and shot indiscriminately into crowds of protesters. Labor protesters were killed in what became known as Bloody Thursday. The strike eventually ended with all West Coast ports unionized. Now a national figure and head of the longshoremen's union, Bridges was widely respected for his incorruptibility and for his relentless pursuit of basic rights for his unionized workers: a living wage and the right to organize.

But in successfully challenging his time's political and economic status quo, Bridges unleashed against himself powerful political forces, from the Pacific Northwest to the corridors of power in Washington, D.C. These forces—governmental, corporate, and private—allied against him and used the immigration system as a vehicle to persecute and punish him. The exact means of accomplishing this end involved labeling noncitizen Bridges a member of the Communist Party. If under American immigration law at the time, Bridges could be proven to be a Communist Party member, then he could be deported for supporting an organization that allegedly sought the overthrow of the government. And if convicted, then the government could remove Bridges from the United States, and, more pointedly, remove him from the national labor dialogue, his voice instantly silenced.

This book tells the story of America's twenty-year legal crusade to label Bridges a communist and deport him through a series of deportation trials. It is a story of government spies paid to infiltrate Bridges' labor movement and act as *agents provocateurs* to incite mob violence so as to create a justification for a brutal, bloody police response. It is a story of government witnesses perjuring themselves to frame Bridges as a communist. It is a story of falsified evidence, witness intimidation, and government reliance on a disgraced and disbarred lawyer who ran with Al Capone. It is a story of government promises of clemency and sentence reductions to prisoners if they would testify that Bridges was a communist. It is a story of serial trials, four in all, and the intrigue of wiretaps, FBI surveillance, and the cunning courtroom cross-examination of witnesses. It is a story of assassination plots. It is a story of biased judges with their fingers on the scales of justice, aggressive prosecutors more concerned with winning than serving justice, and larger-than-life defense lawyers risking prison and disbarment for defending Bridges. It is ultimately then the story of enshrined American values of tolerance, freedom of speech, and due process of law all usurped by an unchecked government's relentless persecution-through-prosecution crusade.

But it is also the story of a lone foreigner who refuses to buckle despite overwhelming odds and adversity.

CHAPTER 1

From Sandy Beaches to Bloody Thursday

Broken bottles under children's feet
Bodies strewn across the dead-end street.
But I won't heed the battle call
It puts my back up, puts my back up against the wall.

"SUNDAY BLOODY SUNDAY," U2 (1983)

Finding His Voice

Harry Bridges was born in Melbourne, Australia, on July 28, 1901, and christened Alfred Renton Bridges. As a youngster, he acquired the name "Harry," the name of a favorite adventuring uncle, a man who had himself seen war and was a progressive unionist who fought for the underprivileged in Australian labor union movements. The acquired name Harry would prove a prescient remarkable point of connection between nephew and uncle.[1]

In contrast to Uncle Harry, young Harry's father was a real
estate manager who administered properties for the wealthy, providing his family a solid middle-class life. Upon graduating from
high school at fourteen, Harry worked for his father, collecting rent
from tenants, all of whom were poor, many of whom were entirely
destitute. Knocking on doors, talking to the tenants, trying to collect rent, and seeing their miserable conditions, young Harry found
it cruel to take their money. Almost immediately, then, he took a
different tack. "He collected rent from tenants who could pay and
loaned money to those who couldn't!" his father once quipped.[2] Later in life, Bridges remarked that collecting rents in Melbourne at
that time had a profound impact on his opinions about politics,
about questions of right and wrong, about society's allocations of
resources.[3]

Political debate occurred regularly in the family home. Harry's
father, a conservative, was often at odds in discussions with Harry's
uncles who were members of Australia's Labor Party. Harry's favorite, Uncle Harry Renton, was a Labor Party official who had traveled
widely and so had both stories of social justice as well as tales of
adventure from his foreign travels. Uncle Harry had volunteered for
the South African Boer War, but reported that when he saw the injustice of the war "he and his comrades threw down their rifles and
came home."[4] Later, Uncle Harry would go off to the First World
War where he died in France. Harry's other uncle, Charles Bridges,
would later be elected a Labor Member of Parliament in New South
Wales, Australia.[5]

A favorite author of Harry's during his childhood was Jack
London, the San Francisco author whose seminal works included
The Call of the Wild (1903), about a dog who survives inhumane,
barbaric treatment at the hands of man, and *The Sea-Wolf* (1904),
an adventure story about a survivor of a shipwreck. London's works
would remarkably, if not eerily, foreshadow many of Harry's life experiences.

When Harry was fifteen or so, having quit the rent collecting business, which probably by that point was of no great disappointment to his father since the rent collections were being loaned to other tenants, he worked for a short period as a clerk in a retail establishment. However, he had no interest in it, and his heart was certainly not in real estate or commercial enterprises.

With his youthful good looks, wavy brown hair, and a slender five-foot-ten-inch frame (and still growing), Harry looked to the sea. Like a character in a London novel and his uncle, Harry yearned not just for adventure, but adventure at sea. He tried to join the Australian Mercantile Marine, but given his age he needed his father's permission. Harry prevailed upon Captain Suffern, president of the Australian Mercantile Marine Board, to come to the Bridges' home and plead his case. Harry's father was not happy, but also knew he had a headstrong son, so he tried to stack the odds against Harry in a ploy to cause him to change his mind.

As Harry's father recounted:

"To test the boy's love of the sea, I hatched a plot with an old Norwegian skipper who ran a ketch between Tasmania and Melbourne. The boat was very small, although seaworthy, and making a stormy crossing in it was guaranteed to test the stoutest heart. During the passage with the young Bridges aboard, a storm arose. That was on the homeward trip, and the boat was blown more than a hundred miles out of its course. Harry was delighted and refused to leave the deck. The skipper expected him to be washed overboard with every wave. After that there was no stopping the boy from going to sea."[6]

His sea legs well under him now, he joined the Mercantile Marine as a sailor at the age of sixteen. And adventure he found. He was in two shipwrecks, one on the famed *Val Marie* off Ninety-Mile Beach in the remote northwest corner of New Zealand. As his father later relayed, "Harry went overboard with my mandolin and kept afloat on it until he was picked up."[7] It is unclear if that mandolin survived, but the mandolin became Harry's preferred instrument, one he played his whole life.

As well as shipwrecks, Harry started learning about labor unions and labor tactics, and he joined the Australian Seamen's Union. Then, within his first year at sea, he joined a general strike:

"I was just a young kid, but I can still remember it. We piled off the ships in Melbourne for a stop-working meeting on the front… we all took torches and marched two or three miles to an army post on the outskirts of Melbourne where they were assembling troops to use against the strikers. They put up soap boxes right in the middle of the post, and striking longshoremen, sailors, and railway men got up and explained to the lads in uniform that the strike was for the principle of unionism. Well we convinced the troops or maybe we scared the authorities so much they didn't dare use the soldiers. Anyway it was a successful demonstration. That was my first big strike."[8]

In 1920, already an active trade unionist in Australia, Bridges shipped off on the *Ysabel*, a ship destined for San Francisco. They were mid-ocean when Easter Monday arrived. Harry and the sailors expected the day off, as it was a recognized day of rest for all workers in Australia. The captain refused. This upset Harry, who was chairman of the ship's on-board union committee. When he arrived in San Francisco in April 1920, he immediately paid the then-required head tax fee for entry and entered the United States, now nineteen years of age, with the intention of finding a new ship to work on, one that would be fairer to him.[9]

Once landed in America, Harry transferred his union membership to the American Federation of Labor (AFL) Sailors' Union of the Pacific. He found work on an American ship and spent the next two years travelling the West Coast as well as the East Coast and the Gulf of Mexico. In 1921, Harry was in New Orleans when a large strike erupted. He joined the strike, ran a picket squad, and was arrested for loitering. The strike destroyed the AFL Sailors' Union, which Bridges blamed in part on the AFL itself. Harry felt that the

AFL, charged with protecting the strikers, had actually sold them and the strike out as well. Harry also briefly joined the Industrial Workers of the World (IWW) in 1921.[10]

In 1921, Harry applied for U.S. citizenship, the first of several citizenship application filings he would eventually make. On one of his sea journeys, he met, in Coos Bay, Oregon, Agnes Brown, whom he later married. To stay home more and avoid long sea journeys, in 1922 Harry took a job in San Francisco as a longshoreman, loading and unloading the cargo that enter ports. But finding steady work was not easy, and this next part of his life formed the fulcrum for Harry's future labor battles.

In those days, Harry went early in the morning to the Embarcadero in San Francisco to find work. The Embarcadero is the eastern waterfront at the Port of San Francisco. Back then, it was the major port in San Francisco where ships were loaded and unloaded. At six every morning, he would join the crowds of men desperate for a day's work. Supply of workers far exceeded the demand for labor, so the hiring foremen had leverage over the putative workers. And they used it: in return for granting work, the foremen would often demand a kick-back, generally 5 to 10 percent of wages.[11]

To add to the indignity, as Harry recounted, "At the moment of eight o'clock, we were herded along by the police to allow the commuters to go across the street from the Ferry Building, more or less like a slave market in the Old World countries."[12] This slave-market analogy is no great exaggeration, for the practice—known as the Shape Up—was an old practice in Great Britain that had drawn strong public condemnation in the British press of the 1800s:

> "He who wishes to behold one of the most extraordinary and least-known scenes of this metropolis should wend his way to the London Dock gates at half-past 7 in the morning…you know by the stream pouring through the gates and the rush toward

particular spots that the 'calling foremen' have made
their appearance...men jump up on the backs of the
others, so as to lift themselves high above the rest,
and attract the notice of him who hires them...Some
cry aloud his surname, some his Christian name,
others call out their own names, to remind him that
they are there...it is a sight to sadden the most cal-
lous, to see thousands of men struggling for only one
day's hire...to look in the faces of that hungry crowd
is to see a sight that must be ever remembered...For
weeks many have gone there, and gone through the
same struggle—the same cries; and have gone away,
after all, without the work they had screamed for."[13]

So appalling was the practice that the Port of London abandoned it in 1891. Yet it was alive and strong in San Francisco in the
1920s. As well as the Shape Up, there was a corollary process called
the Speed Up that existed to control the longshoremen and minimize
their pay. The Speed Up was a process whereby the longshoremen
would regularly work eighteen, twenty-four, even thirty-six hours at
a rapid pace in dangerous conditions to offload cargo. Due to these
twin practices, the output of offloaded tonnage in San Francisco at
the time was greater than any other port city in the world.[14]

Under the Speed Up, if men stopped working, they would be
replaced instantly, and so the men, to maintain a job, worked themselves to exhaustion, sometimes even to death. "The men would
drop on the job and you would pack them off and lay them to one
side—if they had an attack of heart failure, well, they would maybe lay there an hour or two until the ambulance came and picked
them up...I was on the job on three different occasions when men
dropped dead, just—that was the end of them," Bridges explained.[15]

Getting work was harder than just paying the bribes and
surviving the Shape Up and Speed Up practices. To get steady

longshore work, the men needed also to join a special "union" that the shipowners had created and approved. Specifically, the AFL had maintained an International Longshoremen's Association (ILA) Pacific Coast structure, but the shipowners broke that union's coast-wide unity in 1916. San Francisco's dock workers retained an independent union until they lost a strike in 1919. Then, longshoreman Jack Bryan struck a deal with the shipowners: in essence, Bryan would create and manage a "union" in San Francisco and the shipowners agreed to hire exclusively from it, a closed shop. The shipowners accepted the union—because it was favorable to them—and the union issued a Blue Book, which was a registry of all paid "union" members. This "union," known as the Blue Book, controlled San Francisco work flow and wages, but of course on terms the shipowners approved. A worker needed to be listed in the Blue Book to be selected for the privilege of then paying the further bribe to work in dangerous conditions.[16]

The cloak of terror imposed by the employers and shipowners extended to monitoring the conduct of workers with paid spies. If any longshoremen were reported to the Blue Book for complaining about pay or conditions, they would be fired and blacklisted on the entire Pacific Coast. Even daring to complain about work-related injuries would land one on the blacklist. In one instance, Bridges witnessed a 350-pound barrel fall on a man's foot and break it. The man had just returned from a prior injury, and so then was fired and blacklisted for having soft bones. Bridges never heard of the man again.

Men regularly worked with serious injuries as Bridges experienced himself. "I broke my foot in '29 working in the hold. I was standing there on a pile, and we let a load go out, and my foot got jammed between two cases that came together. I worked for a couple days with it—couldn't afford to lay off, you see? But it swelled up so high that I couldn't work..." At the same time, access to the legal system was effectively denied: if a worker received a subpoena to appear in court in a case filed by another injured worker, compliance with the subpoena resulted in blacklisting.[17]

On principle, Harry refused to join the Blue Book, and as a result, constantly struggled to find work. Then, in 1924, the Blue Book union contract was up for renewal, and so an effort was made to restart the original AFL's ILA Pacific Coast District. Harry joined, having never given up hope that a true worker-controlled longshoremen's union could exist, and on Labor Day he and four hundred other workers joined a labor parade. As they marched down Market Street in San Francisco, the Blue Book agents took down all the names of the protesters. The Blue Book union then resecured its contract, and all the protesters, Harry included, were blacklisted. Because Harry was a foreigner, blacklisting was a greater hardship for him than for others. Blacklisted citizens could at least get work from the Army at its transport docks, but not blacklisted foreigners.[18]

By 1925, Harry and Agnes were married and, with young children to feed, Harry eventually gave in and joined the Blue Book. For several years he worked a rapid pace and handled massive projects with large tonnage—sixty- or seventy-foot sheets of steel, as well as massive prefabricated steel—in dangerous conditions. One of his most important jobs in this period involved offloading steel to be used in the construction of two of the most impressive engineering feats of the time, the Golden Gate Bridge and the San Francisco Bay Bridge.[19]

By 1928, the citizenship application Harry had filed in 1921 had to be acted upon. Harry went to the immigration office and secured a hearing date to appear in the United States District Court to swear in as a citizen. The day arrived, and with his witnesses in tow, Harry went to the federal courthouse in San Francisco. However, when he arrived, the court told him that he was actually a few months late, so he would have to reapply and start the process over again. As was later discovered, the court was wrong—Harry had appeared in time. However, the court refused to swear him in and required him to reapply. This apparently innocent paperwork mistake would later have fateful consequences.[20]

Meanwhile, the changing social and economic times, precipitated by the Great Depression, also provoked change on the union front. In 1933, the Blue Book union was challenged as illegal under the newly enacted National Industrial Recovery Act (NIRA), thereby paving the way for the ILA to renew its efforts to build a union and regain some power. The ILA formally issued a new charter and reestablished the ILA Pacific Coast District as a new longshoremen's union, known as "Local 38-79" in San Francisco. However, factions immediately emerged within the ILA in terms of strategy and direction.[21]

These events started grooming Harry. An active trade-unionist since his earliest days in Australia, a believer in the strike as a means to force fair negotiations, a long-term holdout of the Blue Book union, and skeptical of the AFL from his prior experiences, Harry started speaking loudly and publicly for improved rights. "When he came to this country from Australia, he already had an Aussie point of view about the difference between the master class and the slave class, the owning class and the working class. When he got here, he had kind of an instinct for leadership among workers," recounted Sidney Roger, a waterfront journalist of the time.[22] Consequently, with his Australian cockney accent, he argued for a strong union, regularly preaching on the waterfront his Australian-bred ideas of labor unity. Quickly, many of the men on the frontlines started to listen.

In short order, he came to the attention of Secretary of Labor Frances Perkins, the first female cabinet member in history, who would come to deal with Harry many times in the ensuing years. Secretary Perkins later recalled that in the early scene of West Coast labor struggles, "Nobody had heard of him before. Nobody knew him." But, she remarked, "He was one of the first...who seemed to be able to think."[23]

By 1933, there were three major groups vying for control of the ILA. Two were large and powerful factions representing the old guard of union politics, but the third group's voice coalesced around Harry Bridges. Harry was dissatisfied because the union's leaders failed to push for real change, never held meetings, and ran the union in an undemocratic manner. He thus raised money and formed a group within the union so it could be its own faction with its own voice. Because of his prior union experience in Australia, he became the natural leader of those who wanted more radical action. This third group met on Sundays to plan and discuss strategy in a building called Albion Hall and so became known as the Albion Hall group. As one of the Albion Hall members said, "Hell, he knew more about what to do than the rest of us combined." Albion Hall, under Harry Bridges, became the focal point for the small but loud voice of radical labor.[24]

Fundamentally, those in the Albion Hall group wanted an independent union with union control of hiring halls, one that eliminated the Shape Up practices and secured better working conditions. While the larger factions of old-guard control saw litigation through the new national labor laws as the mechanism to effect change, Bridges' approach was a direct challenge: a program of strikes and intentional job slowdowns.[25]

Critically, Bridges also wanted a single powerful union that controlled all the ports of the West Coast. This was critical because in the scenario of small unions at each port, the shipowners could pit ports against each other for work and drive a wedge between the men.[26] "I had also studied the background of the 1916 and 1919 longshore strikes, and one of the things that broke the strikes was the ability of the employers to play one port against the other. Ships are moving plants or warehouses that can pack the goods from one port to the other. It stands to reason that when one port is on strike, and the ship can move a few miles away and be worked by members of the same union, it's ridiculous," Bridges explained.[27]

Harry Bridges arguing his cause. Copyright Underwood Archives/Getty Images.

To spread his ideas, Bridges started touring the West Coast ports and spoke to workers. At the same time, some of the Albion Hall faction were elected to official union positions, including Bridges, who was elected to an ILA Board seat, although not as an officer.[28]

Bridges' concept of union management itself was also different. He argued that a union must function democratically with regular meetings, financial accountings to union members, and a democratic constitution. At the same time, while the other factions were wrapped up in internal policy debates without member meetings, Albion Hall filled the void and quickly started an effective

mobilization program of education and speech on the waterfront, as
well as actual work slowdowns to combat the relentless work pressure. Workers saw Albion Hall actually doing something, and that
in turn enabled it to gain more traction.[29]

Eventually, the government board charged with administering
the new national recovery laws, the National Recovery Administration (NRA), addressed the legal status of the Blue Book. Remarkably, or not as the case may be, in 1933 the government board held
that the Blue Book was a valid union. While in some sense a blow
to the ILA and Bridges' Albion Hall, the government's finding probably was a boon to Bridges because it confirmed what he had been
saying all along: workers who wanted a real union had to take ownership of the problem and create a union themselves, because the
government was not going to help them. Thus, the government's
blessing of the Blue Book cemented Bridges' credibility as a voice
pointing in the right direction.[30]

Power never gives up easily, though, and the Blue Book was no
exception. One morning in September 1933 as longshoremen were
loading a ship owned by the Matson Navigation Company in the
Port of San Francisco, Blue Book officials arrived to verify that the
workers were paid-up in their dues. The Matson Navigation Company was one of the most virulent anti-ILA companies. When the
workers refused to show their Blue Books, tensions escalated. Eventually, the Blue Book officials found four ILA union men working a
ship, and quickly had the men fired from the job and in turn hired
Blue Book replacements.

The fired ILA men went to the Embarcadero, talked with others about what had happened, and pretty soon a large group gathered. Frustration boiled over and men started burning their Blue
Books in an act of defiance against the power of the government-
approved and shipowner-approved Blue Book union. In short order, hundreds of Blue Books were burning, an act of social defiance
as men searched for a peaceful means to express their frustration.

Soon thereafter the ILA Executive Board met to address the situation, and Bridges demanded a full strike on the Matson Navigation Company until the company rehired the ILA men. Fearing the political risks, the ILA disagreed with Bridges' strategy.[31]

Strikers burning their union books in defiance and protest. Copyright UC Berkeley, Bancroft Library.

So Bridges took matters into his own hands: "We went down there one morning, we lined up in the Shape Up, and as the fellows started going to work, we stopped every one of them and said, 'Look, fellows, four guys have been fired for joining the union. Let's have a program where they hire these four fellows back or none of us goes to work.' So everybody stayed out. That affected the docks, and the strike lasted for five days. The Matson Company and the Waterfront Employers Association at that time went up to Skid Row and they hired a bunch of men from the employment halls, and of course we spoke to those men and got most of them to quit."[32]

By now, a localized makeshift strike was underway with Bridges at its helm, a strike in defiance of both the Blue Book and the nervous ILA. Suddenly, the government NRA Board intervened and ordered Matson to rehire the four ILA men. This quickly demonstrated that Bridges' strategy had been correct and that he had the skill to get things done. "That was the end of the fear and intimidation," Bridges later recalled. "You could join the union and...if the company tried to fire you we had enough power to tie up that waterfront in order to enforce the demand. From that time on the union was established, it was recognized, it was in business."[33]

Consequently, by late 1933 the ILA stood as a viable alternative to the Blue Book. And within the ILA, Albion Hall possessed significant status thanks to Bridges' passion and wisdom, which had now firmly cemented him as a leading labor voice. Even then, however, he remained remarkably humble and unassuming, as recounted by Secretary of Labor Perkins: "The fact that he was Australian born, with a British background, to some extent accounted for this sort of humble attitude, poor dressing, no braggadocio, no bravado about him, which is rather uncommon in an American who steps forward to be a spokesman."[34]

But at the same time, various quarters had started to take note of Bridges and his perceived agitation. Government agents working for the NRA Board had sent messages to Washington, D.C., warning that Bridges' strike was communistic in nature and would lead to communist control of the waterfront. The Blue Book union's president—jealous at his loss of power to the new ILA—testified in 1933 at hearings in Washington, D.C., that subversive communists and radicals were at work in the West Coast longshoremen's movement.[35] These communiqués to the halls of power in Washington—all revolving around fears of communism on the waterfront, and specifically about Bridges as an alleged centerpiece of the communist movement—started as a slow trickle in 1933, but events were about to turn that trickle into a raging river.

Things Come to a Head

In February 1934, a convention of the now-reborn Pacific District of the ILA was held in San Francisco. Its focus was on how to get a contract with the shipowners so that the union could secure better wages, hours, and working conditions. Instantly, the rifts between Bridges and the old-line of the ILA were exposed. The ILA old-timers wanted to wait for the government to promulgate some laws that would place government officials in each port to supervise the contractual hiring of longshoremen. Bridges' counter-coalition refused to wait and wanted to create a federation of all longshoremen's unions on the West Coast so they could negotiate directly with shipowners, this time with leverage, and secure a favorable contract, with the threat of strike always in their back pocket. Bridges also demanded the abolition of the antiquated, abhorrent Shape Up practice. As the convention wore on, reports were given to the members in attendance that the shipowners had officially stated that they would not deal with the ILA. This prompted calls for a coast-wide longshoremen's strike as the various delegates for each constituency took to the convention's stage.[36]

After the various delegates had finished speaking, Bridges was the last to take the stage. Lean and six feet tall, rakish in appearance, handsome but not soft, he retained a definite rugged appearance from his seafaring and longshoreman days. Slicked-back dark hair crowned a long, narrow head adorned with a prominent aquiline nose. One attendee described him as having the swagger of a race-track bookie with an intense alertness, and an intelligent, suspicious manner about him. Confident, he spoke in a relatively quiet, matter-of-fact tone, but was intensely defiant, a working man's man, completely unimpressed by, and uninterested in, material wealth.[37]

"He came to the meeting in his working clothes with a cap on the back of his head and a cargo hook sticking out of his back pants pocket," one unionist said of Harry. "For half an hour he walked back and forth, talking with his thumbs hooked in his belt."[38] Drawing from his experiences as a teenage sailor, Bridges understood the power of a union and the power of a strike. He spoke with a firmness echoed by a confident take-it-or-leave-it tone.[39] The thrust of his argument was that the shipowners would never deal with the ILA unless the ILA demonstrated its power with a full strike.

"Now, brother delegates, I want to bring this out forcibly," he started. "We shouldn't take any notice of what the shipowners think or say about us." He continued, raising the stakes in stark, crisp terms, "They would shoot us if they had the chance or could get away with it without being discovered. We are putting them on the block and we should keep them there."[40] His radical approach took root: the union voted and agreed that if the employer class did not agree to their demands, then a strike vote would occur on March 22, with the strike potentially to begin the next day.

However, the ILA's Pacific Coast District president, Bill Lewis, started wavering, and Bridges feared he would not call a strike vote, despite a referendum poll that showed the strike count was 10 to 1 in favor. So Bridges started creating strike teams with the San Franciso and Oakland longshoremen, an organized structure from the dock level on up, at each port. His plan had support and he was elected chairman of the strike committee. As March 22 approached, the employers refused to back down. A vote was forced, and the strike was called for the next day.[41]

The employers and shipowners called in federal reinforcements. President Franklin D. Roosevelt called on the union to halt the looming strike and allow him to try to mediate the dispute with a federal mediation board. The president's call worked, at least temporarily, as Lewis halted the strike pending a possible resolution. By April 1934, the federal mediators offered a complicated, half-measure proposal: hiring halls as a joint venture between employers and labor in each port; union elections under supervision of a regional board; no coast-wide union contract; and wages and hours would be set by another decision-making board of employer and employee representatives.[42]

Bridges denounced the federal mediators' proposal, recognizing that the longshoremen's basic demands would be lost in a legal process designed to derail the union into future legal and procedural wrangling. As longshoremen from the West Coast realized that the ILA's technical leaders lacked Bridges' heart, motivation, and organizational ability, all men looked to Bridges as the beacon of hope. If a contract for fair hours, fair pay, safe working conditions, and the power that came from an organized coast-wide union were to exist, it was now in Harry Bridges' hands to lead the charge. The longshoremen up and down the coast then voted, and all ports— Bellingham, Seattle, Tacoma, Aberdeen, Portland, Astoria, Grays Harbor, San Francisco, Oakland, Stockton, San Pedro, San Diego, as well as the smaller ports—favored a strike.[43]

And so it was that on May 9, 1934, the Great Strike began.

Bloody Thursday

Instantly, twelve to fourteen thousand longshoremen went on strike, paralyzing West Coast shipping.[44] Prepared, the shipowners established recruiting offices in the various port cities to hire strikebreakers to offload the ships. On the strike's second day in San Francisco, over five hundred longshoremen marched on the shipowners' recruiting office. Police arrived and a minor melee ensued, injuring several on each side. The police responded with an ominous policy: "From now on, strikers will be shown no quarter." That ominous policy set the stage for future conflicts.[45]

Picketing longshoremen march with their banners, May 10, 1934. Copyright UC Berkeley, Bancroft Library.

Police controlling the protesting longshoremen. Copyright San Francisco History Center, San Francisco Public Library.

Now on strike, every morning Bridges would have all the lines of strikers meet at the Embarcadero, where he would stand on a box and deliver a daily report from the strike committee. Workers then went off to picket and march, and brutal police responses followed. "We had a hell of a time because picketing was illegal...We'd get out there with our flag, our union banner, and I think we had a couple of drums to march along. Then the cops would move in and beat... us," Bridges recounted.[46]

Within a week, industry had come to a halt in many West Coast cities as other related maritime unions joined the strike. A full maritime strike now existed, and all West Coast ports sat eerily still as no ships entered or left.[47] Secretary of Labor Perkins sent a representative to the West Coast to try to find a resolution. Taking the employers' side, the government representative told the press that the strike was the product of Communist Party elements. The papers, in turn, took the employers' side, reporting that the strike was the product of "communistic agitators" and leaders who were not real Americans, all direct assaults on Harry Bridges.[48] Later, all of the San Francisco and Oakland newspapers banded together and agreed to focus their efforts on protecting the community from "communism."[49] Only two papers supported the strike: the *Western Worker*, published by the local Communist Party, and a local Catholic newspaper called the *Catholic Leader*.[50]

The Communist Party was indeed active on the waterfront, advocating for the strikers to build its political base. But the protesting longshoremen were striking to solve practical day-to-day problems. "The men on the waterfront, myself included, they were seeking an answer to their problems, and the problems were, first of all, job security; the big thing on the waterfront was the fact that the casual nature of the work, you didn't know if you was going to work from one day to another," Bridges explained. "And the various other conditions, the bad working conditions, the Speed Up, the chiseling, the racketeering, the kickbacks and the indignities of the whole thing. So the truth of the matter is that the men on the waterfront, they wanted a solution to their problems, and so did I," Bridges argued.[51]

At the same time, the Communist Party youth section took to the street in San Francisco to protest in support of the strikers. In one incident, there were two to three hundred teenage boys and girls, sixteen to seventeen years old or so, all protesting near the ILA Union Hall. The police blocked the teenagers at each end of the street and then moved in and started beating them. The fleeing teenagers took refuge in the ILA Union Hall. Bridges ordered his men to protect the kids from the police, and then contacted the Communist Party to have them come collect the kids.[52] This act of charity would be used against Bridges down the road.

By the end of May, over thirty thousand men were on strike. The national ILA president, Joseph Ryan, arrived on the West Coast to try to triangulate Harry Bridges out of the equation. Ryan secretly negotiated with the shipowners and the mayor of San Francisco to reach a deal that was palatable to the shipowners: port-by-port unions, no closed shops, and Shape Ups were fine. Ryan also accused Bridges of maintaining a strike and splintering the workers because of a desire to serve Communist Party ideals.[53] Industry was happy.

But Bridges was not. By mid-June, Bridges was chairman of the Joint Marine Strike Committee and although he lacked the technical power of Ryan as ILA president, Bridges nonetheless possessed an unwavering and loud voice against the apparent sell-out deal. "Reports in the newspapers that the strike is settled are absolutely untrue," he stated in dissent, adding that the proposed settlement was unacceptable. In turn, the ILA members voted 10 to 1 to maintain the strike. Ryan left, condemning the strikers as communists taking orders from Moscow. Frustrated, the employers' groups even tried to bribe Bridges, offering him $50,000 cash to call off the strike. Bridges refused.[54]

Quickly, the San Francisco Immigration and Naturalization Service (INS) joined the fray. After receiving reports shortly after the strike began that Bridges was a communist agitator, the local INS officials alerted INS officials in Washington.[55] The commissioner of immigration in D.C., Daniel MacCormack, in turn sent an urgent telegram to local INS officials in May 1934 to investigate "aliens illegally...fomenting longshoreman strike," with "alien" referring to Harry Bridges.[56] The White House was briefed within days.[57] And local immigration officials visited the picket lines, threatening Filipino strikers with deportation if they didn't abandon the strike and get back to work. At the same time, immigration officials interviewed Bridges, who told them, "Look, I have been around here since 1922 or 1923. All this baloney about me just being especially imported on the waterfront in the last few months to stir up a lot of trouble, why, that is a lot of hogwash." The officials left and didn't question him any further.[58]

Secretary of Labor Perkins then came to the West Coast to help find a solution. At one of the meetings with government conciliators, Secretary Perkins met Bridges in person for the first time. She recalled: "He was peculiarly rough looking, though not tough. He was poorly dressed. He had on a tweed-like sort of jacket, very worn, very baggy, the collar sort of lapped over and pinned with a safety pin...He was very, very thin. He stooped so much that I later discovered he was a taller man than my first impression of him had been. In his hand he had a cap, just exactly the kind of cap that British workmen wear."[59]

Government progress was slow, however, and by early July in San Francisco the shipowners had hired more strikebreakers to come in and move cargo from the docks to trucks. Bridges sent an emergency message to all striking workers to picket the entire waterfront so the employers could not remove cargo with strikebreakers, and called on the Teamsters to help prevent strikebreakers aiding the shipowners. This then expanded the focus from the longshoremen to the Teamsters Union, which controlled cargo movement from the docks. The Teamsters joined the ILA, thereby expanding the scope of the strike. The employers in turn went to the mayor and the police to get armed help to control the waterfront and break the picket lines.[60]

A combustible situation was now unfolding. By Tuesday, July 3, 1934, there were over five thousand strikers on the waterfront when the police and fire services of San Francisco came roaring into the waterfront on the Embarcadero, drove the protesters back, and created an armed corridor for strikebreaker trucks to enter and unload the cargo. The strikers in turn started marching on the police and throwing rocks, stemming the ability of the shipowners to move the cargo. Advance police units moved in, wearing gas masks and black helmets, and launched tear gas grenades, clearing the way for other police officers to attack with their batons.

Then, the police opened fire on Harry Bridges and the protesters. One protester was hit in the ankle and another above the eye by a ricocheting bullet that went through a bank window. As the commotion unfolded, Bridges and some of his men went racing around a corner as bullets whizzed past their heads. As Bridges turned the corner, he looked back and saw a police officer still aiming his gun.[61] When the smoke cleared, one strike-breaker, thirty-three-year-old Argonne Riley, was found lying in the gutter. Battered and bloody, Riley was treated by police but then transferred to police custody for being drunk. Late in the evening, Riley started complaining of headaches and shortly thereafter died as a result of a fractured skull from the melee earlier in the day. He was the first San Francisco fatality of the strike.[62]

The next day was July 4, Independence Day, and street tensions simmered. But the Industrial Association, an organization representing the employers and shipowners, declared that July 5 would be the showdown to reopen the port.

Strikers at a warehouse in the Embarcadero area as police launch tear gas grenades during the battles that became known as Bloody Thursday, July 1934. Copyright Bettman/Getty Images.

As dawn broke on Thursday, July 5, 1934, over three thousand protesters were at the docks as cargo trains tried to enter the San Francisco waterfront. Police ordered the protesters to move. They refused and started pelting the police with rocks. The protesters then surrounded the boxcars and set them ablaze. When the fire trucks arrived, police commandeered the hoses and turned them on the protesters, forcing them off the docks and up nearby Rincon Hill. As the protesters retreated up Rincon Hill, the police attacked, firing their guns and launching tear gas grenades. The protesters took the high ground and were able to build a makeshift barricade out of piles of brick and masonry left from a recently demolished building. From their defensive position, the protesters fought back the advancing police officers who charged the hill. Each time the

police crested the hill, the protesters lobbed bricks over their barricade and stopped the advance. The police then prepared to lob
tear gas grenades at the defensive structure on top of the hill. Recognizing the nature of the impending police action, the protesters
escaped. The police launched the tear gas and then broke over the
barricade, only to find it empty of the then-evacuated protesters.
This became known as the Battle of Rincon Hill.[63]

Police respond to strikers. Copyright San Francisco History Center, San Francisco Public Library.

While the Battle of Rincon Hill raged, other protesters moved
to the ILA Union Hall on the Embarcadero. The police in turn cor-
doned them off and started moving in from each side of the street
in a classic pincer movement. With the police launching tear gas
grenades and firing indiscriminately, three protesters fell, bleeding
on the ground.[64] Hundreds were wounded, many with shots to the
back.[65] And as protesters came to help the fallen, the police ordered

them back lest they get the same treatment.[66] As a result of the police attacks, two protesters were dead: Howard Sperry, a striking longshoreman working in a relief kitchen; and Nicholas Counderakis (aka Nick Bordoise), a cook.[67]

That afternoon, fearing the day's events were spinning out of control, California Governor Frank Merriam called in the National Guard and declared a state of emergency. By midnight, the National Guard's steel-helmeted troops controlled the docks and a forced peace descended as fifteen hundred National Guardsmen patrolled the area. Tanks, machine guns, and barricades littered the area rendering the Embarcadero a no man's land. But Bridges did not stand down, although he urged nonviolence by taking to the radio waves to ask the striking men not to fight the National Guard.[68]

When what later became known as Bloody Thursday was over—an apt title appended to the day's events decades before U2 sang of the "Bloody Sunday" that struck Northern Ireland in 1972—the toll in San Francisco was two dead, over thirty shot and wounded, another forty-three beaten and gassed, and over four hundred more injured.[69] The bodies of the two dead men, Sperry and Counderakis, lay in caskets at ILA headquarters, near where they had died. At the actual location of their deaths on the sidewalk near the ILA headquarters, ILA strikers chalked off the area and bordered it with flowers and wreaths as a vivid reminder of the horror, a makeshift memorial that was then protected by ILA strikers.[70]

At the same time, *agents provocateurs* tried to infiltrate the striking committee's headquarters and plant evidence. In one instance, a spy posing as a radical striker delivered hand grenades for ostensible use against the police, but the strike committee saw the trap and dumped the grenades in San Francisco Bay. In another instance, the Waterfront Employers Association, an organization representing the shipowners along with the Industrial Association, even managed to plant a spy in the union as Harry Bridges' secretary.[71]

At the scene of the strikers' deaths, longshoremen chalked off the area and placed wreaths in a makeshift memorial, July 1934. Copyright San Francisco History Center, San Francisco Public Library.

As part of the funeral procession, people gather to honor the fallen strikers on Bloody Thursday. Copyright UC Berkeley, Bancroft Library.

On July 9, Bridges led a funeral procession up Market Street for the two dead protesters. Perhaps with some exaggeration, it is reported that fifty thousand workers marching eight abreast led the funeral procession. Bridges reported fifteen to twenty thousand marched, but regardless of the exact number, the showing was certainly large. Owing to the incendiary situation, the police allowed the procession to proceed.[72] One of the deceased, Sperry, was a veteran and was buried in the Presidio that day by the marching strikers.[73]

Then, Bridges pushed for a general San Francisco strike across all unions as a mass protest against the killings. In turn, other unions started voting to strike, as union workers from other sectors of the economy joined in solidarity with the battered but defiant longshoremen. By mid-July over one hundred different unions had voted to strike in support of Bridges' longshoremen. This general strike began on July 16.[74]

San Francisco virtually shut down. No street cars ran, grocery stores were closed, and only nineteen restaurants remained open. Streets were deserted as gasoline stations had no gasoline to sell. Cars that ran out of gas sat idle in the streets. Mayor Rossi of San Francisco took to the radio waves to plead both for calm and for all parties—strikers and employers alike—to allow federal mediators to find a solution to the controversy.[75] Within four days, the general strike ended—the show of solidarity having made its point—but the longshoremen's strike held firm, with Bridges at the center of the storm. With this turn of events, at last the employers relented. They removed all strikebreakers and agreed to arbitrate a solution before federal mediators. Thus, after nearly three months, on July 31, 1934, the National Guard retreated and the longshoremen returned to work as the arbitration process began.

Within another three months, the arbitration board issued a decision that was a tremendous victory for Bridges and the longshoremen: the longshoremen secured a coast-wide contract, precluding the employers from pitting port against port to depress wages or defeat strikes; six-hour workdays as demanded; a pay raise of not quite the one dollar they sought, but to ninety-five cents; employer-owned hiring halls and Shape Ups were gone forever; new hiring halls with some employer participation; earnings were equalized; and the hiring dispatcher who oversaw the hiring process had to be elected by the union.[76]

After eighty-three days of striking, nine dead, hundreds seriously injured, and a temporary general strike that shut down all San Francisco business, Bridges had achieved the near impossible for his men. He succeeded in achieving a coast-wide union and vastly improved working conditions. He and his men had destroyed the old employer-controlled Blue Book. And the men loved him. Bridges was now widely regarded as the leading voice of radical labor on the West Coast, and was subsequently elected president of the ILA's Pacific Coast District.[77]

The Fight Begins to Squash Bridges' Voice...
Federal Investigations

But those on the other side of the table, having lost the battle, did not see the war as over. From the moment Bridges rose to the forefront, and certainly when the Great Strike began, the communist cry went up against Bridges by private interests representing employers and shipowners, provoking Department of Labor deportation investigations as ordered by Secretary Perkins.[78] Federal INS officials went to the San Francisco Police, who reported that they had nothing about Bridges in their files. After further investigation, all they could report was that Bridges was an excellent longshoreman, very trustworthy, had a good record, never missed a day's work, and his prior employers all spoke highly of him.[79]

During the summer of 1934—within days of the Great Strike beginning—the Department of State had also begun forwarding to the Department of Labor information it could muster bearing on any affiliation between Bridges and the Communist Party, and the INS had begun interviewing witnesses about whether Harry Bridges had communist ties.[80] Remarkably, the same day protester Argonne Riley was killed, on July 3, 1934, the INS in San Francisco was taking sworn testimony from a witness, trying to ascertain if Bridges was a communist. But all the witness could say was that he had seen Bridges reading literature that was allegedly communistic.[81]

Even Bridges' boarding house landlord was interviewed, who reported that Bridges always paid his rent, and was quiet and well behaved. The only detail of note was that he played his mandolin nightly before bed.[82] Government officials then contacted the Australian police to inquire into any communistic leanings in the Bridges family. The Sydney Commissioner of Police reported that "Harry Bridges was well educated and bore an excellent character before he left Australia. He was not in any way connected with the Communist Party…The parents and brother of this man are eminently respectable and are in no way connected with the Communistic Organization."[83] Thus, as of February 1935, the San Francisco Immigration Office concluded that it "had maintained a very close contact with the Crime Prevention Detail from a period long antedating the general strike in San Francisco until the present date," but that nonetheless the investigation "had failed to show that [Bridges] is in any manner connected with the Communist Party."[84] Confronted with a picture of someone hardly seeming a threat to the nation—nor a member of the Communist Party—Secretary Perkins declined to deport Bridges.[85]

However, notwithstanding the federal investigations that yielded no evidence Bridges was a communist, powerful anti-Bridges forces had emerged. These forces ranged from private industry groups such as the conservative American Legion, to the shipowners and employers (represented by the Industrial Association and the Waterfront Employers Association), to state police and government officials in the Pacific Northwest, to congressmen and federal officials in Washington, and even to rival unionists. All rallied around the mantra that Bridges was a Communist Party member working in concert with communists to undermine American democracy and that Secretary Perkins should deport Bridges as un-American.[86]

Silencing voices that challenged the status quo was not new in the 1930s. We can go to the founding of the Republic and witness our embrace of foreigners who speak for the status quo, but also our intolerance if they dare speak too loudly against the mainstream. Englishman Thomas Paine offers a fascinating case in point, experiencing both extremes. His originally anonymous masterpiece *Common Sense* expressed the anger and revulsion of a colonial people at their treatment at the hands of the English king. Paine's writings helped move a nascent nation to declare independence, and moved its men to die for the cause. George Washington cited Paine's work as the seminal publication that provoked "a powerful change in the minds of many men."[87] Indeed, George Washington even relied on Paine's words in war, ordering Paine's words read to his troops on the eve of battle. In turn, John Adams remarked, "Without the pen of the author of *Common Sense*, the sword of Washington would have been raised in vain."[88]

But Paine eventually fell out of vogue and experienced the wrath brought to bear on those who dissented too loudly on American shores. This time his writing was not on topics such as the American Revolution and independence, but rather on religion in *The Age of Reason* in 1793. An attack on organized religion—penned ironically under the First Amendment his earlier writings helped give birth to—Paine soon discovered that his earlier sponsors abandoned him after his writings were published. Samuel Adams decried Paine's work as an effort to "unchristianize the mass of our citizens." John Adams in turn attacked Paine's character, calling him the product of a "wild boar on a bitch wolf."[89]

Notwithstanding Paine's influential writings and foundational participation in American democracy, when he attempted to vote in a congressional election in 1806, the polling inspectors denied him a ballot because he was a foreigner.[90] And when Paine died in New York in 1809, neither the surviving Founding Fathers nor any other American statesman attended his funeral. Notably, only six people attended, two of whom were freed slaves no doubt appreciative for one of Paine's other writings, *African Slavery in America*, one of the first public writings in America that called for the abolition of slavery. Tragically, Paine's pivotal voice, which had played such a large role in the birth of American democracy, ended in an ignominious burial without even a proper eulogy to acknowledge publicly Paine and his offerings to American democracy.[91]

An apt eulogy might have quoted the opening lines from *Common Sense*, words that proved prescient for him and that would prove prescient for many future dissenters, Harry Bridges included:

> "Perhaps the sentiments contained in the following pages are not *yet* sufficiently fashionable to procure them general favor; a long habit of not thinking a thing *wrong*, gives it a superficial appearance of being *right*, and raises at first a formidable outcry in defence of custom. But the tumult soon subsides. Time makes more converts than reason."[92]

Paine's words have echoed through the ages, and a century and a half later his time-reason admonition settled on another noncitizen agitator as government and private forces now allied to use the legal system as the primary weapon in a crusade against Harry Bridges.

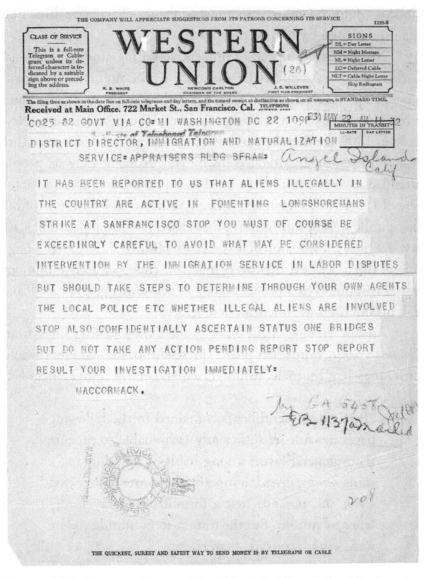

The original INS telegram issued May 1934 about "illegal alien" Harry Bridges (also pictured on cover).

CHAPTER 2

The Gathering Storm (1935-39)

"He was just an inexplicable man who had appeared from the mist."

SECRETARY OF LABOR FRANCES PERKINS, FIRST FEMALE CABINET MEMBER IN AMERICAN HISTORY, REFERRING TO HARRY BRIDGES IN 1934[1]

Assassination?

Had Bridges simply led the West Coast strike and remained content with the union gains, he probably never would have experienced one trial, let alone four. But Bridges was not the type to slink away into the night. Instead, after the successful strike in 1934, Bridges pushed for more rights and more labor reforms. That is, he refused to stay silent. "The union, not the employer, is going to decide on the Pacific Coast whether a man can work or not," he demanded. "Unionism must come first and agreements second," he further declared.[2]

At the University of Washington, Bridges delivered a rousing speech that crystallized his views of a class struggle: "We take the stand that we as workers have nothing in common with the employers. We are in a class struggle, and we subscribe to the belief that if the employer is not in business his products still will be necessary and we still will be providing them when there is no employing class. We frankly believe that day is coming."

This speech in turn provoked significant animus and was routinely cited as evidence of his communistic leanings.[3] Not shy about supporting unpopular causes, Bridges publicly endorsed Upton Sinclair's unsuccessful "End Poverty in California" bid for the 1934 California governorship.[4]

Bridges also sought to unite all the maritime unions into one coalition. At a convention in Seattle in 1935, Bridges rousingly spoke to the audience, convincing the myriad maritime unions to join together and form one coalition. When the meeting ended, Bridges had succeeded. The new coalition was called the Maritime Federation of the Pacific, representing workers from all facets of the maritime industry, and its lasting motto was coined at the convention: "An injury to one is an injury to all."[5]

Behind this premise lay concern for serious socio-political change: Bridges tolerated no racial discrimination in the union, a progressive stance in the 1930s.[6] Even during the 1934 strike, Bridges had traveled to black churches to speak where he implored the black community to join him on the picket line.[7] Bridges' belief was decidedly simple in hindsight: a union could survive employer threats and strikebreakers if its members stuck together in a transparent democratic union where everyone got the same amount of work regardless of race, religion, or politics. "If there are 4,000 men working, one man is entitled to one four-thousandth of the work," Bridges proclaimed. This democratic structure eliminated the disunity that had plagued unions for years. "That is the whole secret of that," Bridges remarked. "There is nothing more to it than that."[8]

Bridges' loud dissenting voice won the admiration of his workers. Indeed, at one point in 1935, Bridges became ill and was rushed to the St. Francis Hospital in San Francisco for emergency surgery. While Bridges was in the operating room, hundreds of supporters anxiously waited long into the night to hear the eventual news of the surgery's success. Flowers poured into the hospital, reportedly more than had ever been received by the hospital for any one patient.[9] He recovered and returned to the union.

By 1936, the arbitrated 1934 agreement that ended the Great Strike was up for renegotiation. Each side felt that the other had violated the terms that resolved the 1934 strike, and the major point of dispute was over the hiring halls. After the 1934 strike, labor had taken de facto control of hiring, which aggrieved the employers; reciprocally, the longshoremen wanted formally to have complete control over hiring and wanted proper overtime pay. The battle lines drawn, the employers demanded a new arbitration, looking to undo the longshoremen's gains of 1934.

Fearing that arbitrators would side with employers this time, Bridges called another strike in October 1936. This time there was no violence. All ports on the West Coast, however, again shut down. The strike lasted ninety-eight days, longer than the Great Strike of 1934, and ended with a negotiated resolution that had each side claiming gains. Bridges' longshoremen netted better job security, but got neither the complete, unfettered control they sought nor new wages. Bridges, nonetheless, came out of the strike in a position of tremendous support within the union, having retained the gains from 1934.[10]

Harry Bridges in 1936. Copyright San Francisco History Center, San Francisco Public Library.

By 1937, the Pacific Coast District of the ILA union, which Bridges still headed, seceded from the ILA and became the International Longshore and Warehouse Union (ILWU), with Bridges as its president. Bridges led this secession because he wanted a union that was entirely progressive, militant in its focus on the rank and file, and incorruptible. The ILWU then affiliated with the powerful Committee for Industrial Organization (renamed as the Congress of Industrial Organizations in 1938 and known by its acronym, CIO), a national federation of industrial unions that rivaled the AFL in the 1930s. In short order, John L. Lewis, the president of the CIO, appointed Bridges as the West Coast regional director.[11]

In a few short years, Bridges had risen from passionate and outspoken longshoreman to leader of the new ILWU. Yet Bridges drew a meager salary and insisted other ILWU leaders do the same—salaries that were significantly smaller than those of any other comparable national union leaders. "It is good union policy that officers should not earn so much that they drift away from the members," he argued in his Australian accent. Bridges lived in a modest five-room blue-collar home, and refused any trappings of wealth. Bridges' refusal to take the spoils of labor leadership that others readily feasted upon helped earn him a reputation for incorruptibility.[12]

Bridges' refusal to take financial advantage is illustrated in one famed story. A local Cadillac dealer with stringent franchise obligations to General Motors had to get rid of old cars at a loss to make room for the new models. An admirer of the ILWU and Bridges, the dealer offered the cars to Bridges and his executives at a steep discount, but Bridges refused to take the offer, not comfortable driving a Cadillac.[13] Indeed, even with his fame, power, and ability to command real financial resources to himself, if he chose to take advantage of the union, Bridges was in 1937 borrowing to survive and remained behind on his taxes and car payments to Ford.[14] No doubt, this kind of incorruptibility is what inspired deep loyalty within the ILWU.[15]

In July 1937, Bridges graced the cover of *Time* magazine—the first Australian to do so—and was the centerpiece of an article detailing his humble nature and labor successes. *Time* published the contention that Bridges had already endured "close to persecution." This, before he had even seen any of his four trials to come. That same year, *Time* reported, Bridges spoke to a rally of union workers at Madison Square Garden in New York, where, his oratory powers significantly improved, he held spellbound an audience of fifteen thousand for one hour as he spoke extemporaneously. The only noticeable change in his appearance was that he now wore good suits and owned a good hat.[16]

Bridges' modesty in his success and the massive loyalty of the ILWU men only served to increase the angst in his enemies. One night, a dozen or so prominent San Francisco business leaders, representing shipowners and the business community, got together to discuss what to do about Bridges and the waterfront situation. Quickly, tempers flared and the men started discussing the need to secure the "disappearance" of Bridges. One of the attendees, Paul Smith, a prominent *San Francisco Chronicle* newspaper editor, refused to participate and left, indicating his outrage and promising to tell Bridges about the nascent assassination plot. The remaining attendees insisted Smith had interpreted them too literally—they had discussed murder only to show how impractical such a solution was, they asserted. Yet even thirty years later, Smith remained convinced that he had averted an assassination plot.[17]

With overt assassination off the table, the focus shifted in full force to Bridges' status as a noncitizen. Under American immigration law of the time, if a noncitizen was affiliated with an organization that advocated the overthrow of the government, then he could be deported. The Communist Party was one of the primary organizations that triggered governmental deportation actions. Thus, if Bridges could be proven a member of the Communist Party with concurrent evidence that the Communist Party advocated the overthrow of the government, then Bridges could be deported and his radical voice for labor permanently silenced.[18]

The Knowles-Keegan-Doyle Axis:
A Private-Governmental Anti-Bridges
Coalition Forms

In the mid-1930s, several figures on the West Coast emerged as the leading anti-Bridges crusaders focused on establishing that Bridges was a Communist Party member. Key among them, if not the ringleader, was Harper Knowles, a man in his late thirties with tightly trimmed hair shaved so short as to be almost bald above the ears and around the nape of his neck. A San Franciscan member of the American Legion, he often had an American Legion cap perched atop his head. At that time, the American Legion was a conservative organization made up of male veterans and male descendants of male veterans, with chapters all across America. The American Legion promoted the ideology of Americanism, which was a belief in all things American, an ideology that required devotion and loyalty to American culture, customs, and government. The Legion sought to impact public policy to achieve its generally conservative aims, often in the realm of veterans' affairs.[19]

Many of its West Coast members were distressed at the Great Strike and the radical elements they believed were taking over the West Coast. By the time the strike had ended, the American Legion believed as a matter of policy that dangerous communist agitators were threatening the American way of life. Consequently, by 1935 the American Legion had created its own Subversive Activities Commission, a private-sector precursor to the federal House Un-American Activities Committee (HUAC) that was formed in 1938.[20]

Knowles became the chairman of the Legion's Subversive Activities Commission, which was headquartered in the Veterans Building in San Francisco. Under his command, the Subversive Activities Commission employed hundreds of informants across the West Coast, all charged both with reporting on supposed radicals in their local towns and communities and collecting radical literature, all of which information was stored in an elaborate, pre-computer, indexed database tracking hundreds of individuals and organizations deemed radical. Organized around a complex political structure with twenty-four districts, each with its own subcommittee, all units gathered data and reported to Knowles.[21] One person in particular, in San Francisco, who was the subject of the American Legion's watchful eye, was Harry Bridges.

Harper Knowles, one of the original architects of the actions against Bridges, testifies before HUAC in the 1930s charging Bridges with membership in the Communist Party. Library of Congress, Prints & Photographs Division, photography by Harris & Ewing, LC-DIG-hec-25149.

As chairman of the Legion's Subversive Activities Commission, Knowles sent an endless stream of letters to Secretary Perkins and the United States government, all claiming that Bridges was a Communist Party member. Long on accusations, against both the Department of Labor as a communist coddler and Bridges, but short on evidence, the letters included snippets of Bridges' speeches and unsubstantiated allegations of Bridges' alleged ties to the Communist Party. Arrogant and presumptuous in tone, one December 1935 letter instructed the Department of Labor on its legal functions and duties and demanded that Bridges be deported. In short, Knowles was desperately trying to convince the Department of Labor to initiate deportation proceedings against Bridges, notwithstanding the Department of Labor's prior investigations that yielded no evidence that Bridges was a communist.[22]

Eventually, somebody made a report to the San Francisco Police that Bridges attended radical meetings in a private home in the Embarcadero area. These musings suddenly were trumpeted by employers on the waterfront, amplifying public proclamations that Bridges was a radical and a communist. Specific claims were in turn published in the papers. And as Secretary Perkins later reminisced, "There was no evidence. It was all hearsay. Nobody ever did know where the police got this information that he had been to these meetings...This was the first time we had ever heard this. Otherwise he was just an inexplicable man who had appeared from the mist."[23] Nonetheless, specific allegations of Bridges' alleged ties to communists had gone public.

As Secretary Perkins later explained, "I personally did not believe that Bridges was a communist when I received this information. As soon as he became successful at the close of that strike and won it, all kinds of ill-natured rumors began to float around him. They began to say he was a Red, this, and that, but there was nothing very definite. I still had the police department report of San Francisco that showed nothing but a perfectly clear background."[24]

Secretary of Labor Frances Perkins testifies before Congress. Library of Congress, Prints & Photographs Division, photography by Harris & Ewing, LC-H2-B-6995.

Knowles, however, continued his American Legion letter-writing campaign until 1936, when a leaked Department of Labor report quoted senior government officials essentially mocking Knowles for his "intemperate and overbearing" crusade of unsubstantiated charges entirely lacking in evidence. Widely distributed at an American Legion Annual Convention, the public humiliation certainly impacted Knowles. But not as one might expect.[25]

Rather than capitulate, Knowles ramped up his battle against Bridges and settled upon new, more aggressive tactics. Abandoning the letter-writing campaign as the sole front of attack (although he continued to issue his missives), Knowles decided he needed more powerful allies. He cast around for government help, and in the Portland police department and prosecutor's office, he found detectives who were members of the local American Legion Subversive Activities Commission in Oregon, making them a perfect partner for Knowles.[26]

Specifically, Knowles formed a relationship with two state officials, Captain John Keegan, chief of detectives, and Stanley "Larry" Doyle, special prosecutor for Oregon. Each became a major player in the deportation case that would soon unfold. Now firmly embedded with Portland police and prosecutors, Knowles began to work in a coordinated manner with Keegan and Doyle, tying the private-sector conservative American Legion to government officials in the quest to show that Bridges was a communist.

In his mid-fifties, bespectacled and with a distinguished mop of silver hair, Keegan, chief detective in charge of the Red Squad (squads focused on ferreting out communists), began investigating Bridges in earnest in the spring of 1937 when Bridges attended a convention in Portland. A recording device was placed in Bridges' hotel room, but it was discovered by Bridges, who had some fun with it. He called some press members and let them in on an organized joke to get the local police riled up. Bridges scripted a conversation with fellow unionists where they lauded the recent Russian accomplishment of flying over the North Pole and talked about getting the Russian government to drop bags of rubles into America so they could foment a domestic revolution.[27] One can only imagine the feverish excitement of the Portland police thinking that they had uncovered the holy grail of evidence against Bridges, only to have the joke turned on them by a recoiling press corps.

After Bridges left Portland, Keegan, at Knowles' urging, widened his investigation into California. Keegan sent one of his detectives, Detective Browne, to California to meet with other alleged informants who had information supposedly supporting the contention that Bridges was a communist. Captain Keegan paid for these investigative trips with state money—jaunts that had nothing to do with Oregon law and everything to do with gathering evidence to give to the federal government to push it to deport Bridges. Detective Browne in turn made multiple trips to California to interview and secure statements from alleged witnesses.[28]

Keegan's compatriot was Stanley Doyle, a special prosecutor of the State of Oregon, who also had been declared by the Oregon governor a "special agent" and issued a formal badge.[29] Doyle was a high-ranking Legionnaire and a member of a secret Legion society known as the Forty and Eight or "40 et 8," which was shorthand for "Forty Men and Eight Horses," a symbolic reference to World War I boxcars that could hold forty men or eight horses.[30] Mustachioed like Adolf Hitler, six-foot-four with a double chin, Doyle was already a famed, if not notorious, prosecutor in Oregon. He had prosecuted and convicted a communist in a highly publicized 1935 criminal case called *Oregon v. DeJonge*, a case where Doyle attempted to bribe a witness to change testimony to get a conviction.[31]

Witnesses Come Forward

By 1937, Doyle and Keegan, working with Knowles, had procured witnesses who would say that Bridges was a Communist Party member. One witness Doyle procured was Laurence Milner, a major in the Oregon National Guard Reserves. Middle-aged and hawk-nosed, Milner had served in World War I and for a time was custodian of the Multnomah County Armory. Eventually, in 1933, the State of Oregon's Military Department hired him to investigate subversive activities. His task was to run undercover operations: to pose as a communist and infiltrate communist organizations.[32]

Milner successfully infiltrated various labor and communist groups, but his undercover pursuits were also tinged with violence. During some of the West Coast strikes in 1934, he was an *agent provocateur* of mob violence, where he proudly claimed to have taught strikers how to defeat charging police officers. As such, he encouraged strikers to attack the Portland police and defend with violence. Of course it did not end well for the strikers on the front lines, which lines did not include the *agent provocateur* Milner.[33]

Doyle's recruitment in 1937 of Milner as an anti-Bridges witness was truly remarkable, because Milner was the very witness Doyle had tried to bribe in the *DeJonge* trial! In that case, Milner was undercover in DeJonge's group and had testified that DeJonge was not a communist. Doyle asked him to change his testimony and say DeJonge was a communist. Doyle offered to help Milner get financial remuneration from the state if he so testified. Milner refused to go as far as Doyle wanted, but, playing the double agent, never reported the attempted bribe to DeJonge's lawyer so as to maintain his cover. Had Milner reported the facts, DeJonge would certainly have escaped a conviction. But Milner, ever the double agent, stayed silent, and DeJonge was convicted.[34] Doyle's bribery never came to light during the trial, and so Milner continued on as an embedded secret agent in the unions, casting around for communists he could destroy, and playing the *agent provocateur* in the West Coast labor struggles.

Now, a few years later, Doyle approached Milner again. This time Milner was ready to blow his cover in what would be the pinnacle of his undercover operations: destroying Harry Bridges. Thus, Milner gave Prosecutor Doyle and Captain Keegan an affidavit swearing that while undercover he had seen Bridges at official Communist Party events.[35]

Knowles also referred Captain Keegan and Prosecutor Doyle to John Leech of Los Angeles. Long and slender, with the air of a cowboy, Leech had made a meager and unsuccessful living as a painter in the 1920s, and by the early 1930s had a family and was destitute. By 1933, he was living in California in one of the shanty Hoovervilles, a collection of shacks filled with the unemployed suffering through the Great Depression, when the California police

burned some of the shacks down. Leech then became a member of
the Communist Party and rose through its ranks. He even ran for
the California State Assembly as the Communist Party candidate in
1934, and for Congress in 1936, losing each election.[36]

Harper Knowles in his American Legion hat (left), John Keegan (center), and John Leech (right),
all part of the team claiming Harry Bridges was a Communist Party member. Courtesy of ILWU,
San Francisco.

Knowles and Keegan now descended on Leech. Captain Keegan again sent Detective Browne to Los Angeles to interview Leech.
In June 1937, Detective Browne arrived at the Leech home. Browne
showed his badge and explained he was a detective in Oregon working for Captain Keegan. After much banter, Browne trying to ascertain whether Leech would cooperate, and Leech playing coy regarding fears of Communist Party reprisals, Detective Browne eventually
offered to pay for Leech's travel to Portland if he would offer sworn

testimony that Bridges was a communist. Leech was non-committal, and Browne left promising to return the next day.[37]

By chance, one of Leech's Communist Party friends named Bundy came by and Leech told him what had happened. The Communist Party swiftly prepared an affidavit for Leech to sign, attesting to the fact of Browne's visit, the offer of money for testimony, and the fact that Bridges was not, to Leech's knowledge, a communist. Leech signed it. The next day Bundy hid in Leech's house and listened as Browne returned. Eavesdropping from behind the kitchen door, Bundy heard Browne offer $1,000 for testimony. When Leech refused, Browne increased the offer to $2,000. Browne then said he had traveled to Los Angeles with $10,000 and was prepared to spend more, but he needed an affidavit. Leech, however, refused.[38]

But the Keegan-Doyle axis had not given up on Leech. A few weeks later, Special Prosecutor Doyle himself traveled to Los Angeles to talk to Leech. Stepping off one of the old streetcars that used to crisscross Los Angeles outside the Leech home, Doyle approached the house. When Leech opened the door, Doyle flashed his badge and explained his status as a special agent of the State of Oregon. Doyle now offered to pay to move Leech and his family to Portland and to get Leech a job there if he would testify under oath that Bridges was a communist. This time, Leech capitulated. A week later, Leech and his family were driving to Portland with their life belongings.

Once in Portland, Leech went to the INS's Portland office and, with Doyle present, along with local police officials, gave a sworn affidavit that he knew Bridges to be a communist and had seen Bridges at communist meetings. Leech's signature was formally witnessed by two others who signed the affidavit attesting to Leech's signature. Interestingly, Doyle insisted on signing the affidavit also, despite the absence of a line for a third witness. His unnecessary signature, scrawled across the bottom of the affidavit, reads as one who marked his territory and declared ownership of his find, Leech. In short order, a job was procured for Leech.[39]

Knowles, working with Captain Keegan and Special Prosecutor Doyle in this unholy trinity, had by the summer of 1937 now secured affidavits from Milner and Leech, each of whom swore they had seen Bridges at Communist Party events and that Bridges was a communist. Special Prosecutor Doyle, in August 1937, even boasted in a sworn statement to the INS that "as a special agent for the State of Oregon" he had been engaged for two years in "the assembling of positive affirmative evidence" and had himself procured other witnesses.[40]

Doyle even put forth a document he claimed was a copy of Harry Bridges' secret Communist Party Membership Card, issued in the name of "Harry Dorgan." Dorgan was Bridges' mother's maiden name, and so the assertion was that Bridges used his mother's maiden name as an alias.[41] Doyle claimed that he obtained the secret document from an unidentified person who broke into Harry Bridges' hotel room at Doyle's request, found the card, removed it, and gave it to Doyle.[42] Whether Doyle would ever prove such a claim would become a major aspect of the future trials.

Doyle's Staggering Connections to the Federal Government, from Secret, Never-Before-Published Documents

In 1937, Doyle approached INS Division Chief of the Pacific Northwest Raphael Bonham. Doyle told Bonham he could produce specific evidence, including the Communist Party Membership Card. Bonham, a small man with mouse-gray hair and beady eyes, was bewitched.[43] Indeed, since late 1934 to early 1935 Bonham had been trying to find proof that Bridges was a communist, despite the fact that Bonham was not in San Francisco, where Bridges lived, and was instead in the Seattle INS office. Bonham even admitted in internal governmental correspondence (which would remain classified for decades) that he had authorized an effort to secure Bridges' fingerprints without Bridges' consent or knowledge.[44]

Doyle thus had a natural ally in Bonham. In a secret letter, Doyle boasted to Bonham that he could produce even more witnesses if he (Doyle) provided legal services to those witnesses.[45] With Doyle as a special prosecutor, the seeming inference from Doyle's claim was that he would cut deals or give people breaks in the criminal justice system if they would attest to certain facts.

State official Doyle and federal official Bonham worked together closely enough that Doyle even referred to Raphael Bonham in correspondence as "my dear Rafe."[46] Energetically charged for the cause, Bonham in turn relentlessly pursued Bridges, even investigating Bridges' private life to make the case that he was living with Agnes but not properly married. In Bonham's words, Bridges' alleged "adulterous cohabitation" would undermine any claim of good moral character, especially regarding application for citizenship.[47]

Doyle, however, was not only courting Bonham and the Pacific Northwest INS officials. The tentacles of his spy network reached much higher. Specifically, Doyle was sending secret communiqués to United States Senator Arthur Vandenberg, asserting that Doyle—an Oregon prosecutor—had a spy inside Bridges' union and was intercepting and stealing Bridges' mail. Doyle even sent Senator Vandenberg copies of the stolen materials.[48] Vandenberg in turn sent confidential letters to Doyle thanking him for the secret information.[49] None of Doyle's conduct—tied to some of the highest officials in the federal government—was revealed at the time to Bridges or his legal defense team, as the documents were secreted away. It is only now, nearly a century later, that these archived documents have been discovered, discussed, and published, here, for the very first time.

The alleged proof that Harry Bridges was a Communist Party member, a membership book in the name of "Harry Dorgan." Whether the book was real or fake became a central issue in the ensuing years.

Bonham Pushes for a Deportation Warrant and Matters Explode

By 1937, Bonham and other West Coast federal immigration officials possessed the actual affidavits of witnesses forwarded to them by the Knowles-Keegan-Doyle connection. Believing the affidavits, and believing the "Harry Dorgan" Communist Party Membership Card was real, Bonham, in fall 1937, telegraphed Washington asking for immediate authority to issue a warrant for Bridges' arrest and deportation.[50] Given leaks to the press, newspapers reported about the evidence right after the West Coast immigration officials secured the evidence.[51] At the same time, Governor Martin of Oregon publicly claimed the evidence proved Harry Bridges was a Communist Party member, and demanded that President Roosevelt deport him.[52]

Secretary Perkins was surprised by the entire episode. After all, it was odd for Portland and Seattle local officials to be at the center of an investigation into a resident of San Francisco. Coupled with the fact that Oregon state officials had secured incriminating evidence (he's a communist) contrary to the exculpatory findings of the San Francisco officials in Bridges' backyard (no evidence he's a communist), the material seemed highly dubious.[53] Nonetheless, Secretary Perkins called in the solicitor general, the commissioner of immigration, and attorneys within the Department of Labor to discuss the evidence. "None of us was very much impressed by the evidence, or by the character of Milner, who had produced this evidence. We had never heard of anything like this *agent provocateur* and secret agency apparently operating on its own [the American Legion's Subversive Activities Commission]," she explained.[54]

But Congress's agitation at the failure to deport Bridges was growing, and this started pushing matters out of Secretary

Perkins' hands. During a closed session of the Senate Commerce Committee in February 1938, the affidavits were discussed as Secretary Perkins updated the Commerce Committee on the Bridges investigation. Rather than keep the matter secret and confidential, as Perkins had been told would be the case, Senator Royal Copeland of New York, the Commerce Committee chairman, immediately held a press conference and issued public statements that evidence of Bridges' communistic ties existed and a prosecution would follow.

"There is in this country one Harry Bridges, an alien and an avowed communist. He is the leader of a movement on the Pacific Coast that I believe is dangerous and subversive...the Labor Department has enough evidence on Harry Bridges to make a prima facie case for his deportation," Senator Copeland announced.[55]

At the same time, Bonham, even though ostensibly an employee under Secretary Perkins in the Department of Labor, improperly leaked to Special Prosecutor Doyle, Captain Keegan, and the public that the federal government in fact had sufficient evidence to prosecute Bridges.[56] Bonham's improper leak, coupled with Senator Copeland's statements, added to the public pressure to initiate a deportation proceeding. In turn, Harry Bridges demanded to speak to Senator Copeland's Commerce Committee, but the committee refused to allow him to speak and defend himself against the charges.[57]

A Warrant Is Issued

Bridges saw the flames of public animosity fanning against him, and so he next took the offensive with a courageous and unexpected move. Two days after Senator Copeland's press conference, Bridges telegraphed Secretary Perkins and actually demanded a deportation hearing! This was itself a remarkable event. An accused party, especially where there is mass animosity—from public and governmental quarters alike—rarely, if ever, asks for his arrest, arraignment, and trial. But Bridges, convinced that the evidence would prove him righteous, demanded a deportation hearing. He did this even though his trial would unfold not before a jury of his peers, but instead before a government-appointed immigration officer chosen by the executive (the same branch of government trying to deport him).

Given this environment, Secretary Perkins issued a warrant for Bridges' arrest and deportation with a trial set for April 1938. The warrant charged Bridges with entering the country and having been a member of an organization that sought the overthrow of the American government by force.

Once a legal process begins, the sides polarize. Whatever Secretary Perkins once believed, or continued to believe, the prosecution was now under way. Handed to government lawyers within the immigration department, the lawyers now had a case, and they wanted to win. Bridges had his own lawyers, and they too wanted to win. However, they also had a vague target they were fighting against: an intentionally opaque charge of an affiliation with an organization, no explanation even of which organization, when he affiliated, what he did exactly, or when, where, or with whom he had colluded. Thus, Bridges asked for a bill of particulars.[58]

A bill of particulars is a formal written charge issued by the government when a person is charged with unlawful activity. In almost every criminal prosecution at the time, the government was required to provide a bill of particulars so the accused would know exactly the charge, as well as the evidence and witnesses the government would use to prove its case. This enabled the accused to start preparing his defense and test the veracity of the witnesses and the documentary evidence.[59] Given the gravity of the charge against Bridges—a proceeding that threatened to remove him from the country he had lived in since his late teens—it was almost inconceivable that his lawyers would not be provided the specifics of the charges and the witnesses that the government would use to prove its case. However, when Bridges' legal defense team repeatedly asked for a bill of particulars, the government refused, offering only that the organization they would allege Bridges was affiliated with was the Communist Party of the United States.

As unearthed files from the National Archives now demonstrate, government lawyers intentionally chose not to give a bill of particulars for purely political reasons: they feared being seen as fair towards the accused, so rather than experience public criticism from the anti-Bridges quarters, they punished Bridges and denied him basic due process in the form of a bill of particulars.[60] This placed the defense at a decided disadvantage and the government at a decided advantage.

A Detour: "Impeach Secretary Perkins"

Secretary Perkins' job was complicated in the spring of 1938 when a federal appellate court in Texas, in a case entitled *United States v. Strecker*, ruled that prior membership in the Communist Party was not a basis to deport a person. *Strecker* involved a Polish immigrant who, during the Great Depression, joined the Communist Party in 1932. He paid dues for a few months, and then left the party. In 1933, he applied for citizenship and told the INS official about his brief encounter with the Communist Party. The INS's response was to deport him. Strecker appealed and the Texas federal appeals court, the Fifth Circuit Court of Appeals, strongly rebuked the government. "It seems…to be a kind of Pecksniffian righteousness, savoring strongly of hypocrisy and party bigotry, to assume and find that merely because [one] joined the Communist Party of America, he is an advocate of, or belongs to, a party which advocates the overthrow by force and violence of the government of the United States."[61]

Given *Strecker's* holding that prior membership in the Communist Party did not justify deportation, Secretary Perkins, in April

1938, had to halt Bridges' deportation case until the Supreme Court resolved the legal question. Indeed, due to *Strecker*, all deportation cases involving alleged communists were suddenly in legal limbo.[62]

The moment Secretary Perkins halted Bridges' deportation case, loud cries went up in Washington and around the country saying that Secretary Perkins had intentionally railroaded the Bridges deportation case by using the *Strecker* decision as pretext to protect Bridges.[63] Shockingly, Secretary Perkins' employee Bonham from the Pacific Northwest, who had been working with the Keegan-Knowles-Doyle axis, again joined in the efforts to undermine Secretary Perkins' decision. Specifically, Bonham telegraphed Secretary Perkins' office that in his opinion the trial should proceed.[64] When Secretary Perkins chose to wait for the Supreme Court to resolve the governing law in the *Strecker* case, Bonham leaked his telegraph into the public record. This gross act of defiance and breach of basic organizational hierarchy norms required a formal rebuke for Bonham's "excessive zeal and bad judgment" because he was too "keenly devoted to his duty as he sees it," as opposed to what the law and facts dictated.[65]

In short order, the American Legion, in May 1938, issued a national proclamation demanding that the Department of Labor continue with the deportation case. Its resolution charged Harry Bridges with "fomenting strikes," "membership in the Communist Party," and an "intention to attempt overthrow of the American Government by force." It thus demanded the "immediate prosecution" of Harry Bridges.[66]

In a remarkable twist of near comic absurdity worthy of a Peter Sellers movie, Harry Bridges, at this very time, had been asked to speak publicly in Los Angeles. While Bridges was preparing to speak, a color guard of American Legionnaires suddenly appeared at the event. Overflowing with zeal and anger, the Legionnaires marched onto the stage to joust publicly with Bridges, disrupt his speech, and charge him with un-American behavior. The Legionnaires, dressed in their full color guard uniforms adorned with medals, stepped onto the stage just as Bridges was about to speak. Interrupting the proceedings, the leading Legionnaire grabbed the microphone from Bridges and euphorically commanded, "We're going to open this meeting with the Pledge of Allegiance to the Flag! Repeat after me."

But as the excited Legionnaire started the Pledge of Allegiance, he suddenly could not remember the words and began stuttering and faltering. Bridges in turn calmly walked over to him, took the microphone, held his hand over his heart, and led the audience in the Pledge. When the audience had finished the Pledge, Bridges turned to the be-medalled Legionnaires and admonished them, "You know, when I say that pledge, it comes from here," motioning his hand over his heart.[67] Humiliated, the Legionnaire color guard left.

That public event aside, the massive public pressure did not subside. Even the *New York Times* succumbed and published an editorial calling for Secretary Perkins to proceed with the Bridges case irrespective of *Strecker*.[68] Secretary Perkins, however, refused to budge, and the case was now delayed pending the Supreme Court's ruling in the *Strecker* case of whether past membership in the Communist Party justified deportation.[69]

But while there was a lull in the case, congressional pressure against Bridges now exploded. On May 26, 1938, Martin Dies, a Democratic congressman from Texas, introduced a resolution to create the House Un-American Activities Committee (HUAC) under his leadership. Described as "physically a giant, very young, ambitious, and cocksure," Dies spoke on the House floor where he specifically commended the American Legion for endorsing HUAC's creation.[70] Indeed, HUAC was itself a federal, governmental version of the American Legion's earlier, private-sector Subversive Activities Commission chaired by Knowles.

Congressman Martin Dies (center), HUAC's leader, with Harper Knowles (left) and Rep. Joe Starnes of Mississippi. Library of Congress, Prints & Photographs Division, photography by Harris & Ewing, LC-H22-D-4804.

It is a fact nearly forgotten to history that during the House debate about whether to create HUAC, the subject of the need to create it so as to specifically target Harry Bridges arose. In particular, Representative J. Will Taylor of Tennessee railed against Harry Bridges and the too-friendly treatment he had received from Secretary Perkins, concluding in feverous rapture that, "We must preserve America for Americans. For the descendants of the heroes of Concord, Valley Forge, and Kings Mountain to fold their arms in indolence and allow this great country to be wrecked and overthrown by influences imported from Russia would be the greatest tragedy that history has yet recorded."[71]

That same day, the resolution passed, and HUAC sprang into existence to investigate subversive activities. Known interchangeably as HUAC or the Dies Committee, it was now charged with the formal mandate to unearth un-American activities in all corners of American life. In turn, the American Legion boasted that its efforts at rooting out subversive elements—chief among them Harry Bridges—decisively led to HUAC's creation.[72]

A few months later, in August 1938, HUAC opened its probe into alleged un-American activities. Out of the gate, investigators immediately started an investigation into Harry Bridges.[73] One of the first witnesses the Dies Committee called was none other than Harper Knowles, chair of the Legion's Subversive Activities Commission. Knowles testified before HUAC for three days, from October 24 to 26, 1938, and at the beginning of the very first day, Congressman Dies himself quoted the notorious Bonham telegram as evidence of lenient treatment afforded Bridges by Secretary Perkins. Knowles argued that the West Coast had become "a matter of absolute lawlessness and a reign of terror, directed by the Communist Party, as part of the Communist Party program." Knowles was permitted to read into the Congressional Record an obviously oxymoronic "indictment" issued from the private American Legion, which charged Bridges with violations of federal criminal laws.[74] HUAC also received a copy of the alleged Communist Party Membership Card in the name of Harry Dorgan.[75]

Congressional and public wrath, however, reached beyond Bridges. Quickly, Congressman Dies and HUAC charged Secretary Perkins with failing her deportation duties as secretary of labor by delaying a deportation trial until the Supreme Court decided the *Strecker* case. Secretary Perkins responded with a lengthy letter explaining the need to have Supreme Court clarity. She asked Congressman Dies to let the legal system take its course under the Constitution: "The fact that Communists are unpopular, and I agree in this, does not justify us in placing within that category every other unpopular person, nor in deporting them without a scrupulous regard for the due process of law, the clear and certain ruling of the courts and the facts in the case."[76]

But Secretary Perkins' words fell on deaf ears. As 1938 passed to 1939, Chairman Dies launched an aggressive charge of public condemnation against Secretary Perkins when he declared, "She's flirting with impeachment."[77] In short order, on January 24, 1939, Representative J. Parnell Thomas of New Jersey, a Republican HUAC member under Representative Dies, rose in the House and without any advance warning to Secretary Perkins suddenly declared the beginning of an impeachment proceeding.

"On my own responsibility as a member of the House of Representatives, I impeach Francis Perkins, secretary of labor of the United States; James Houghteling, commissioner of the Immigration and Naturalization Service of the Department of Labor; and Gerard Reilly, solicitor of the Department of Labor for high crimes and misdemeanors in violation of the Constitution and the laws of the United States," Representative Thomas declared.

Congressman Thomas further thundered that "they did willfully, unlawfully, and feloniously conspire, confederate, and agree together from on or about September 1, 1937, to and including this date, to commit offenses against the United States and to defraud the United States by failing, neglecting, and refusing to enforce the immigration laws." Congressman Thomas charged one and only one violation, namely the failure to deport Harry Bridges.[78] No other so-called "crimes" were mentioned; the entire impeachment revolved around the mandolin-playing Harry Bridges.

Representative Thomas's scathing oral remarks were followed by a fifty-six-page resolution that outlined and quoted volumes of evidence that he and other congressional representatives had been compiling, including copies of the affidavits already secured by the Knowles-Keegan-Doyle inquests, all of which purported to prove that Bridges was a communist and that Secretary Perkins was intentionally hindering the investigation. As a public and well-publicized resolution from Congress, it charged Perkins with "impertinence and want of respect for the officials of the Department of Labor," supported the Portland-Seattle immigration officials over their superiors in the Department of Labor, and quoted Captain Keegan's affidavit and similar testimony that he had by then given to HUAC.[79]

The matter was then referred to the Judiciary Committee to investigate and potentially initiate impeachment proceedings for high crimes and misdemeanors.[80] Secretary Perkins demanded public hearings so that the charges and "evidence" would be transparent to all. But the Judiciary Committee refused. Witnesses were called. "I was generally condemned for not having immediately deported Bridges," Secretary Perkins recalled. Indeed, when Representative Thomas berated Secretary Perkins in the hearings, he trembled in anger with a shaking voice.[81]

The next month, February 1939, the Supreme Court heard arguments in the *Strecker* case. From the tenor of the marathon three-day oral argument, it was clear that the Texas appellate court's *Strecker* decision would fall and so deportations of communists would resume, at least in some capacity.

Secretary Perkins defends herself before the Judiciary Committee, February 8, 1939. Library of Congress, Prints & Photographs Division, photography by Harris & Ewing, LC-H22-D-5760.

The light was now at the end of the tunnel, and the deportation case would be back on track. Having played the impeachment-threat card to pressure Secretary Perkins and to sway public opinion against her, and where the deportation case would now inevitably resume anyway given the impending *Strecker* reversal, the Judiciary Committee opted for an easy-out with a two-prong decision on March 24, 1939. The Judiciary Committee held that the evidence was insufficient to impeach Secretary Perkins—thereby averting a crisis provoked by having to prove a basis to impeach government officials for high crimes and misdemeanors—but at the same time its Republican members issued a public censure, proclaiming that Secretary Perkins had "been lenient and indulgent to Harry Bridges in the conduct of his deportation case to an unprecedented extent."[82] The censure was a clear missive aimed at Secretary Perkins' department to help ensure a vicious deportation assault on Bridges. Impeachment averted, even many years later the scars remained, as Secretary Perkins remarked on the episode: "You see in some of the members of Congress the makings of one of the most prejudiced, ignorant, irresponsible, and inattentive juries imaginable."[83]

Days later, the Supreme Court issued its decision in the *Strecker* case. The Supreme Court held that the federal deportation laws as written indeed permitted deportation where the noncitizen had a present (at the time of arrest) membership in the Communist Party and the party advocated the overthrow of the American government.[84]

Now instantly back on track, Bridges' deportation trial, the culmination of private and governmental investigations and pressure since 1934, was set for July 10, 1939.

CHAPTER 3

All Rise: The First Trial

"Even while they are tyrannical, they still claim to be humanitarian. I should regret my taking the risks of coming in the first place."

CHINESE IMMIGRANT WRITING CARVED INTO THE WALL AT ANGEL ISLAND, EARLY TWENTIETH CENTURY, DETAINED AUTHOR UNKNOWN[1]

Angel Island is a small island in the San Francisco Bay, about six miles offshore. Lush and green like the mainland, Angel Island is both significantly larger and farther offshore from San Francisco than its decidedly more famous sister, Alcatraz Island. Angel Island originally housed military arsenals and infantry garrisons, serving as a departure point for military campaigns against Native Americans in the nineteenth century. By the twentieth century, Angel Island was home to the Angel Island Immigration Station, charged with processing immigrants arriving primarily from the Far East. Known as the Ellis Island of the West Coast, in the early twentieth century over one million Chinese immigrants passed through Angel Island as their entry point into the United States, many of whom spent weeks, months, and even years detained on the island as their cases languished due to the then-existing federal Chinese Exclusion Act. This was the site selected by Secretary Perkins for the Bridges deportation trial.

Once the site was selected, the next issue Secretary Perkins had to decide was who should be the trier of fact, that is who should be the judge of Harry Bridges' fate? This itself reveals a curious aspect to the immigration justice system. In traditional federal courts under Article III of the Constitution, federal judges are selected by the president, approved by the Senate, and appointed for life within the co-equal third branch of government, the judicial branch. Generally taken from the ranks of esteemed and qualified lawyers, federal judges receive lifetime tenure to aid their independence and neutrality from the political whims of the day. Rather than have a neutral, federal judge from the co-equal judicial branch decide an immigrant's fate, however, immigrants are in the executive branch and executive-controlled court system where the executive appoints the immigration judges, who in turn decide the fate of the very people that the executive decides it wants to deport. The executive also appoints the lawyers to prosecute the deportation, but at the same time the executive does not provide a lawyer to the deportee. As circular as this may seem, it remains true, even though the Supreme Court has long held that deportation cases trigger fundamental constitutional liberty interests.[2] Although judicial branch federal courts normally adjudicate the contours of constitutional liberty rights—as stated by one of the most important, foundational constitutional opinions in American history: "it is emphatically the province and duty of the judicial department to say what the law is"—immigration cases remain in the executive's grip and executive judges decide the cases.[3] This state of affairs is as true today as it was in 1939, and it gives rise to the obvious ability to stack the deck if the political powers in the executive branch stray from the straight and narrow, or forget the cornerstone of due process: ensuring a fair, balanced hearing.

Secretary Perkins confronted a dilemma in deciding who to appoint as the judge. She believed the ranking officers within the INS in Washington were seen as pro-Bridges, while the ranking West Coast INS officials were seen as anti-Bridges. Trying to avoid controversy, she chose a distinguished and respected lawyer with, in her words, standing "such that his judgment would be beyond suspicion of possible influence."[4] Thus, Secretary Perkins settled on the dean of the Harvard Law School, James Landis, who agreed to act as the arbiter of the Harry Bridges deportation trial. Before taking the Harvard Deanship, Landis had worked extensively in the New Deal's new administrative state, where he had been a member of the Federal Trade Commission and chairman of the Securities and Exchange Commission. Referred to with his Harvard Law School title, Dean Landis was seen as a respectable, learned man, a person with extensive experience dealing with the administrative state, and a fair and balanced jurist. Indeed, Dean Landis was widely believed to be the next Supreme Court Justice.[5] Interestingly, his physical appearance matched his credentials, for his receding blond hairline sat atop a large forehead on a face with a solid chin and large protruding ears, and a boyish, square forty-year-old face that exuded calmness. His medium frame was even adorned by a sophisticated East Coast three-piece suit, a gold watch and chain dangling from the vest.

James Landis, Dean of Harvard Law School and trial examiner. Copyright San Francisco History Center, San Francisco Public Library.

Originally, the government decided the trial was to be a non-public event. But between the massive press outcry and Harry Bridges' demands for a public trial, the government abandoned a secret proceeding in favor of an open one with press access. Even after allowing access to major press outlets, other papers and journalists pressured for access, so additional press passes were provided. Seats were at a premium, as the trial generated significant public interest.[6] It appears this was the first fully public immigration hearing in American history.

Harry Bridges with daughter Jacqueline Betty (left) and attorney Carol King (right) appear for the first day of trial on July 10, 1939. Copyright San Francisco History Center, San Francisco Public Library.

On the morning of July 10, 1939, a large cast of characters convened at Pier 5 in San Francisco for the thirty-minute ferry ride to Angel Island. Harry Bridges had his fourteen-year-old daughter, Betty, with him, along with his lawyers, Carol King from New

York and Richard Gladstein and Aubrey Grossman from a local San Francisco law firm. The government had its prosecutors, including Thomas Shoemaker from Washington and Bonham from the Seattle INS office. Joined by members of the press and other attendees, they waited at Pier 5 to take the ferry to Angel Island for the first day of trial. As they all waited, the press peppered questions at everyone, including young Betty. Asked how she would handle her father being deported, Betty replied, "If they deport Daddy to Australia, it'll have to be a double deportation. I won't be left behind."[7]

While Betty and Bridges' lawyers were answering questions, Bridges quietly approached the government prosecutor, Shoemaker, freshly arrived from Washington to prosecute the case, and extended his hand. "Glad to see you, sir. I hope you'll enjoy your visit to San Francisco," Bridges offered.

Shoemaker, a tall, solid man in his late forties with shaved short hair on the side of his head and a tuft of longer hair on top, and an emerging belly in his midriff, shook Bridges' hand. Later, Shoemaker asked others to relay a message: "Tell Mr. Bridges how much I appreciate the greeting he gave me this morning. I like that sort of thing." Then, Shoemaker remarked privately, "I never have been able to understand why we can't be good sports about these things. I'm an old ball player. Got professional offers you know. Well, we used to scrap and razz each other on the field, but after the game was over we could always go out and have dinner together. Any man who couldn't wasn't worth a damn...I like a man to be a good sport and that was a sporting thing for Bridges to do."[8]

But Shoemaker's sport was Bridges' life. That Shoemaker saw the contest as a sport between men was the first sign that the prosecutor's worldview was off. Federal prosecutors work for the executive to prosecute cases, but unlike private civil litigants who essentially fight only to win, federal prosecutors are held to a different standard given their awesome power. Federal prosecutors are required to ensure justice is accomplished, and accomplishing justice is not necessarily synonymous with winning a case. The official motto and seal of the Department of Justice is *Qui Pro Domina Justitia Sequitur*, a Latin phrase that translates as, "To prosecute on behalf of Justice or Lady Justice."[9] Lady Justice in modern and ancient iconography is generally a blindfolded woman holding scales of justice. A metaphorical construct, Lady Justice connotes blind justice, which blindness affords objectivity thus providing moral force to the law. Justice is not sport. No doubt, how blind Lady Justice would be was the central question on Harry Bridges' mind as he climbed onto the ferry.

Thomas Shoemaker, lead prosecutor for the government. Copyright San Francisco History Center, San Francisco Public Library.

As the ferry arrived at Angel Island's sandy beach, the spectators and participants made their way from the pier to the makeshift courtroom located in the main immigration building. The 483-square-foot courtroom was packed, with three press tables behind the lawyers' tables. A makeshift phone and telegraph room had been built to allow the press rapid communication of the day's events to their main outlets.[10]

Once inside, Dean Landis addressed various preliminary matters including identifying the specific questions before him: Was Harry Bridges a current member of the Communist Party? If so, was the Communist Party an organization that advocated overthrow of the United States government? Then, Dean Landis fired the starting bullet: "You may proceed, Mr. Shoemaker."[11]

The Trial Begins

Shoemaker unexpectedly dispensed with an opening statement, and with lightning speed called Bridges to the stand, another unexpected move. He immediately asked whether Bridges was now or ever had been a member of the Communist Party. Bridges denied the charge. Having taken the element of surprise, and having secured Bridges' denial of Communist Party membership under penalty of perjury, Shoemaker as quickly dismissed Bridges. Given Bridges' multiple, prior sworn denials of Communist Party membership, Shoemaker's move was entirely unnecessary and instead was designed to unsettle the defense and create some theatre.[12]

However, as Shoemaker then tried to call his first government witness, Bridges' lawyer, Carol King, leapt up and took the stage, looking to launch her own fireworks. Described by the *New York Times* as a "short, stocky woman of great energy," King had short brown curly hair and thick round glasses.[13] "I would like to take this opportunity," she said, "to make an opening statement on behalf of the alien before the evidence goes any further."[14] And as Shoemaker had done to her, King now pushed Shoemaker aside and took the offensive to outline for Dean Landis her perception of what the trial was really about.

"Since 1934 Harry Bridges has been a stormy petrel around whom has raged such a storm as only the most violent labor struggles engender," King began. As she continued, she argued that the case was a classic frame-up by powerful interests: "This case is a product of employer plans and employer money." Central among them was Knowles, she alleged: "As a modern Voltaire might say, 'If there were no evidence, Knowles would find it necessary to create some.' ...They began to offer large sums of money for affidavits against Bridges. They resorted to blackmail..." Her voice rising, King then squarely alleged that the people ranged from those in the private realm to those in state government, and all the way to those in federal government. She finished with a crescendo: "The mainspring of the whole conspiracy is Larry Doyle, who has supported himself by this case for several years. It is he who does the dirty work of perjuring witnesses so [the government employees'] hands may remain clean."[15]

With that, King rested her opening, and Shoemaker was now able to call the first government witness.

The Government's Evidence from the Knowles-Keegan-Doyle Axis

Shoemaker's first witness was the spy, Major Laurence Milner of Oregon. Milner possessed a seemingly illustrious background as a World War I company captain of the 364th Infantry, and special investigator of the Military Intelligence Department of the Oregon National Guard. Also a member of the American Legion, his specific role was to go undercover and infiltrate and spy on alleged communist groups.[16]

Milner testified that he had professed his support to the Communist Party by attending meetings and donating money, and as such had grown in rank and become a trusted member of the party in the Pacific Northwest.[17] He lamented that his undercover work had cost him his friends and relationships, including his membership in the American Legion, but that he'd done it to serve the higher cause of ferreting out communists.[18] While a spy, he stated, he learned that Harry Bridges was a Communist Party member, and that, because of Bridges' importance, the party decided that Bridges should not be seen in public with known, high-ranking party members. Milner explained that he saw Bridges pay his Communist Party dues, and on several occasions drove Bridges between

Seattle and San Francisco, where communist issues were discussed with other Communist Party members. Indeed, Milner added, Bridges was known as "Comrade Bridges" within party circles. Further, Milner testified that Bridges had remarked, upon seeing military battleships in the harbor, "We will see a day when we can sink those damn things because they are the enemy of the workers." Milner also asserted that he had drafted fourteen hundred reports of his Communist Party surveillance work, and he brought seventy-seven of them to the trial, which he relied on to refresh his memory.[19]

Milner was an extremely impressive witness, whose testimony constituted solid evidence, if believed, that placed Bridges at Communist Party events and showed him to be a dues-paying formal member. Bridges' lawyers, thus, had to focus on Milner's honesty and credibility to destroy any belief Dean Landis placed in his testimony. Gladstein, a spritely man with a round head and svelte black mustache, took the reins of this cross-examination, and because of Milner's involvement with Doyle in the notorious *DeJonge* trial, his cross-examination focused on that issue.

In the *DeJonge* criminal trial, as discussed above, Milner had been a character witness for the defense. Milner testified that DeJonge was a good guy, not a communist, even though Milner fully believed DeJonge was a communist. Milner lied under oath because he wanted to protect his status as an undercover agent (certainly not to help DeJonge) and ingratiate himself with the communists he was infiltrating. During the trial, Doyle approached Milner and indicated that he knew Milner was an undercover agent but that he wanted Milner to tell the truth about DeJonge. Doyle even offered to help Milner get retirement benefits if Milner would shift his testimony. When people reported that Doyle had approached Milner, Milner told DeJonge's lawyers that Doyle had just chatted with him briefly but had not said anything significant. And Milner then went back on the stand and reiterated exactly that, swearing that Doyle had not promised him anything for testimony. DeJonge was in turn convicted and sent to prison for seven years.[20]

Now in Harry Bridges' trial, Milner immediately testified that everything he had said in the *DeJonge* trial was in fact true. When pushed about how he had lied under oath in the *DeJonge* trial, Milner asserted confusion about the events. But he then unraveled as he admitted, on cross-examination, that Doyle had indeed offered him compensation for changing his testimony, and he admitted that he had lied in the *DeJonge* trial when he denied that Doyle had promised him anything or that Doyle tried to get him to change his testimony.[21]

As Gladstein pressed, Milner became self-righteous:

"And in order to achieve your ends, you were willing to take any means, including perjury?" Gladstein asked.

"I had to do it," Milner contended.

"You did do it?" Gladstein pressed.

"I did do it, *you bet*," Milner emphatically proclaimed, proudly adding that he "lied many a time, because I was working for an outfit that did the same thing," the "outfit" being, in his mind, the Communist Party.

"To carry your work, in other words, Major, you considered a lot of things much more important than giving truthful testimony, isn't that true?" Gladstein inquired.

"I considered it my duty as a military intelligence officer to do anything to gain my purpose without being disclosed. *And I did it*," Milner proudly proclaimed.[22]

Gladstein then moved to the fourteen hundred reports Milner claimed to have. Milner testified first that he had them, but that he refused to bring them to the trial, as they were hidden in a secret location.[23] Gladstein wanted all the reports because they could contain material that Milner had recorded that in fact refuted his trial claim that Harry Bridges was a Communist Party member. But in response to the request for them, Major Milner suddenly said he did not have them.[24] Then, Shoemaker objected and vehemently argued that the records were private Oregon state records that even the federal government could not compel Oregon to disclose.[25] Dean Landis eventually sided with Shoemaker and ordered the testimony to continue without the reports. To this day, no one knows what exculpatory evidence Milner possibly secreted away in the over thirteen hundred missing reports.

Harry Bridges with lawyers Richard Gladstein (left) and Aubrey Grossman (center). Copyright San Francisco History Center, San Francisco Public Library.

As the cross-examination continued, Milner was forced to concede one other fact: As the Great Strike of 1934 unfolded, Milner had used his military training to teach union members to fight the police in street warfare. But on the day of the street violence, when two protesters employed Milner's training and were killed by the police, Milner, he nonchalantly testified, had stayed home in bed.[26]

Bridges' lawyers felt confident they had turned the tables on Shoemaker, and asked Dean Landis to issue perjury charges against Milner for his blatant lies. Agreeing, Dean Landis indicated that he was handing the file to the Department of Labor's chief counsel to assess a perjury prosecution.[27] Rather than let it rest, Shoemaker then argued at length that Milner had not lied and instead made a few minor "mis-statements," a prosecutor's lawyerly euphemism for "lied." Not impressed, Dean Landis quizzically and sarcastically shot back, "a man says no when he means yes."[28] With that, Milner's testimony was over.

Shoemaker's first witness proved a debacle for the government. By the time Milner was off the stand, he had admitted that he had perjured himself in the earlier *DeJonge* case, and it was obvious he had again perjured himself in this case when he claimed to have never lied in the *DeJonge* case. What is more, he had perjured himself so as to protect Doyle. He even firmly asserted that he had the right to perjure himself so as to serve the higher cause of being a spy. Perjury abounded.

Shaken at such a disastrous beginning to its case, the government turned to a different witness, John Leech, a man who the government contended had been a member of the Communist Party with Harry Bridges.

Leech, the Alleged Former Communist Party Member

Leech, as explained earlier, was a part-time drifter and Communist Party member originally from Los Angeles. Colorfully dressed, Leech was described as having worn a tan checkered suit with a bright orange handkerchief in the breast pocket, a pink

rosebud in his lapel, and gray and pink socks.[29] His testimony regarding Harry Bridges centered around three alleged Communist
Party meetings.

The first, in San Francisco in 1936, was attended by the Los
Angeles Communist Party delegation, which included Leech. He
testified that Bridges attended from the San Francisco delegation
and gave a speech.

Then, a few months later, Leech claimed, the delegates again
met at a second meeting to vote on the national Communist Party Central Committee candidates. At that election, Bridges was allegedly elected to the Central Committee.[30]

The third Communist Party meeting allegedly occurred in
San Francisco, and Bridges, present with others, allegedly developed
a plan to urge the repeal of certain state criminal anti-syndicalism
laws.[31]

At the time, state anti-syndicalism laws were laws that crim-
inalized conduct aimed at achieving economic or social changes
through sabotage, violence, or other such acts. Many states had such
laws in the post-World War I period, and California's Criminal Syndicalism Act of 1919 alone led to over five hundred arrests and 164
convictions within five years of its enactment.[32] After the Cold War,
most of these laws were repealed or declared unconstitutional because so many people were really being jailed for speech-related activities, although to this day California's Education Code still allows
public teachers to be fired for engaging in criminal syndicalism.[33]
In the 1930s, however, communists challenged the anti-syndicalism
laws, and so Leech's testimony, if believed, could constitute circum-
stantial evidence of Communist Party affiliation.

Although Harry Bridges later testified that he was not even
in the state on some of the days of the alleged meetings and had
never seen Leech before Leech walked into the courtroom—
thereby undermining Leech's honesty—his lawyers focused their
attack on Leech's character and credibility.[34] As developed on

cross-examination and explained above: Special Prosecutor Doyle recruited Leech in Los Angeles and moved Leech and his family to Portland; government officials promised a job for Leech based upon his testimony under oath that Bridges was a communist; Leech agreed and once ensconced in Portland gave a sworn affidavit that he knew Bridges was a communist and had seen Bridges at communist meetings; in short order, the promised job was procured for Leech.[35]

Having admitted that he traded testimony for financial support, Leech's problems on the witness stand only continued. Before he signed Doyle's affidavit, Leech had also signed an earlier affidavit proclaiming that he did not know Harry Bridges to be a Communist Party member and that Detective Browne (working under Captain Keegan) had attempted to bribe him to state Bridges was a communist. When this earlier affidavit was shown to him on cross-examination, Leech at first claimed the signature was not his. But Bridges' lawyers then called handwriting experts to the stand who testified that it was unequivocally Leech's signature, forcing Leech to then concede that he may have signed it after all.[36]

At this point, Leech had lied about his signature and had signed two affidavits saying diametrically opposite things; and Doyle had rewarded him for the one that said Harry Bridges was a Communist Party member. By the time Leech was off the stand, he seemed a dubious witness, but he had offered specific facts that tied Harry Bridges to Communist Party meetings. How Dean Landis would evaluate the testimony was anyone's guess at this point.

One clear fact, however, emerged: Special Prosecutor Doyle played the central role in procuring Leech's testimony, as he had with Milner before.

The Communist Party Membership Card

As the second week of trial began, Shoemaker sought to demonstrate that Harry Bridges was a card-carrying Communist Party member by producing the alleged "Harry Dorgan" Communist Party Membership Card. This alleged secret membership card had appeared out of thin air, via Doyle, some years earlier, and was trumpeted in the HUAC hearings. The government's theory was a convoluted one, namely that the card had been stolen from Bridges' hotel room by an unidentified associate of Doyle's while Bridges was out of the room. Delivered to Doyle, in turn Doyle gave it to Captain Keegan.[37] However, the government had no witness who could actually testify to having entered the room and taken the alleged card. In the law's terms, this is known as a "foundation" and "authentication."[38] Before a document can be accepted as evidence, it must be authenticated by someone who can explain what it is and where it came from—its chain of title, so to speak.[39] Absent such proof, a document cannot exist in the trial. Unable to prove exactly where the card came from and hence if it was even real, Shoemaker had to concede that he could not actually get the card into evidence, and so Dean Landis refused to accept it as actual evidence.[40]

The truth about the so-called "Harry Dorgan" card confounds reason. INS officials had already concluded a full year earlier, by July 1938, that the "Harry Dorgan" membership card was a forgery. Even Bonham knew. He had been told in no uncertain terms in the summer of 1938 by the INS's inspector-in-charge that the Dorgan card was not "authentic." Even Shoemaker believed the card a "phony," a fact he later told the FBI. The internal government documents that prove the government's knowledge of this remained classified until recently, and so Shoemaker's attempt to get the membership card into evidence was a knowing attempt to get forged evidence into the record.[41]

At this point, the central architect of so much "evidence," Stanley Doyle, had still not testified, but suddenly he had disappeared and gone into hiding. As the trial progressed, he was eventually found in Minnesota attending, no less, an American Legion convention.[42] Doyle was in turn served with a subpoena issued by Dean Landis at Bridges' request. Because the immigration trial occurred in an executive court, Dean Landis lacked the same subpoena power to compel witnesses to attend a hearing, the type of subpoena power that federal or state judges possess. In other words, Dean Landis could issue a subpoena but he lacked the judicial power of imprisonment that generally forces compliance. Thus, Bridges' defense team secured help from the United States Attorney's Office in Minnesota to try to force Doyle to attend trial on Angel Island. At this point, Doyle was one of those witnesses who causes defense lawyers to fight amongst themselves for the opportunity to take on the witness stand. But until Doyle could be forced to California, Bridges' legal team had to march on.

In turn, Shoemaker now shifted to a witness from the ranks of labor, a lawyer for labor unions.

Sapiro...and Al Capone

All trials, if tried well by the lawyers, have climactic moments as the story unfolds, moments where key witnesses are broken on cross-examination or where their credibility is blown apart. Well-tried cases are like stories, the evidence and arguments incrementally mount and push the viewer towards a conclusion, and, as with plots, there is often a peak moment that breaks the tension and illuminates the now-assumed, near-inevitable conclusion. Aaron Sapiro was to be that climactic witness.

Aaron Sapiro, 1939. Courtesy of ILWU, San Francisco.

Called to the stand by Shoemaker, Sapiro smoothly testified that he was a lawyer and represented the Sailors' Union in legal battles against various employers. Sapiro explained that he worked with one of Bridges' competitors, Harry Lundeberg, who was also vying for control on the West Coast. At a meeting with Bridges, Sapiro testified that Bridges claimed that he "controlled the Communist Party and the Communist Party controlled the unions in the Maritime Federation on the Pacific Coast." Sapiro also alleged that Bridges claimed that he could, through the Communist Party, "destroy any man they wanted within 24 hours." Sapiro saw this as a threat against him for supporting Bridges' adversary, Lundeberg.[43] Sapiro then testified many had told him that Bridges was a leading communist and a member of the Communist Party Central Committee.[44] Although hearsay, in immigration court the rules of evidence are lax. Thus, if Dean Landis believed either Sapiro's alleged first-hand testimony or third-hand hearsay, it could corroborate the government's central claim: direct proof that Bridges was a party member, an admission from Bridges himself coupled with consistent, albeit hearsay, third-party statements. At last, Dean Landis had heard potentially solid, and highly damning, evidence from an apparently reputable lawyer. Yet like prior witnesses, it hinged entirely on Sapiro's credibility and honesty.

Cross-examination of Sapiro began like a bomb detonating. Sapiro was immediately shown a document from a New York federal court. The document was a formal federal criminal indictment, a document common in any attorney's office. However, this indictment charged jury tampering against none other than Sapiro himself. Jury tampering for anyone, especially a lawyer, is about as serious an ethical and legal transgression as one can imagine. Lawyers represent their clients and do their best to win, but the rules and laws of the courts demand that the litigation process be played fairly. Lawyers are often referred to as "officers of the court" precisely because they have a higher obligation than the average citizen to ensure that ethical rules designed to promote the integrity of the process not be broken in pursuit of their clients' causes. For lawyers, juries are sacred, untouchable, and supposed to be impervious to any communications outside the participation of the court and all parties. So when Bridges' lawyers pounced on Sapiro with the indictment, it instantly raised massive questions about Sapiro's honesty and Shoemaker's integrity in using Sapiro as a central witness.

Remarkably, Sapiro's problems then went deeper. Bridges' lawyers next confronted Sapiro with a federal judge's court order of disbarment from the practice of law in the New York federal courts because of the jury tampering. The disbarment order bespoke a judge outraged at conduct beyond comprehension: "In other words, he [Sapiro] was content that justice should be improperly influenced, if not polluted, at its source. This, in my judgment, when one considers Sapiro's experience and intelligence, was a serious offense...To put the matter differently, bribery was suggested, if not actually offered...To my mind, this constituted nothing less than corrupt misconduct."[45]

On cross-examination, then, the evidence established that Sapiro had known of juror tampering to help get his client a favorable verdict, he hid it from the court, and the court even believed that Sapiro had been involved in juror bribing as the means of tampering. Thus, within the first few minutes, Sapiro's credibility was already in tatters.

Sapiro, the once polished, silver-tongued lawyer when testifying for the government, was now acerbic and testy, fighting with Bridges' lawyers every step of the way.[46] From the indictment/disbarment for jury tampering, Bridges' lawyers then showed Sapiro another indictment filed against him! The idea that any lawyer—but especially one posing as a witness and asking a court to take his word on a question deciding someone's fate—has had two indictments filed against him is simply astounding. Like dynamite detonating a building, this one charged Sapiro and none other than Al Capone with bombing, acid-throwing, and strike-fomenting by violence.[47] At this point, Dean Landis was certainly stunned about Sapiro's presence.

Bridges' lawyers then unmasked the fact that Sapiro had met on several occasions with the Seattle immigration officials who had worked with the Knowles-Keegan-Doyle axis. When Sapiro was shown a carbon copy of a letter he received from Captain Keegan (a document Bridges' lawyers managed to discover), Sapiro, bruised and testy, responded by objecting as if he were the trial lawyer and not the witness![48] Worn out, even Prosecutor Shoemaker did not object, and the letter was then read, a letter that made clear Sapiro was working both with Doyle and Captain Keegan.[49] Sapiro was then released as a witness.

What was unknown to the participants at the time, however, was just how far Sapiro and Captain Keegan had gone in their efforts to manufacture evidence. In the California Surveillance Archives at the J. Paul Leonard Library in San Francisco, there are folders filled with Knowles' documents about his secret spy network. Now available to the public, one such document is a secret report from an undercover spy. In that report, dated October 17, 1937, the unnamed undercover operative reported to Knowles that Captain Keegan had audio recordings of Bridges from a hotel room where Bridges apparently had an extramarital affair with a married woman. Captain Keegan in turn told Sapiro that he would give the recordings to Sapiro "if Sapiro would make an affidavit that Bridges had asked him to join the party." Sapiro would then use the recordings to represent the husband of the woman and sue Bridges for alienation of affection. Remarkably, in the same report, the undercover operative also reported that Sapiro met with federal INS officials from the Pacific Northwest in a hotel lobby, where Sapiro asked for the federal file on Bridges so he could see what missing links existed in the evidence, which links Sapiro would then fill with his own testimony.[50]

Even without access to such staggering evidence that in the 1930s remained secreted away in Knowles' secret files, Sapiro's disreputable background and obvious enmity towards Bridges were certainly, as of that day, the trial's climactic moment. After all, a lawyer who was indicted with Al Capone for bomb-making is not an everyday occurrence in any case, but such a lawyer is hardly, if ever, a central witness that the government seeks to rest the righteousness of its cause upon.

But some remarkable trials, like good books or movies, manage not simply to traverse from climax to conclusion, but instead escalate to another surprise moment of emotional intensity. And when

Bridges' defense team, now at full speed starting their defense case, called Earl King and Ernest Ramsay, new climactic peaks lingered on the horizon.

The Trial Moves to San Quentin Prison

Bridges' defense team had long centered part of their case on two witnesses for the defense, Earl King and Ernest Ramsay. King and Ramsay were leaders in the 1930s of the Marine Firemen, Oilers, Watertenders and Wipers Association (MFOW), a small maritime union that represented the ship workers who tended ship engine rooms. Given their prominent union role, they had occasion to meet Bridges in union circles.

But they also had massive criminal problems stemming from a murder case. The case started in 1936, when Chief Engineer George Alberts was murdered on his ship docked in the Alameda harbor. The California state criminal authorities indicted King and Ramsay (and others) for the murder, contending that the murder was the result of a dispute between King-Ramsay's union and Alberts over work and pay issues. Basically, the State contended, King and Ramsay sent goons to beat Alberts up. As the confrontation intensified, it spun out of control, culminating in Alberts' murder, the State contended. The King-Ramsay trial was itself one of the most sensational, highly publicized trials in San Francisco in the 1930s and seen by many as a proxy for the social battles between radical labor and entrenched power. The MFOW and the Bay Area maritime unions certainly saw the trial as one of framed prosecutions of radical labor leaders.

The King-Ramsay trial lasted three months, coincided with the 1936-37 maritime strike, and ultimately resulted in murder convictions for King and Ramsay and life sentences in the infamous San Quentin Prison. Many years later, after Harry Bridges' deportation trial, it came to light that one of the female King-Ramsay jurors had been having an affair with one of the male assistant district attorneys, and that she had lied during jury selection about her alleged absence of connections to the prosecutors. What is more, she had even loaned the assistant district attorney large sums of money during the time of the King-Ramsay trial.[51]

Stanley "Larry" Doyle, who visited Earl King and Ernest Ramsay at San Quentin Prison. Courtesy of ILWU, San Francisco.

None of the King-Ramsay trial intrigue was known to the Bridges legal defense team in 1939, however, and so they needed testimony from two convicted murderers, people who in most trials, for obvious reasons, have little credibility. The idea that convicted murderers could afford hope to Bridges was itself curious, occasioned by the remarkable fact that while incarcerated in San Quentin both King and Ramsay had received a common visitor, none other than Special Prosecutor Doyle. To secure the King-Ramsay testimony about their meeting with Doyle, the entire trial had to move from Angel Island to San Quentin.

A makeshift courtroom was established, and Dean Landis first swore King in. As King recounted, he was in his cell one day when a prison runner came and gave him a slip to go to the guard captain's office. He was surprised, as such a slip was normally for legal visitors, and although his murder conviction was on appeal he was not expecting a visit from his attorney. He made his way across the prison grounds and arrived at the captain's office. As he entered, he saw a man he had never met before waiting for him, alone. The man flashed a gold badge that read "Special Agent, State of Oregon." The man then introduced himself as Special Prosecutor Doyle.

Immediately, Doyle began talking about how he had been a union man himself in Canada, in an apparent ploy to pander to the pro-union leanings of King. Suspicious, King recounted how he too had come from Canada, but asked why Doyle had come to see him.

"How would you like to get out of here? There is a way that you might be able to get out," Doyle directly offered.

"I am always glad to hear anything once," King suspiciously replied.

"I am the man who prosecuted the *DeJonge* case. Now I want to get Mr. Bridges out of this country. I am working on Bridges and I am going to get him," Doyle boasted. "If you will help me, I have got connections. I have spoken to a number of gentlemen and if you will testify against Bridges, state that you sat in top fraction meetings of the Communist Party at places and times I can give you—I will give you the addresses and dates—we will get you to come up to Oregon. We will have a hearing behind closed doors. If you will testify to that, your testimony will be very convincing and it will be clinching and we can deport him. If you will do that, I have spoken to Earl Warren [the governor] and the lieutenant governor, and we will give you a parole to Canada."

"Well, let's hear the rest of it. Suppose I don't?" King replied.

"Well, if you don't, you are going to be in a tough spot. If you don't we are going to hang another murder on you in case you win your appeal," Doyle declared. "Your best bet is to do as we want you to do, to testify against Bridges and go on up to Oregon. I am working very closely with the Immigration Department in Oregon. If you do this for us, why, the gentleman I mentioned will speak on your behalf and will get you a parole to Canada," Doyle asserted.

"Well, I can give you my answer right now," King angrily retorted.

"Well, don't do it. Think it over awhile," Doyle angled.

"It won't make any difference how long I think it over. The answer will still be the same. The answer is no," King guaranteed.

"What is the matter with you? Are you crazy?" Doyle asked.

"Well, I don't know; I don't think so," King answered.

"Don't you know what you are facing if you don't do as I ask you?" Doyle threatened.

"Quite possibly, yes," King honestly answered, no doubt aware of the grave consequences he could face. "If you want, I can explain why I won't do it."

In the makeshift prison courtroom, King then emotionally explained what he had said to Doyle at the prison meeting. "Well, I am about 45 years of age. I have been to a lot of places, and done near pretty much everything I wanted to do, had a good time, had good friends," he began.

"Nobody can make me perjure myself. I am not going to lie against Harry Bridges just to get out of here. I don't care what happens to me now. I only got my self-respect left; I am going to keep that. Nobody is going to take that away," King offered, sobbing as he broke down in tears on the stand.

As King started crying, Dean Landis ordered a five-minute break, recognizing the emotional impact of the events and King's veracity. The convicted murderer King was unwilling to trade Bridges' life for his freedom, insistent that all he had left was one part of his basic human dignity—his word—and that he would not sell his dignity and self-respect even to buy his freedom. The subsequent trial transcripts as recorded by the official stenographer poignantly note at this point, "Witness visibly moved and sobbed audibly."[52]

In turn, Ramsay offered the same factual testimony as King, having himself also received Doyle as a visitor with Doyle offering clemency for positive testimony, but pinned murder convictions for any refusal to cooperate.[53]

Despite cross-examination, neither King nor Ramsay were tripped up, and Doyle's tactics were exposed. Only Doyle could rebut the King-Ramsay testimony, but still Doyle refused to attend the trial. And as King and Ramsay returned to their prison cells, the trial returned to Angel Island. But the toll was also affecting Bridges, who developed ulcers due to the stress and was reduced to eating baby food to soothe his inflamed stomach.[54]

Back to Angel Island: Garfield King

Carol King and Richard Gladstein did not want to rest entirely on the testimony of convicted murderers for claims that Doyle would probably deny, so they also called Garfield King to the stand. Garfield King was Earl King's brother and a reputable Canadian barrister. Remarkably, as Garfield would explain, he too had experienced American governmental pressure to corral his brother Earl into fingering Bridges as a communist. But, unlike Earl, who was pressured by Oregon state official Doyle, Garfield experienced federal official Bonham's advances in Vancouver, Canada.

In particular, Bonham told Garfield that there appeared to be some doubt as to the guilt of Earl King. This immediately interested Garfield. Yet Bonham then took an ominous turn: "If Garfield King would advise his brother to furnish evidence, or affidavit that Harry Bridges was a member of the Communist Party, he, Mr. Bonham, could possibly use his influence to secure Earl King a pardon."[55]

Raphael Bonham, INS division chief of the Pacific Northwest, July 13, 1939. Copyright San Francisco History Center, San Francisco Public Library.

Garfield's testimony was gripping. Bonham, seated in the prosecutor's chair, listened intently as Garfield testified how Bonham in fact believed Earl King may be innocent, but wanted Garfield to use his lawyerly skills to convince his brother Earl to finger Bridges, at which point Bonham would aid the release of the apparently innocent King. This now tied federal officials into the practice of offering rewards for testimony, and in massively unseemly circumstances no less. As Garfield testified, Bonham was surely squirming inside. Yet when Garfield finished testifying, Bonham remained quiet. In fact, the government lawyers did not even attempt to dispute on cross-examination Garfield King's testimony about Bonham's advances.[56]

The entire event left Dean Landis incredulous. "[W]ithholding action that might release an assumedly innocent man from jail unless he produced certain testimony," Dean Landis stated, was part of a "devious and unusual" ploy.[57] As experienced trial lawyers, Carol King and Richard Gladstein certainly felt better about their case now that the King-Ramsay escapades had come to light. At full speed, yet still unable to get Doyle to the trial, they now turned to the original architect of the long-standing campaign, Harper Knowles.

Harper Knowles and the American Legion

Harry Bridges' lawyers had long focused on Harper Knowles as part of the central conspiracy to paint Harry Bridges as a Communist Party member. As head of the American Legion's Subversive Activities Commission, Knowles had long lobbied the government to deport Bridges through his HUAC appearances and letter-writing campaign. Now Bridges' lawyers sought to tie Knowles to Doyle and other government officials to establish the connected hubs of the broad campaign against Bridges. Of course, the remarkable evidence of undercover informants and Keegan-Sapiro deals remained buried in Knowles' secret files, as discussed above, and so was not available to the defense lawyers in the 1930s. King and Gladstein then had to make the case with whatever evidence they could muster.

In his late thirties and dapper, Knowles had slicked-back hair with a slight widow's peak. As he took the stand, he explained that his duties for the American Legion involved collecting information on subversive movements and people. Communists and people with perceived communistic tendencies were the major focus of the Legion's watchful eye. Once a person was identified as possessing communist tendencies, the Legion would then watch and track the person.[58] Under Knowles' control, the Legion had hundreds of informants generating data on thousands of people. These informants were, in essence, labor spies. Knowles could even secure official state driver's licenses with fictitious names for his undercover spies.[59] Before the era of computers, this large volume of data collected by

Knowles was indexed in an internal, complex cross-referenced file system.[60] Knowles controlled this database and would share the information with both state and federal officials as well as private industry, but when pressed on the stand he refused to tell Bridges' lawyers the location of his database.[61]

Knowles admitted he knew Doyle and had become friends with him.[62] Doyle in turn gave Knowles reports on Harry Bridges, but when asked where the reports were located, Knowles again refused to say.[63] Doyle even admitted to Knowles that he knew Sapiro and discussed the Bridges case with the now-infamous Sapiro.[64] As Bridges' lawyers pushed this Knowles-Doyle-Sapiro connection, Knowles explained that Doyle interviewed a witness to secure evidence against Harry Bridges in a conversation that remarkably, and eerily, mentioned the "King frame up."[65] Then one day, Doyle procured a Communist Party Membership Book in the name of "Harry Dorgan," claiming to Knowles that it was Harry Bridges' secret Communist Party Membership Book.[66] Eventually, Knowles admitted that he, Doyle, and INS official Bonham met together to discuss the evidence against Harry Bridges.[67]

As Gladstein's examination of Knowles continued, the pressure began to intensify. Gladstein surprised Knowles with a copy of a letter that Doyle had sent Knowles, in which Doyle said he was getting ready for a new "set up." Knowles at first professed ignorance about the letter and what the "set up" referred to, but Gladstein did not let go.

"Does that mean that they might have told you that they had a 'set up' to work on the Bridges case…Is that your answer?"

Knowles refused to answer, so Gladstein again demanded, "Will you please answer the question?"

"This is a question difficult to answer, I think," Knowles cagily offered.

Frustrated, Dean Landis then took over and asked if the "set up" related to Harry Bridges, to which Knowles finally admitted "it possibly could." Dean Landis, now questioning Knowles himself in an effort to get to the truth of this "set up," asked if Knowles had "an idea as to what the setup is?"

"Very hazy," Knowles sheepishly answered.

"Very hazy?" Dean Landis responded in amazement.

"I don't know," Knowles evasively offered.

"But you do remember what it is?" Dean Landis asked.

"No," Knowles offered, now shifting positions again.

At this point, Dean Landis almost jumped out of his chair. "Curious! Curious discrimination there! I am afraid I don't gather your use of the English language. You are willing to say you don't know what it is, but still you have ideas as to what it was."[68] That the "set up" referred to the Harry Bridges case was clear from the cagey exchange; that the same witness mentioned the "King frame up," where King was serving life for a murder he contended had been pinned on him, only added to the suspicion circling around Knowles and Doyle.

Broken, Knowles finally admitted that it was possible that Doyle offered another witness money to swear an affidavit against Harry Bridges.[69]

In all, Knowles spent over three days on the witness stand as Bridges' lawyers poked and prodded his testimony in their effort to show Dean Landis both that Knowles had a long-standing agenda in conjunction with private economic interests, and that Knowles fed government agencies material to advance the prosecution against Bridges. By the time Knowles was off the stand, no one knew exactly how Dean Landis would view the totality of Knowles' testimony, although his expressed frustration at Knowles' intentional caginess over the "set up" references was certainly a tea leaf all were trying to read.

Captain Keegan

After Knowles, Bridges' legal team needed to tie a government official into the broad campaign against Bridges. Milner had been one spoke tied to Special Prosecutor Doyle, but Milner's involvement had been limited in time, and Doyle was still refusing to attend as a witness. Bridges' lawyers needed to show deeper, root government involvement in the quest against Bridges. Confronting that issue, Gladstein called Captain Keegan of the Portland police to the stand.

Captain Keegan was a good ol' boy in the pejorative sense, a man whose English was often sub-par, as he was routinely oblivious to proper tenses. As chief detective of the Portland police, Captain Keegan was another of Doyle's friends. Captain Keegan testified that he assigned one of his underlings and fellow Legionnaire, Detective Browne, to find evidence of Bridges' Communist Party involvement. Dutifully, Browne set off with Doyle to California, and the duo secured the Leech affidavit already discussed.[70] Then, Doyle and Browne, with Captain Keegan's knowledge, placed a bugging device (a dictaphone) in Bridges' hotel room in Portland while Bridges was visiting the city.[71] The wiretapping yielded nothing for the deportation case.

As Gladstein pressed Keegan, the thrust of Bridges' defense theory became clear. Captain Keegan, in Portland, Oregon, was sending his detectives to Los Angeles to look for evidence that Bridges was a Communist Party member. Captain Keegan would not tell the LAPD he was sending his men down there. Nor did he share his findings with the LAPD. Instead, he shared them with the INS in Oregon and Washington, even though the Portland police had no jurisdiction over federal deportation matters.[72] He did not even share the findings with the San Francisco INS, which was in Harry Bridges' backyard. Similarly, Captain Keegan would investigate in

San Francisco without notifying the SFPD. In fact, Captain Keegan even used Portland city money to pay none other than Aaron Sapiro to travel to Portland to give statements against Bridges.[73] And in his zeal, Captain Keegan had even investigated Bridges for alleged adultery, a quintessentially local issue for Bridges' home city or state, if at all.[74] Eventually, as the Portland police's role in the evidence quest unraveled, Captain Keegan admitted that he had been instructed by the chief of police to cooperate with private Legionnaire Knowles "to the fullest extent."[75]

A private-public partnership, emanating from the Pacific Northwest and built along the Knowles-Keegan-Doyle axis, had now emerged. But whether any of this mattered to Dean Landis was anyone's guess. After all, if under the law Harry Bridges was a Communist Party member, then he could be deported. The motivations of the forces against him could well be coordinated and ill, but those forces could also be correct on the ultimate factual question confronting Dean Landis. Demonstrating that the evidence was weak and the product of ill motivation was one approach to defending the case, but not necessarily enough to win. To truly win, Harry Bridges had to now carry his own water and prove that he was indeed not a Communist Party member. Remarkably, in this long trial over Bridges' fate, which had consumed almost two months, Harry Bridges had not yet even told his life story. Nor had Dean Landis' glaring eyes assessed Bridges' credibility. But now, at last, on the heels of evidence of coordinated public and private efforts, Bridges' turn to testify arrived, his chance to convince everyone that he was not a Communist Party member.

Harry Bridges Testifies

Bridges shared his life story, his active trade unionism from his teenage days in Australia, and his perception that Australia's union movement was ahead of the United States, causing him to be seen here as too progressive. He explained that fundamentally his only concern was better conditions for his men and protecting labor. "I get a little irritated when my views are ascribed to the Communist Party, because I had them before the Communist Party came into being," he said, referring to his early days in the labor movement in Australia.[76]

Harry Bridges testifies. Copyright San Francisco History Center, San Francisco Public Library.

Indeed, he argued, he lacked the grand political vision of a mass takeover of American democracy. Why? Because he was too concerned with the difficult details of work and wages to worry about such macro issues: "We have enough trouble on our hands at this time even getting the right to organize, the right to recognition, the right to have our trade unions, or even to get a 10-cent-an-hour increase in wages."[77]

Bridges' narrative was pretty simple. The waterfront working conditions were abhorrent—Shape Ups, Speed Ups, insufficient living wages, dangerous working conditions, kickbacks, and terror—and he wanted answers to these basic, day-to-day problems that he and the longshoremen confronted, not grand theoretical answers to political problems of a national orientation. He said of the Communist Party: "As far as I have delved into them they are pretty much a matter of theory, and our hands are full with practical matters…I generally stay with the practical matters."[78]

Bridges continued: "There is no one, when it comes to the best policy of the longshoremen on the waterfront, that knows more about what is best for us than we ourselves. It is ridiculous and not intelligent to believe that we would go to anybody that practices theory to ask them about such things. We are the experts on the waterfront; there are none better."[79]

Bridges' testimony was positive, if Dean Landis believed it. The government's case now hanging in the balance, Shoemaker's last chance was to break Bridges on the stand in cross-examination.

As Shoemaker began, Bridges had to admit that he willingly accepted help in his pursuit of union justice, regardless of where the help came from and even if it came from communists. In particular, Bridges conceded that he gladly accepted help from the communist publication *Western Worker*, and even encouraged people to subscribe because the paper was pro-union and supported his efforts. Indeed, the paper along with a Catholic paper were the only papers that published pro-union stories during the Great Strike of 1934, so he gladly accepted whatever help he could get.[80]

As Shoemaker marched on, he methodically focused on Bridges' personal and professional relationships. Bridges had to admit that he had many friends and associates who were bona fide communists. And at times, he conceded, he had actively sought the help of the Communist Party when it would advocate for labor's goals.[81]

Shoemaker then surprised Bridges with evidence that Bridges had been to the Communist Party headquarters before. But Shoemaker's surprise quickly unraveled as Bridges turned the tables on Shoemaker: "I specifically recall another meeting and that was at the time of the riots on the waterfront, where there were some two hundred or three hundred people shot, gassed, and clubbed, and we were moving them to hospitals, and here and there. A lot of our people were at [the Communist Party headquarters], that being a kind of hospital...There is a large room up there and there were some hundred people laying on the floor, generally pretty well beaten up or shot, and a lot of our fellows were among them."[82]

In short, the Communist Party headquarters had been a makeshift hospital to handle victims of the police abuse during the Great Strike of 1934. Harry Bridges' presence there showed his basic humanity, not nefarious communist activities.

Finally, Shoemaker came around to Bridges' political beliefs. Bridges was an open book and did not play the evasive game of Knowles or Keegan. Bridges readily admitted that his political convictions were essentially Marxist in nature, believing that the government should take ownership of the major means of production in society. He candidly asserted that he believed government would mismanage the assets, but no more than private enterprise. While Shoemaker was thrilled that he had scored some points on the major issue of ideology, Bridges then explained that all this theoretical talk was of no particular interest to him, because in the present he had too many far more mundane issues to attend to: "It seems to me that it might be all very well to talk about [government ownership of means of production], but before we can get to the point where we can talk about it…[I am focused on] getting 5 cents or 10 cents an hour a day more…I am not concerned with that. I believe it will be thirty or forty years hence, and I do not think I will be around. There are plenty of things to be done today…simple recognition of trade unions…"[83]

Indeed, Bridges further explained that in reality he thought the Communist Party was engaged in folly, because the existing capitalist system was too strong to ever be broken by a bunch of philosophical communists. As such, Bridges believed that their aims were so fantastical that the government should not even dignify their efforts with suppression.[84]

Bridges then starkly testified to his pragmatic philosophy about the rights of workers against the power of corporations: "The chain stores and the big corporations are spreading all the time and engulfing and eliminating the small businessman, generally known as the middle class…these large corporations are getting control of everything…I think you will probably have about 30,000,000 people on relief…and the big corporations will deny them relief. But they won't answer the question 'Are they going to starve to death?' They will say, 'It is none of our business. We are sorry, but it is none of our business.' It is our business in the trade unions to do something about it. It is a condition before us and we have to do something about it. I cannot ignore it. This is a struggle between the two classes…The only thing I see to do about it right now is to organize the trade unions and we will head off a little bit of it."[85]

As Shoemaker then tried to categorize the Great Strike of 1934 as a Communist Party power move with bloodshed caused by Harry Bridges, it was Harry Bridges who shot back, again angry but clear and practical:

"I have never run into one union worker yet that started this use of tear gas, of police clubs, or anything like that. It is always started by the employers, or their *provocateurs*. Never once have I found a group of workers that relished the idea of running up against guns, and the police line, the National Guard or anything else. Today in every section of the country, there are people being shot down, not for revolutionary activity, but because they are trying to strike and picket and get increased wages."[86]

On that note, Bridges' testimony about his political beliefs ended. After three grueling days of cross-examination, of explaining his political, practical, and philosophical beliefs, Bridges' testimony was finally over, and with it the trial too, for all practical purposes, was over.[87]

Had Shoemaker scored some points? No doubt. Harry Bridges could not avoid the fact that his political beliefs could fairly be labeled Marxist. He advocated political and economic positions that certainly lined up closely to the Communist Party. He admitted friendly relations with many well-known Communist Party members. He had sought help from the Communist Party when it helped his labor cause. But did the evidence prove that he was in fact an official Communist Party member? Harry Bridges' fate now hung on how Dean Landis would see the evidence on that specific question.

But Where Is Doyle?

The nagging Doyle issue had still not been resolved. Eventually located and subject to legal proceedings to force him back to California, Doyle announced that he would not attend unless he was provided witness compensation.[88] Then, on September 13, 1939, Doyle finally arrived in San Francisco with a lawyer. By then, however, the trial had ended, and Dean Landis had returned to Harvard. Thus, a deputy examiner was appointed to take Doyle's testimony in a deposition setting in downtown San Francisco.

As Doyle arrived with a lawyer to represent him, he refused to take the stand unless he received his witness fees, travel fees, and compensation for lost income. The deputy examiner and Doyle's lawyer fought about whether Doyle should receive compensation, and if so, how much. After half a day arguing about it, the deputy examiner required Bridges to pay Doyle $131.00. A check for $131.00 was handed to Doyle.[89]

Doyle was then sworn in. But before Gladstein could even ask a question, Doyle immediately insisted that he receive assurance the check would not bounce. When Gladstein promised funds were there to protect it, Doyle's lawyer then jumped up and explained that Doyle would not answer any questions! Exasperated, everyone started arguing, and Doyle explained that he had insisted that he be paid his witness fees to attend and take the stand, but not to testify. Now Doyle claimed he would not testify because the hearing was in a private deposition setting instead of the trial setting. Doyle, in short, demanded that he have the same public setting that every other witness had, a setting he knew was not available because he had refused to attend when the trial was actually occurring.[90]

Angered, Gladstein insisted he answer questions or return the check. But Doyle refused to return the check (having sneakily secured the promise it would not bounce) and refused to answer questions. The deputy examiner, confused and frustrated, instructed Doyle to testify, but Doyle refused, arguing it was his right to insist on the same "setting" other witnesses received. Bridges' lawyers then decided to go before the local federal judge to get an order compelling Doyle to testify.[91]

The parties raced to the local federal judge to explain the situation. That same day, the federal judge issued an order that required Doyle to testify. A few hours later, they returned to the deputy examiner, who then asked Doyle to take the stand and testify. Doyle took the stand, but the circus antics began anew. Doyle again refused to testify, arguing that he was entitled to more money for his witness fees and lost income. Doyle claimed that the federal judge, hours earlier, had indicated that Doyle should be paid all his claimed fees, not just $131.00, but that the judge had accidentally forgot to put it in the order. The deputy examiner again could not get Doyle to testify, and so the parties went back to the federal judge to address the money issue. But the federal judge could not be found, so Doyle steadfastly refused to testify until he received more money.[92]

Tempers flared, and Bridges' lawyers exploded at the ongoing charade. "I think it ought to be clear in everybody's minds that Mr. Doyle is not here with any intention to testify…He is not here for the purpose of giving full and complete testimony as the order requires…We are not going to give Mr. Doyle a single cent until he has taken the stand and testified fully and completely…He has lied about everything," Gladstein charged.[93]

"You are a cockeyed liar! I am not going to be called a liar by a 'commie,'" Doyle yelled, accusing Gladstein of being a communist.

As Gladstein tried to speak, Doyle interrupted: "Just a moment! I want to beg your pardon for telling that 'commie' what I think he is."[94]

The proceeding devolved into a shouting match between the lawyers. After arguing for one full day and half of the next, Doyle had erected constant procedural reasons not to testify. The net result: One of the leading anti-Bridges crusaders had to be dragged halfway across the country under subpoena, but was still entirely unwilling to testify. This was Doyle's chance to prove the Harry Dorgan card was really stolen from Bridges' hotel room, but he refused to make such a statement under penalty of perjury. Ultimately, unable to get the federal judge reinvolved, the deputy examiner simply gave up, finding the financial and procedural demands of the acerbic lawyer Doyle too much.

Technically, then, the last words uttered in the trial were when the deputy examiner turned to Shoemaker and asked whether, since Doyle was present in court and had been a government agent,

Shoemaker wished to call Doyle as a government witness instead. Shoemaker curtly responded, "I don't think under the circumstances...that I care to call Mr. Doyle." With those words, the Harry Bridges deportation trial finally ended.[95]

In many ways, Doyle's silence and the government's refusal to call Doyle as a witness encapsulated much of the larger issues at play. A powerful ending for Bridges' side, Doyle's recalcitrant silence was deafening, an obvious marker for the government's realization that by now Doyle—a state official and one of the original architects of the campaign to prove Bridges was a communist—would only damage the government's case even more if allowed to testify.

During the eleven-week trial, the government in all called thirty-two witnesses. Bridges called twenty-seven witnesses for his defense. Many of the witnesses were experts on the issues of communist ideology, Marxism and Leninism, the Communist Party of America, and whether the Communist Party of America sought the overthrow of the American government. Many others were character witnesses or minor factual witnesses offering uncorroborated assertions, often hearsay, that they had reason to believe Harry Bridges was a Communist Party member because of various interactions. One witness even arrived at court with a gun, to everyone's amazement. None of the other witnesses, however, offered the government any real evidence beyond the central evidence from the Knowles-Keegan-Doyle axis and the Sapiro story; and none of Bridges' other witnesses did anything other than corroborate Bridges' central contention that he was not a Communist Party member, as well as vouch for his good character. When finished, the transcript was a staggering 7,724 pages long with 274 exhibits.[96] The matter was finally in Dean Landis' hands to decide.

The Verdict

Dean Landis spent several months analyzing the record, and issued a 150-page written decision on December 28, 1939. The central legal issue before Dean Landis was whether Bridges was presently a Communist Party member. On that issue, Dean Landis decided that the government had failed to prove its deportation case. Harry Bridges won!

Fundamentally, Dean Landis rejected almost all of the government's witnesses because he simply could not believe their testimony. For example, Dean Landis completely rejected the government's very first witness, the perjurer Milner. Even years later in his memoirs, Dean Landis recalled how in the first three solid days of testimony, the government had not managed to give him any evidence: "Well, I was disappointed in these three days of trial, not being able to have even an iota of proof in three days."[97]

Dean Landis then addressed Sapiro in his decision, and was nothing short of appalled: "Something more than the word of a disbarred and repudiated attorney seems required to carry such a burden of proof."[98] Remarkably, over twenty-five years later, when Dean Landis gave his oral memoirs, he discussed the Sapiro testimony and recalled it vividly, the brutal cross-examination of Sapiro seared into his memory. Sapiro's "direct stuff wasn't very good. Then they opened up on him in cross. The cross-examination went substantially like this: Mr. Sapiro, were you a member of the New York Bar? Yes. Are you now a member of the New York Bar? No. Were you disbarred? Yes...Did you become a member of the Illinois Bar? Yes. And were you at one time indicted? Yes. And was the indictment for racketeering? Yes. Were these some of your co-defendants and they went down the line, Al Capone..."[99]

That Dean Landis had such recall of the event decades later demonstrated just how profound the impact had been on him at the time. Lawyers and judges see many witnesses and many trials in the course of their careers, and inevitably with the passage of time many of the details are forgotten. But truly remarkable trial experiences remain imprinted, as had the government's failed effort to use Sapiro to deport Harry Bridges.

Dean Landis also methodically dissected the Knowles-Keegan-Doyle axis and the evidence, rejecting on credibility grounds almost all of it. He found that Knowles, Keegan, and Leech all had massive credibility problems, and all had worked with Doyle, who was now known to be entirely unscrupulous, so much so that he used every procedural argument a lawyer could mount to avoid exposing himself to testifying under oath. Dean Landis also found Knowles to have lied under oath: "He was neither a candid nor a forthright witness. His memory tended too frequently to become beclouded when answers might have proven to be revealing."[100] As to Captain Keegan, he found, albeit reluctantly, that a high-ranking government official was equally untrustworthy: "To question the testimony of such a significant law enforcement official as Keegan is a serious matter; but the conclusion is inescapable that his testimony is far from reliable."[101] And as to Leech, Landis concluded that he was "afflicted with verbal hemophilia. It seemed impossible for him to ever answer straight-forward questions simply."[102] In short, Dean Landis outlined a public-private partnership, one where the architects of the evidence were willing to lie in court to achieve their agenda.[103]

Finally, Dean Landis scrutinized Harry Bridges' testimony, finding that Bridges was a practical trade-unionist, too consumed with securing basic rights for his men to be concerned about a grand communistic agenda. Ultimately, Dean Landis found that Bridges lacked formal ties to the Communist Party, was willing to accept their help when he could, but also rejected their help when it clashed with his union aims. In short, Dean Landis found Harry

Bridges was neither affiliated with nor a member of the Communist Party of America.[104]

Secretary Perkins accepted Dean Landis' findings, did not appeal, and canceled the deportation warrant. "This report contains a complete analysis of the issue involved and of the testimony presented at the hearing," Secretary Perkins found. "The trial examiner's analysis of the testimony given by the witnesses and his evaluation of it is clear and comprehensive," she concluded.[105]

Bridges and his lawyers were ecstatic. Gladstein, whom Doyle had attacked as a "commie," publicly praised Dean Landis for having the courage to vindicate Bridges, given the hostile environment.[106] However, unbeknownst to Bridges or his lawyers, the government had not given up. Someone in the government had watched the trial attendees and compiled a list of the suspected Communist Party members who attended the trial. In particular, in the National Archives in San Bruno, California, there is a typed document created by an unnamed "inspector-in-charge" dated September 13, 1939, identifying a lengthy list of fifty-nine suspected communists attending the trial. Bridges' lawyers were placed on that list—King, Gladstein, and Grossman perched at the top—something that would come back to haunt them and Harry Bridges in future days, although at the time none of them knew such a list existed.[107]

Ignorance is bliss, and with 1939 coming to a close, Bridges told reporters: "I have long desired to become an American citizen. Now that the obstacles have been cleared away, I shall seek naturalization at the earliest opportunity."[108] Vindicated, he could now enter the new decade and at last become a citizen and move on with his life, right? Not so, as it turns out.

CHAPTER 4

Reloaded: Take Two

"It is dangerous to be right in matters on which the established authorities are wrong."

VOLTAIRE, *THE AGE OF LOUIS XIV* (1751)

As 1939 passed to 1940, Harry Bridges filled out his application for citizenship, submitted it, and waited. But in the smoke-filled corridors of Washington, D.C., many shared a different New Year's resolution as 1939 gave way to 1940: Rewrite the immigration laws to target Harry Bridges. Indeed, on December 30, 1939, a mere two days after Dean Landis issued his decision, senators in Congress decried the ruling and argued that Harry Bridges should still be deported.[1]

Changing the Immigration Laws

Within months, Representative Leonard Allen of Louisiana had introduced a bill that directly targeted Harry Bridges. Known as House Resolution (H.R.) 9766, the proposed bill stated: "That notwithstanding any other provision of law, the Attorney General be, and is hereby, authorized and directed to take into custody forthwith and deport forthwith to Australia, the country of which he is a citizen or subject, Harry Renton Bridges, whose presence in this country the Congress deems hurtful."[2] Unprecedented, the bill targeted one person, Harry Bridges, for arrest and immediate deportation. Not as unprecedented, this bill was originally sponsored by the American Legion, which had not given up the quest against Bridges.[3]

Because the bill targeted one person, it raised immediate questions under the Constitution, which prohibits what are known as bills of attainder. A bill of attainder is a law that directs the punishment of a specific person. The Constitution's framers prohibited bills of attainder because they sought to avoid trial by legislature and instead wanted trials to be within the judicial branch. For the Constitution's framers, thus, precluding bills of attainder served a separation of powers purpose by safeguarding against politically driven legislative excesses.[4]

Bridges decried the House's bill as unconstitutional. Although he demanded a hearing before any law was enacted that automatically deported him, Congress refused to grant him a hearing.[5] Instead, Representative Allen took his bill to the floor of the Congress for debate and vote on June 13, 1940.

As the debate on the House floor began, the political rhetoric was instantly acidic. Representative William Colmer from Mississippi decried Bridges as un-American: "He has not comported himself in the manner that has met with the approval of American citizens generally. He has been a disturbing factor and ought to be deported from this country…having aligned himself with the communistic element within the country, he has not comported himself with proper respect for the institutions of our country and its government."[6]

Representative Colmer then went further and argued that even if Harry Bridges was a citizen, he should be interned. As he finished, the House erupted in applause.[7]

Representative Dies, head of HUAC, then sarcastically argued that the bill was constitutional because deporting Bridges imposed no punishment on him at all. "I do not think that it can be justly said that the deportation of Harry Bridges constitutes punishment. He has shown that he does not appreciate the hospitality which America has extended to him as a guest. He has shown that he does not believe in our form of government…In view of this attitude, it should be a favor to Mr. Bridges to get him out of the country that he does not like."[8]

Then, in the middle of the debate, one congressman proposed an amendment to tighten the bill's noose: eliminate any right of habeas corpus for Harry Bridges such that he would have no conceivable basis to seek judicial branch help against the illegal bill of attainder.[9] In short, the amendment proposed to exempt Harry Bridges from the Constitution's protection.

Another congressman simply proposed sending Bridges to his death by returning him to the British Commonwealth to join the front lines in the raging war against the Nazis: "The British government, of which Harry Bridges is a subject, can use him to good advantage in the fighting lines…"[10]

Passing the baton, Representative Thomas Ford of California next argued that the bill deporting Harry Bridges was designed to "make America safe for Americans," a sentiment that yielded more applause from the House floor.[11]

Even many opponents of the bill were quick to demonstrate their disdain for Bridges and communists while still arguing for fair procedures. "I am not here defending communists and I want that clearly understood...I am only appealing to your sense of justice that a man ought to have his day in court and he should be given a hearing," argued Representative Samuel Dickstein of New York. As he finished his remarks, no applause emanated from the House.[12]

Some strongly supported Bridges, arguing that a bill deporting one man without even a hearing was unprecedented in American immigration law.[13] Yet, when Representative Vito Marcantonio tried to read into the record a letter written by Harry Bridges himself, suddenly other congressmen objected to Bridges' written defense even becoming part of the congressional record.[14] After multiple objections and arguments, Representative Marcantonio eventually managed to read Bridges' letter into the record.[15]

By the end of debate on June 13, 1940, the House voted overwhelmingly, 330-42, to adopt as law H.R. 9766, fitted with the amendment eliminating any habeas corpus right for Bridges. As passed, the bill mandated that Harry Bridges immediately be deported without any further hearing, notwithstanding his vindication before Dean Landis.

This was a massive event in the arc of the Bridges deportation trials. By now, the complex private and local state government enterprise masterminded by Knowles, Doyle, and Keegan had generated the impetus for the first trial. And although the trial failed, those actors had oiled the machinery and started the wheels of the United States government turning. Once in motion, the need for the complex intrigue of private and local officials was significantly reduced, if not eliminated. In this sense, although the Knowles-Keegan-Doyle axis failed in the first deportation trial, its architects succeeded in beginning the process they desired. House Bill 9766 was testament to their success, and federal officials were now in charge and singularly focused on the enterprise to deport Bridges. This is not to say that private actors were entirely muted, for they were not, as will be seen shortly, but never again were they to enjoy such a central role in the enterprise.

To become law, H.R. 9766 had to survive the Senate and then President Roosevelt's veto power. Legal scholars generally saw the bill as an unconstitutional bill of attainder, as did Attorney General Robert Jackson.[16] But it was an election year, and Harry Bridges was extremely unpopular. President Roosevelt, thus, did not want to be forced to veto the bill given the political headwinds, so the attorney general raced to find a political compromise. Any compromise would have to be a facially neutral law to avoid bill of attainder problems, but also expand the immigration law to facilitate a new prosecution of Bridges to satiate the House. In short, if H.R. 9766 could be dropped in favor of a different law that could deport Bridges, one that did not name him literally and personally, then Jackson could head off the need to have the president veto a clearly popular bill.[17]

This sent everyone back to existing immigration law and the Supreme Court's recent *Strecker* decision. *Strecker* had narrowed the ability of the government to deport communists, because it ruled that, under the extant immigration statutes, the government could deport only people who were current Communist Party members at the time of arrest. Thus, even if the person had been an admitted Communist Party member, but had repudiated such beliefs before arrest, then the prosecution was legally infirm.[18] Because of *Strecker*, Dean Landis had analyzed the question of whether Bridges was a Communist Party member in the 1938 time frame. Accordingly, Jackson and others in Congress sought to amend the immigration statutes to allow the government to deport a person who had *ever at any time* been a member of or affiliated with the Communist Party.

This was the compromise that could still satiate the House and allow Jackson to kill the unconstitutional H.R. 9766 bill of attainder. Sponsored by Representative Howard Smith of Virginia, this new immigration law would not mention Bridges personally, but would allow for Bridges to be rearrested and retried. The new law allowed deportation of any alien who "at the time of entering the United States, or...at any time thereafter" was a member of or affiliated with the Communist Party.[19] This law would not be vetoed by President Roosevelt. Attorney General Jackson, in charge of the Department of Justice and any prosecution, would in turn enlist J. Edgar Hoover and the FBI to manage all investigatory efforts regarding Bridges. And Jackson promised senators that he would appoint a judge "of real judicial stature and experience," implying (to the senators he was coddling, at least) that he would get a judge unlikely to land where Dean Landis had.[20]

On June 22, 1940, the new bill passed the House, 382-4, with Representative Smith cementing the eponymously named Smith Act's aim at Harry Bridges, even if Bridges was no longer mentioned by name in the law: "It is my joy to announce that this bill...changes the law so that the Department of Justice should have little trouble in deporting Harry Bridges."[21] The Senate in turn approved it, and President Roosevelt signed it into law on June 28, 1940.[22]

But changing the scope of the deportation laws alone would not necessarily guarantee Bridges' conviction and appease the congressional forces who wanted Bridges deported. Rather, legal changes to eliminate Secretary Perkins from the equation were also demanded. Specifically, President Roosevelt asked Congress in May 1940 to transfer the INS from the Department of Labor to the Department of Justice.[23] Although the shift was justified as necessary for national security on the eve of World War II, President Roosevelt had, only months earlier, already submitted a governmental reorganization plan that lacked this shift. However, that was before Dean Landis' December 1939 decision.[24] By May 1940, after Dean Landis' decision, there was a growing unhappy chorus in Congress regarding Secretary Perkins' handling of communist deportation cases. Removing Secretary Perkins' control over immigration and granting it to the Department of Justice, aided by the FBI, would appease Congress.[25]

Congress was eager to accept. For example, on May 22, 1940, while the INS's potential shift from Labor to Justice was pending before the Senate, Senator Robert Reynolds argued that the transfer should be approved in conjunction with the amendments to immigration law, specifically to afford a renewed attack on Harry Bridges, especially in light of the participation of J. Edgar Hoover's FBI.[26] Similarly, on May 27, 1940, Representative John Taber took to the House floor and demanded that the reorganization occur so as to remove Secretary Perkins and the Department of Labor from the immigration equation: "We are going to vote for this reorganization plan because the president has not the patriotism nor the courage to remove the secretary of labor, a notorious incompetent, and one who for the last seven years has steadily and steadfastly failed and refused to enforce the immigration law, and continuously admitted and kept here those who were not entitled to stay."[27]

In short order, the new change was enacted as law, now placing the INS under the control of the attorney general and the investigative arm of the FBI.[28] Secretary Perkins was forever removed from the equation, her role in the deportation saga officially concluded. This legal change—one that transferred deportation hearings from the Department of Labor, which addressed immigration through a labor prism, to the Department of Justice, which necessarily addressed issues through a harsher criminal justice prism—would have consequences for decades to come, consequences that are felt to this day.

Groundwork for the New Trial

The national immigration laws now doubly amended in August 1940, Attorney General Jackson ordered J. Edgar Hoover to investigate Harry Bridges.[29] This investigation was so important to

J. Edgar Hoover that he traveled to San Francisco to oversee personally the investigation's launch.[30] At the same time, Hoover demanded that the FBI receive broader wiretapping powers over subversives
and aliens. Jackson approved Hoover's request for those suspected
of subversive activities against the United States, especially aliens.[31]

After a multi-month investigation, J. Edgar Hoover delivered
his confidential report to Attorney General Jackson, in late 1940. At
the same time, before the attorney general could publicly review or
act on the investigation, Hoover told the press that "beyond a doubt
Bridges is a Red" and that the investigation confirmed "Bridges is
a communist."[32] Although presumably Jackson would have ordered
the new trial anyway, given the converging pressures of Congress
and Hoover's FBI, Hoover's preemptive press announcement was
designed to fan the public flames to ensure that the prosecution indeed would move forward. The Department of Justice, in turn, on
February 14, 1941, issued a new arrest warrant, with a trial set for a
mere six weeks later, on March 31, 1941.[33]

The FBI also had Bridges' lawyers in its crosshairs. In late
1940, J. Edgar Hoover sent a then-secret letter to the deputy director of the FBI instructing that in the event of any national emergency, Richard Gladstein should be arrested and placed in "custodial
detention."[34] Gladstein, of course, was oblivious to such a directive,
but was soon to experience the governmental and public scorn saved
for lawyers who defended alleged communists.

With Attorney General Robert Jackson in charge, this time
the Justice Department appointed the trial examiner. Eschewing the
approach of Secretary Perkins, to find a jurist who would appear
neutral and unbiased to all, Attorney General Jackson appointed
an old friend of his, a New York state judge named Charles Sears.[35]
Judge Sears had long served in the New York trial courts and for one
year on the New York Court of Appeals in Buffalo and had been a
Republican delegate to the New York State Constitutional Convention earlier in his career.

With only six weeks to prepare a defense, Bridges asked Judge Sears for an extension. The FBI and INS investigators had spent many months, if not years, preparing their case. Judge Sears denied Bridges' request, finding six weeks ample time to prepare a defense.[36] This is itself the first fingerprint of a judge who has strayed from an unscrupulous focus on basic fairness. It would not be the last. Unable to find child care arrangements on such short notice, Bridges' lead trial lawyer, the single mother Carol King, simply withdrew her teenage son from school and brought him to California from her home in New York for the months of trial.[37] As with the first trial, King was again joined by Gladstein and Grossman from San Francisco.

Judge Sears commenced the hearings on March 31, 1941, in the Federal Building in downtown San Francisco. Unlike the Angel Island hearings, this time the FBI and uniformed Immigration Border Patrol agents blanketed the building.[38]

The Second Trial Begins

Not surprisingly, the government adopted an entirely new strategy the second time around. First, the government called in new trial lawyers from the Department of Justice. Its lead lawyer was Albert Del Guercio, a man who boasted, accurately yet bizarrely, that he looked like Benito Mussolini.[39] Second, recognizing that Bridges' defense theory in the first case had succeeded, Del Guercio now sought to present a case based on all new witnesses. Part of Del Guercio's approach involved eliminating reliance on, and much reference to, the American Legion and other private interests. With a whole new roster of witnesses, the second offensive began.

The government had one major foundation to its case: witness testimony tying Harry Bridges to Communist Party events. Specifically, the government relied principally on testimony from Harry Lundeberg, one of Bridges' rival unionists, and James O'Neil, an alleged former Communist Party member. None of the witnesses had any connection to Knowles, Doyle, or Keegan, although Lundeberg had worked with Sapiro.

Prosecutor Del Guercio Begins

Like Shoemaker in the first trial, Del Guercio sought to start the trial by immediately calling Bridges to the stand. This time, King was prepared, and the moment Del Guercio made his move, King leapt up and objected and had a lengthy legal brief ready to challenge the government's right to engage in this strategy. Once that issue was resolved, the government began calling its witnesses in earnest.

Prosecutor Del Guercio, the man in charge of the second deportation trial. Copyright San Francisco History Center, San Francisco Public Library.

The Rival Harry Lundeberg

Born in Sweden in 1901, Harry Lundeberg had traveled the world as a sailor. Blond and blue-eyed with a crescent moon chin and small button nose, Lundeberg rose through a rival union, the Sailors' Union of the Pacific, which was also trying to secure some power on the waterfront for their sailors.[40]

Lundeberg's testimony about Bridges' alleged Communist Party ties, as elicited by Del Guercio, centered around an alleged dinner party at Bridges' home sometime in 1935. Lundeberg explained that at Bridges' home he met Sam Darcy, who was a high-ranking Communist Party official. But when Del Guercio asked Lundeberg to explain who said what at the dinner party, Lundeberg testified, "Well, I don't remember the details."[41]

Unsatisfied, Del Guercio pushed him again. This time, Lundeberg testified that Darcy asked him to join the Communist Party, to which Bridges allegedly interjected, "You don't have to be afraid because nobody has to know you are a member of the Communist Party if you join."[42]

Still unsatisfied, Del Guercio again asked Lundeberg what Bridges had said. Now Lundeberg offered the most dramatic version yet in his rendition of the alleged dinner party events, testifying that Bridges admitted, "You don't have to be afraid because I am one too."[43] If believed, Lundeberg's testimony was a devastating admission by Bridges that he was in fact a Communist Party member.

But when Gladstein took the podium to cross-examine, he probably had a lawyer's sense that something was amiss. For example, Gladstein knew that Lundeberg had long been an enemy of Bridges. Yet Lundeberg never testified in the first trial to these remarkable events that amounted to admissions of Communist Party membership. And Gladstein also knew that the FBI had left no stone unturned, so this evidence, if true, should have been identified earlier—indeed trumpeted in the HUAC hearings. Moreover, Lundeberg's story on the witness stand had evolved in the space of minutes at Del Guercio's prodding.

Harry Lundeberg, whose testimony against Bridges evolved while on the witness stand. Copyright San Francisco History Center, San Francisco Public Library.

Of course, Gladstein could work only with the information he and his investigators had uncovered about Lundeberg. That material did not include the FBI's investigative reports or interviews with Lundeberg. But Del Guercio had those files. And those FBI files, now uncovered decades later, show that as early as August 1940 the FBI knew that Lundeberg was "very bitter towards Bridges and would like to get him out of the labor movement."[44] Yet the government not only refused to give Bridges' lawyers these files—despite their express request—but even told Judge Sears that it did not possess such documents. This is remarkable, because those interviews directly bore on Lundeberg's bias against the accused, and thus centrally revolved around basic fairness to allow Lundeberg's honesty to be tested in open court. Without them, Gladstein confronted the Herculean task of trying to convince the hostile Lundeberg to admit he hated Bridges.[45]

Without the secret evidence of Lundeberg's admitted bias, Gladstein started cautiously. He began on the issue of Lundeberg's bias, safer ground to spar with the witness on, until he developed a sense for Lundeberg's strength under cross-examination. Gladstein wanted to prove that Lundeberg harbored a clear bias against Bridges, because that would undermine the credibility of Lundeberg's seemingly fantastic, evolving tale of the dinner party. Thus, Gladstein first established that Lundeberg was an AFL man, the enemy union to the CIO, which housed Bridges' union. In that capacity, Lundeberg had strategically ordered a strike on a ship to trigger the firing of Bridges' longshoremen.[46] Lundeberg also then admitted that he had numerous trade union disputes with Bridges because they each saw union matters differently.[47]

When pressed on their differences during the Great Strike of 1934, Lundeberg abjectly refused to credit Bridges with success for the strike's outcome, as if Bridges was a mere footnote to the events: "As a matter of fact, if it hadn't been for the Teamsters we would not have won the strike in 1934; they are the ones that won the strike for us." Finally, Gladstein proved that Lundeberg was a known, rabid anti-communist. This raised the curious question of why Bridges, assuming he had secret Communist Party membership, would encourage a rival unionist to join the very party that his rival publicly vilified.[48] By now, Gladstein demonstrated that Lundeberg harbored a bias, rendering his testimony somewhat dubious. But because he had been denied access to documentary proof, he had not clearly established the true depth of Lundeberg's bias.

Gladstein then circled back to the key testimony, the alleged dinner party admission. As Gladstein peeled away at the tidbit of testimony that Lundeberg had offered when questioned by Del Guercio, Lundeberg suddenly sounded a little vague about the events, given the profound significance of them:

"Who was present when this discussion took place?"

"Only me and Bridges and Darcy."

"In what room of the house?"

"Oh, I don't know, I guess it was the kitchen, I can't recall."

"Before or after supper?"

"Well I guess it was—I don't know whether it was before or after. It was during that night when we were there talking."

"When you came into the house you say you didn't bring anybody to the house with you?"

"Not that I remember."

"Where were you at the time the invitation [to dinner] was extended?"

"I don't know. It must have been around the waterfront somewhere, probably around the Sailors' Union Hall."[49]

Lundeberg's vague memory then sparked Gladstein to begin a new line of questioning:

"Have you ever told anybody about this?"

"Oh, I have mentioned that from time to time."

"This particular admission, Mr. Lundeberg?"

"Oh, I mentioned it to a lot of sailors from time to time."

"All right, who is the first person you mentioned it to?"

"Oh, I can't remember whom I have mentioned it to."[50]

Gladstein knew he was onto something: Bridges admits to his rival that he is a Communist Party member, and the rival tells a few unknown sailors, but can't remember the name of even one of them? It was too fantastic to believe, given the serious nature of the alleged admission, and so Gladstein had the lawyer's sense to know that the testimony sounded fishy.

So Gladstein pushed harder about which government agents Lundeberg had spoken to and what had been said. Lundeberg first admitted that he had spoken to none other than Prosecutor Shoemaker during the first trial in 1939, but he had not told Shoemaker this stunning alleged admission.[51] Lundeberg then admitted that he had spoken to the FBI for half an hour in 1940, but again he had not told the FBI either.[52] He then admitted that he met with the government prosecutor, Del Guercio, in early 1941, and yet again he had not said anything to Del Guercio at this third encounter.[53]

Gladstein knew this did not add up, so he pressed to find out where and how this alleged dinner party admission suddenly appeared in Lundeberg's meetings with government agents. And as Gladstein pressed, Lundeberg finally admitted that he had gone to see Del Guercio a mere twelve hours before his current testimony!

Gladstein certainly now had the adrenaline rush of a lawyer cross-examining a witness and smelling blood. Lundeberg admitted that the night before Del Guercio was angry at him for avoiding government subpoenas. Del Guercio asked Lundeberg if he thought he could "get by with playing around with the United States government and not answer." Del Guercio then instructed him: "You have got to go and testify tomorrow or else you might get into trouble with the law."[54] Facing apparent government threats the night before he was to testify, Lundeberg then, for the first time ever, suddenly told government agents about the alleged admission at the dinner party.[55]

By the time Gladstein's cross-examination ended, Lundeberg had admitted that he had been interviewed by Shoemaker in the first trial, by the FBI repeatedly (and at length), and by Del Guercio ahead of the second trial, and in all of those interviews—all of which focused on one issue: was Bridges a Communist Party member?—Lundeberg never once mentioned his supposed dinner meeting where Bridges made the alleged monumental confession. Instead, the first time Lundeberg ever mentioned the event to the government investigators or lawyers was the very night before he took the witness stand, while experiencing Del Guercio's pressure. Gladstein took his seat, no doubt thrilled that he had destroyed Lundeberg's credibility, even establishing that his testimony may have been falsely concocted due to Del Guercio's pressure against the witness.

When Del Guercio returned to the podium for redirect, he confronted a tactical decision that confronts trial lawyers with collapsed witnesses: do you seek to put the pieces back together again and risk it reimploding, making the disaster even worse, or do you opt for containment to minimize the damage? Either choice is risky. The former, if it fails, only highlights and reconfirms the disastrous testimony, but if it succeeds, can save the day. The latter approach potentially implies to the judge either that you know there is a problem with your witness, or, the lawyer hopes, that there is no problem and the issue is not even worth discussing. Del Guercio chose the latter and made no attempt to rehabilitate Lundeberg on the alleged confession or refute the now-exposed pressure he had brought to bear on Lundeberg.[56] With that, Lundeberg was excused. Gladstein and the entire defense team surely thought they had won that round, but no one knew if Judge Sears agreed.

James D. O'Neil

James D. O'Neil was perhaps the most confounding, indeed megalomanic, witness in all twenty years of the Harry Bridges deportation trials. Drawn from the broadcasting and newspaper ranks and wearing flimsy, thin-framed oval glasses above his bulbous nose and thick, fatty neck, he was a radio broadcaster who came to work as an editor for a San Francisco labor paper. By his account, the Maritime Federation Executive Board was meeting to pick a new editor for the Voice of the Federation paper on a New Year's Eve in the 1930s, when he suddenly appeared at the board meeting, typed up his qualifications on the spot with one of their typewriters, and secured the job over the two qualified, finalist candidates under consideration that day. O'Neil later claimed that the Communist Party became angry at him because he had too much influence over Harry Bridges, so he withdrew from the Communist Party, leaving it "0 to 0 in the last of the 9th as far as I was concerned."[57] There is no evidence the Communist Party, on the other hand, even cared enough about O'Neil to keep score.

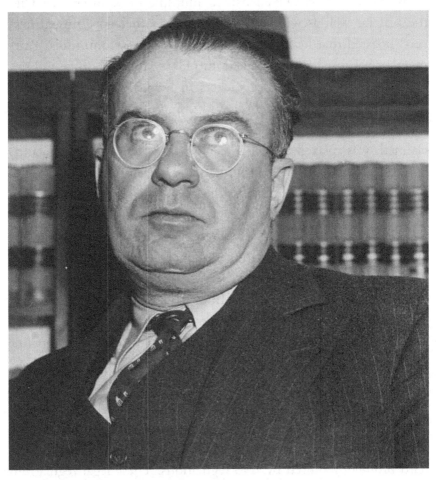

James O'Neil, witness against Harry Bridges. The Board of Immigration Appeals concluded he played the role of Judas and Ananias. Courtesy of ILWU, San Francisco.

Prosecutor Del Guercio called O'Neil as a witness to offer testimony that Harry Bridges was a Communist Party member, but O'Neil was a disaster from the start. Once on the stand, O'Neil immediately testified that he had *no* knowledge of Harry Bridges being a Communist Party member and claimed he had never told the government that he knew Harry Bridges to be a Communist Party member.[58]

Del Guercio was incensed. Del Guercio alleged, and it appears probably true, that O'Neil had in multiple prior interviews with the FBI (as well as with Del Guercio and other government lawyers) boasted that he knew Harry Bridges was a Communist Party member because he once walked into Harry Bridges' office and saw Harry Bridges pasting dues stickers in his little Communist Party Membership Book in 1937. Witnessing this, O'Neil claimed he told Bridges, "You goddamn fool! You are nuts." But Bridges, he claimed, was relaxed with his feet on the desk and nonchalantly continued pasting stickers in his book. A megalomaniac to the end, O'Neil thus boasted that he was the only living person who had visual evidence that Harry Bridges was a Communist Party member.[59]

Then, after O'Neil left these government interviews, he claimed that he told Harry Bridges of the FBI's questioning, but said he offered no damaging evidence. Allegedly, Harry Bridges then offered O'Neil a job on the Harry Bridges Legal Defense Committee. O'Neil then called the FBI and, recounting the job offer, offered to play the double-agent spy role for the FBI by providing a "pipeline to all of the activities transpiring in regard to the [Harry Bridges] Defense Fund."[60]

Yet none of O'Neil's alleged statements to the FBI investigators, made no less with INS lawyers present and spanning several meetings, were recorded in an affidavit for him to sign, the standard protocol required by INS regulations. These legal regulations required that such evidence be recorded and signed under penalty of perjury if it was ever to be used to establish such facts in a hearing.

Inexplicably, the government failed to do so, and when O'Neil suddenly asserted on the stand that he had never made such statements, Del Guercio's case became an evidentiary mess because he lacked a written, signed statement that he could use to impeach O'Neil.[61]

Panicked, Del Guercio sought to prove O'Neil had really made the statements, and so he called government witnesses from those meetings to the stand, including one of the trial lawyers for the government in the very deportation trial under way, as well as a stenographer. The government lawyer who testified was Lemuel Schofield, one of the trial lawyers working with Del Guercio. Schofield testified that O'Neil had made the statements about witnessing Harry Bridges pasting stickers in a Communist Party Membership Book. Schofield reiterated that O'Neil had claimed to be the only living person with visual evidence of this fact. O'Neil then told Schofield, and others, that he would not testify because the consequences could be too severe for him.[62] In turn, the young stenographer who had taken notes of the alleged meeting corroborated what O'Neil had said to the government investigators.[63] But O'Neil denied making the statement.

No doubt nervous that O'Neil had abandoned his prior story, Del Guercio thrashed around and suddenly switched to an aggressive, dramatic attack against Bridges' lawyers. Del Guercio insisted that O'Neil had told him that Gladstein was a top-ranking Communist Party member. Even if true, it was totally irrelevant: Gladstein was an American citizen, had every right to be a member of the Communist Party, and was not on trial.

Incensed, Del Guercio glared at Gladstein and grunted, "Huh, you don't deny it do you?"

"I certainly do. And you are a fool!" Gladstein angrily retorted.

Del Guercio, apparently then in a low breath, cursed or insulted Gladstein, at which point Gladstein demanded he say it out loud.

With the bravado of a kid in a playground fight, Del Guercio charged, "You heard me!"[64]

Del Guercio's decision to attack publicly the accused's lawyers—to justify Bridges' deportation because of Gladstein's alleged political beliefs—was a specific embodiment of the general overarching directive from the FBI and government to place lawyer-citizens on watchlists and even to arrest and detain them in the event of a national emergency, irrespective of whether the individual had even committed a crime.

Judge Sears quickly regained control of the proceedings, did not punish or reprimand Del Guercio, and turned O'Neil over to Gladstein for cross-examination. But Gladstein was clearly caught off-guard by O'Neil's alleged statements to the FBI about the alleged dues sticker incident. Despite a quick effort to try to show that the FBI had made the whole thing up, it appeared more likely than not that O'Neil had made those grand statements to government investigators. It was hard to believe that the government had offered perjured testimony about the prior statements, down to convincing a female stenographer to perjure herself, knowing that O'Neil, hardly a heavyweight witness in any event, would never agree to the statements at trial. Concerned and cautious himself, Gladstein did not question O'Neil for more than a few minutes and quickly sat down.[65]

Gladstein recognized that the battle lines with O'Neil would have to be drawn around the sheer absurdity of his claims, which, if O'Neil had made them, also meant that he was an admitted perjurer before Judge Sears (when he now denied saying them), itself heavily damaging to his credibility. Accordingly, the two embedded questions for Judge Sears became whether O'Neil really had made such earlier statements (despite under penalty of perjury denying them) and, more importantly, even if O'Neil did make such statements, what does a trier of fact make of his amazing story? How Judge Sears would assess these questions was anyone's guess, but his extreme laxness regarding Del Guercio's demeanor was certainly concerning to Bridges' lawyers.

Maurice Cannalonga and Alleged
FBI Intimidation

The government also called Maurice Cannalonga as a former Communist Party member, someone who was supposed to testify that he had seen Harry Bridges at Communist Party meetings. Olive-skinned, with dark oval eyes and a thick mop of wavy black hair, Cannalonga looked like a Godfather-in-training, wearing a black double-breasted suit with a black shirt, black vest, and a black tie adorned with bright white polka dots. Even his thick horn-rimmed glasses were fashionably black.

As Cannalonga began, he testified that in 1937 he had been at Communist Party meetings where Harry Bridges had been present, and in 1940 he signed an affidavit for the FBI attesting to these facts.[66]

Maurice Cannalonga, who testified to FBI pressure in 1941. Courtesy of ILWU, San Francisco.

However, almost immediately thereafter, Cannalonga collapsed as a witness. In response to Del Guercio's own questions, Cannalonga suddenly said that he had in fact been threatened by the FBI. Still further, he testified that the government had offered to pay his expenses as well as sending him to the World's Fair, all if he would testify. In turn, Del Guercio manically, if not comically, tried to resuscitate Cannalonga. In one exchange, Del Guercio asked Cannalonga if his statement that Harry Bridges had been at Communist Party events was voluntarily made. Cannalonga's remarkable response: "Yes and no."[67] For a trial lawyer, Cannalonga's testimony is the equivalent of a pilot's controls suddenly freezing up.

As Del Guercio pushed to resuscitate Cannalonga, his testimony only unraveled further, because Cannalonga now testified that he had given a declaration in 1937 stating that the government had pressured him to put Harry Bridges at Communist Party events, indeed that the government had essentially bribed him, but that he had refused to say Harry Bridges was a Communist Party member.[68] Thus, his 1940 affidavit for Del Guercio was fatally at odds with prior, sworn affidavits, and Cannalonga clearly believed he had been pressured, if not bribed, by the FBI. As Cannalonga left the courthouse, a cigarette dangling from his mouth, Bridges' lawyers certainly felt they had won that round, too.

Bridges Testifies Again

As in the first trial, Bridges testified and explained that his political beliefs were focused on helping the union, not grand communistic designs, and that the "communist" charge was one leveled against all the union men simply because they dared strike: "[T]he entire strike leadership, and practically the entire rank and file on strike, were attacked as communists. So the accusation of being a communist doesn't, or at that time didn't, mean a great deal to any of us. It was passed off as a little more employers' propaganda."[69]

Bridges contended that the "communist" charge was really demeaning because it implied the longshoremen lacked the intelligence to recognize a bad situation and seek remedial help through a labor union organization, as if they were hoodwinked into wanting decent wages, safe working conditions, and the right to organize by way of a political game orchestrated by the Communist Party. "The government has tried, in my opinion, to infer that the entire union, in effect, during 1934 was taking communist support and that, therefore, for that reason and others that are offered by the government it was a communist strike instead of a bona fide fight for trade union conditions," Bridges said.[70]

Del Guercio, however, aggressively tried to paint Bridges' views as official Communist Party ones, sparking verbal battles with Bridges:

"You had received orders from the Communist Party to support this strike...isn't that what happened?" Del Guercio barked.

"You are just a fool," Bridges boldly retorted.

"Did you also state 'the striking workers should know that they have demonstrated solidarity'?" Del Guercio demanded.

"They have to," Bridges explained.

"You got that from the "Communist Manifesto"—solidarity—didn't you?" Del Guercio argued, trying to say that Bridges' utterance of the word "solidarity" proved he was a communist because only communists used the word.

When Del Guercio made the "solidarity" charge, all the people in the court, spectators included, broke into laughter at the sheer absurdity of the idea that anyone who used the word "solidarity" must be a closet communist.[71]

Harry Bridges testifies in May 1941. Copyright San Francisco History Center, San Francisco Public Library.

Del Guercio's demeaning, angry, near petulant attitude ran through his entire examination of Bridges, during which he constantly played sophomoric word games in attempts to paint Bridges as a dangerous communist. For example, when Bridges testified that his uncle in Australia was elected to the Australian Parliament on a non-communist ticket, Del Guercio sarcastically quipped, "A black sheep."[72] Or when Bridges testified that during the Great Strike he gladly accepted positive press for his case from the local communist paper because it was one of only two papers that reported the strikers' side of things, Del Guercio suddenly argued that Bridges was, by his court testimony, now soliciting subscriptions to communist papers, thereby proving his communist stripes.[73] On another occasion, Del Guercio attacked Bridges for not doing any "manual work" and, instead, "living off the union," seemingly oblivious to the fact that Bridges had always lived modestly, never earning more than the highest paid union worker.[74] Del Guercio even made a point of asking Bridges who knew more communists, Bridges or Del Guercio, an obviously grandstanding question.[75]

Del Guercio's toxicity even drew Judge Sears' admonishment, yet even then Del Guercio remained defiantly demeaning:

"Don't scold the witness," Judge Sears warned Del Guercio.

"Sir?" Del Guercio replied.

"Don't scold him," Judge Sears reiterated.

"He couldn't be scolded by me," Del Guercio began. "I am just a…well, I am not a 'big shot.'"[76]

By the time Del Guercio was done, he had spent three days questioning Bridges. But the gist of his argument boiled down to one basic syllogism: Harry Bridges supported the Great Strike of 1934 and accepted advertising and moral support from the Communist Party; the Communist Party supported the Great Strike of 1934 and provided help to the strikers; therefore Harry Bridges was a member of the Communist Party. Encapsulating this issue, Del Guercio asked:

"Now, did you oppose a general strike?"

"No, I was for it."

"You were for it?"

"Yes."

"Was the Communist Party for a general strike?"

"I think it was," Bridges answered.[77] Of course, the fact that all people have two eyes and the fact that dogs also have two eyes does not make a person a dog. But the viability of Del Guercio's argument now lay in Judge Sears' hands.

The Trial Ends

By the time the ten-week trial was over, dozens of witnesses had testified, all new and distinct from the first trial, hundreds of exhibits had been admitted, and the transcript was a blistering 7,546 pages long. How Del Guercio's caustic zeal would play before Judge Sears was up in the air.

From the defense's perspective, although the government had used a new roster of witnesses, much of its strategy remained the same. Witness intimidation and threats again ran rampant, the defense argued, as seen with Cannalonga. Whereas in the first trial, the bribes and threats came from state government officials (Doyle-Keegan), now federal officials and the FBI were at the center of alleged improprieties—threats and possible bribing (Cannalonga)—coupled with biased witnesses and witnesses such as O'Neil and Lundeberg, each of whom offered diametrically opposite stories. And whereas in the first trial, the government relied upon biased witnesses from the private American Legion, now the government resorted to biased witnesses closer to Bridges' home. Ultimately, while Bridges' lawyer Carol King thought Judge Sears would reach the same result as Dean Landis, she also saw such venom in Del Guercio and Schofield that she feared this would not be the end of the line for Bridges even if he won.[78] Everything now rested in Judge Sears' hands.

The FBI Wiretaps Bridges' Hotel Room

After the parties rested, Bridges went to New York on union business, a regular destination in July and August 1941 for his repeat union business trips. Each time, he stayed at the same hotel, but soon noticed that he was always given the same room, Room 1027. Feeling suspicious, he asked for a different room, but the hotel manager evasively told him none were available. Back in Room 1027 once again, he investigated a number of oddities. He looked under the crack in the door between his room and the room next door, Room 1025. He saw wires and equipment that he believed were bugging equipment. Industrious, he then secured some binoculars and went to the roof of the hotel across the street. Room 1025's windows were open, and inside he saw wiretapping equipment and several men wearing earphones. Bridges rented a room at that new hotel and again watched Room 1025.

For fun, Bridges placed a prearranged bogus call to a friend to have an urgent meeting with the "Big One" at the corner drugstore fifteen minutes hence. He then left his hotel room and ducked into a phone booth across the street and watched the FBI men from Room 1025 come charging out. He then went to the drugstore, sat at the counter, and ordered a milkshake. In due course, the FBI agents came into the drugstore and took a seat, as Harry Bridges sat smiling and drinking a milkshake.[79]

Bridges then invited press contacts to his new hotel room across the street from Room 1025 and they too witnessed men in Room 1025 with earphones and wiretapping equipment. Bridges then went back to Room 1027 and inside the room he found a strange object attached to the phone wires. He reported this to the hotel manager, and then heard the occupants of Room 1025 suddenly closing up. He went out into the hallway, but the Room 1025 occupants had fled. One of the press photographers managed to take a photograph of the back of a man hurriedly leaving Room 1025. After forcing his way into Room 1025, Bridges saw wiretapping equipment, wires, hoses, and some carbon paper that read "Evelle Younger, Special Agent." It turns out that Evelle Younger was indeed an FBI agent who later became a member of the Office of Strategic Services (OSS), the precursor agency to the CIA.[80]

Fun and games aside, Bridges' lawyers went back to Judge Sears to report the illegal wiretaps and assess whether the FBI had also intercepted Bridges' privileged conversations with his lawyers during the trial. The government argued that post-trial events were irrelevant. But it noticeably did not provide evidence that it never wiretapped Bridges.[81]

Judge Sears agreed with the government and found that even if the government illegally wiretapped, there was no evidence that the wiretapping occurred before or during the hearing. In short, anything that happened after the hearing was not his business, even if it violated the law: "The mere showing of subsequent violation of Communications Law does not warrant an investigation."[82] Judge Sears' decision was the legal version of an ostrich sticking its head in the sand, willfully oblivious to the events on the ground.

Unbeknownst to any of the participants at the time, however, and now known only because FBI files have been declassified, J. Edgar Hoover personally signed an affidavit under penalty of perjury claiming the FBI had never engaged in any wiretapping, and the FBI's Assistant Director E.J. Connelley signed the same affidavit.[83] However, government lawyers, in preparing their defense, sent a memo to Hoover indicating that they did not want to use his declaration and would try to win in other ways.[84] When the dots are connected, it seems that Hoover lied in his declaration, the government lawyers knew it, and they were concerned about submitting such a document to Judge Sears. After all, as well as mounting the legal arguments they did raise—namely, that the wiretapping was irrelevant because it was post-hearing—there is no better defense than the facts—specifically, to offer the FBI director's factual statement categorically denying the acts. Recognizing that if discovery began into the events, Hoover's affidavit would likely be shown to be false (because there were too many witnesses), the lawyers wisely aimed for the technical legal defense only and avoided the facts. But history now shows that Hoover and Connelley willingly signed an affidavit that, given the facts, appears completely false. In true cloak-and-dagger fashion, Hoover demanded the return of the original, signed affidavits, which he in turn ordered his secretary to: "Place in safe to be held for me. H."[85] Of course, the pregnant question is whether illegal wiretapping occurred before or during the hearing, as a flex of the powers Attorney General Jackson had given Hoover in 1940, with the mandate to ferret out subversives. History has not yet definitively answered that question one way or the other.

But at that time, none of this was known. Secured away in Hoover's safe, the documents would not see the light of day for generations. And just as Judge Sears refused to look into the FBI's conduct, he issued his verdict.

The Verdict

Judge Sears issued a lengthy opinion on September 26, 1941. Unlike Dean Landis' decision that first addressed whether there was evidence of Harry Bridges' connection to the Communist Party, Judge Sears spent the first eighty pages of his opinion establishing that the Communist Party was a menace.[86] This itself spelled trouble for Bridges, because Dean Landis' approach is the logical one. If on the narrow factual question Bridges was not a member, then there was no need to address the more complex policy question of whether the Communist Party advocated overthrow of the American government. So when Judge Sears addressed that question first, it implied analytically that he would then find a path to justify the conclusion Bridges was a Communist Party member. And, in turn, Judge Sears concluded that indeed Harry Bridges was a Communist Party member and was affiliated with the Communist Party, and so he ordered Harry Bridges deported.[87]

Judge Sears' decision rested entirely on O'Neil's and Lundeberg's testimonies. Remarkably, Judge Sears rejected many of the government's other witnesses as lacking credibility. That is, Judge Sears, like Dean Landis before him, found that the government put numerous other witnesses on the stand who were inherently unbelievable—liars. Judge Sears failed to address how Lundeberg and O'Neil could so readily be believed, given this remarkable finding that the government regularly offered lying witnesses.

As to O'Neil, Judge Sears believed that O'Neil's testimony given to the INS and FBI indeed occurred, and that his testimony at this trial, denying the alleged prior statements, was perjurious. In short, Judge Sears believed O'Neil was a perjurer—which generally means a witness is not believable in any way, shape, or form—but nonetheless believed O'Neil's alleged, unsworn prior statements not only occurred but

Judge Charles Sears, the appointed trial examiner for the second trial. He ordered Harry Bridges deported. Copyright San Francisco History Center, San Francisco Public Library.

were also absolutely true. He did not grapple with the staggering inherent contradiction, nor the critical question of whether O'Neil's amazing claims were really believable on their merits. Heads: the government wins; tails: Harry Bridges loses.[88]

As to Lundeberg, Judge Sears believed Lundeberg's testimony, despite Lundeberg's obvious disdain for Bridges. Judge Sears simply ruled that while Lundeberg had a reason to lie and claim Harry Bridges admitted his Communist Party ties, Bridges had a greater reason to lie about it because he was fighting for his life. "Lundeberg is strongly biased against the alien. On the other hand, Bridges himself is the most interested of all witnesses in his own behalf," Judge

Sears declared.[89] When one pauses to consider that nugget of judicial reasoning, it yields the conclusion that an accused can never be believed over others who have a demonstrated motive to lie because, by definition, the accused always has a greater motive to lie; thus, no accused can ever be believed. Heads: the government wins; tails: Harry Bridges loses.

As to Cannalonga, Judge Sears stated that he did not place any reliance on Cannalonga, a witness whom he also found "clearly falsified" testimony at times.[90] While Judge Sears' treatment of Cannalonga neatly boxed his testimony up as irrelevant to the decision, it did not address the deeper issue Cannalonga's testimony created: Was the FBI pressuring witnesses? Like the FBI's wiretapping, Judge Sears simply sidestepped that issue, a critical issue that raised questions about the legitimacy of the entire prosecution. Heads: the government wins; tails: Harry Bridges loses.

Bridges and his team were deflated. They believed the two witnesses Judge Sears relied on were remarkably weak witnesses with dubious testimony too thin to justify deportation. The government had offered other witnesses that Judge Sears found lacking in credibility and honesty. Testimony of FBI threats existed. But they still lost.

Devastated, the lawyers prepared to appeal, and Bridges continued running the union on the West Coast.

CHAPTER 5

Political Intrigue and Supreme Court Appeals

The bosses brought a trial to deport him over the sea,
But the judge said, "He's an honest man, I got to set him
free."
Then they brought another trial to frame him if they can
But right by Harry Bridges stands every working man!

"THE BALLAD OF HARRY BRIDGES," BY PETE SEEGER,
LEE HAYS, AND MILLARD LAMPELL (1942)

Bridges Appeals Within the Department of Justice

Bridges immediately appealed Judge Sears' decision to the Board of Immigration Appeals (BIA). The BIA is the appellate arm of the immigration courts, comprised of a panel of immigration appellate judges who assess the validity of the immigration trial findings. The BIA in turn appointed five immigration specialists to analyze the record and decide the case. After the BIA analyzed Judge Sears' September 1941 decision, it wrote its own ninety-nine-page opinion in January 1942, where all five BIA members unanimously agreed that no evidence supported Judge Sears' conclusions.[1] Consequently, the BIA reversed Judge Sears' deportation order, saving Harry Bridges.

The BIA focused heavily on O'Neil and Lundeberg, the two witnesses Judge Sears had relied upon for his conclusions. As to Lundeberg, the BIA was concerned with his testimony because he was an admitted long-term enemy of Bridges, going back to the early union days in 1934-35. On top of that, Lundeberg's testimony evolved from describing a dinner where Bridges had said nothing, to describing a dinner where Bridges had said Lundeberg could be a secret member, to describing a dinner where Bridges had admitted he, too, was a secret member. The shifting story, coupled with it never having been told to interviewers in three prior interviews in all the earlier years, made it simply too hard to believe, especially on the heels of apparent pressure from Del Guercio.[2]

As to O'Neil, the BIA dissected O'Neil's testimony in great detail and agreed that O'Neil probably made the statements about witnessing Harry Bridges putting stickers in a membership book. But the BIA's careful assessment led it to conclude that O'Neil was a megalomaniac, a deeply unreliable witness (and a willing perjurer by definition) who believed that he was central to the massive socio-legal events at hand. The reality is that he was a small-time editor of a paper, not a labor leader, nor a labor confidant, and not important in the labor struggles at issue, barely a footnote to history.

Practically, the idea that Harry Bridges was a top Communist Party leader—one who knew he was under investigation with government and private enterprise trying to paint him as a communist—yet would also pay dues to some Communist Party tax collector and then paste little stickers in a membership book to prove he paid his dues, and would do so openly in an office that O'Neil could just walk into unannounced at any time, was too fantastical to believe. O'Neil had certainly lied so that he could appear as a central player in the drama of the day.

"O'Neil played Ananias as well as Judas," the five BIA judges found, with Ananias being a Biblical reference to the disciple Ananias who was sent by Jesus to restore sight to someone—as O'Neil believed that only he could save America and prove Bridges was a communist.[3]

By all accounts, when Bridges won before the BIA, he and his lawyers assumed the matter was at last resolved.[4] This is because the BIA was supposed to be the end of the line for immigration decisions within the executive branch, primarily because the BIA was supposed to be quasi-judicial so as to remove it from the executive as much as possible. In particular, the BIA "was made a larger body with quasi-judicial jurisdiction and to a degree independent of this service [INS within the Department of Justice under the Attorney General]."[5] After all, if the executive can, through the attorney general, decide who to deport and also freely review the deportation judge's deportation decision, the attorney general is then both prosecutor and judge in the same case.

By now, Attorney General Jackson, who had started this process in 1940, had been appointed to the United States Supreme Court. The new attorney general was Francis Biddle. And in a surprise ping-pong move, Attorney General Biddle, in May 1942, suddenly stepped in, reversed the BIA, and reinstated Judge Sears' deportation decision. In the 1940s, it was exceptionally rare for the attorney general to hear any appeal from the BIA, which was supposed to happen in very limited and specific circumstances.[6] Remarkably, there is no evidence that the government lawyers even appealed the BIA's decision to Biddle! Rather, Biddle simply reached out and reversed the BIA's decision of his own accord, rendering his action more political than legal.[7]

The backstory as to how Biddle managed to take the case from the BIA is itself important, and further illuminates how those in government pursued their anti-Bridges bias as far as possible. As mentioned above, INS Commissioner Schofield had testified at trial that he heard O'Neil tell the government agents in an interview that he saw Bridges pasting dues stickers in a communist membership book. Despite his bias and probable conflict as an interested witness, Schofield, in February 1942, wrote Biddle a scathing indictment of the BIA's decision and urged Biddle to reverse it. And when Biddle issued his decision in May, it largely tracked Schofield's memorandum.[8] This is doubly remarkable. First, Schofield was a witness in the trial, which generally counsels against also acting as the lawyer in the proceeding, as it raises questions about one's potential for impartiality. Second, Schofield was now almost ghostwriting the decision for the very proceeding in which he had testified.

Biddle made this move despite seemingly knowing that President Roosevelt did not approve of such action. More cynically, one could conclude that Biddle appeared to recognize that President Roosevelt was cornered by the political headwinds. Before Biddle announced his decision, he went to President Roosevelt and told him what he was about to do, specifically not asking for the president's advice. After listening to Biddle, President Roosevelt whistled, drew on his cigarette, and sat deep in thought. After pondering for a while, President Roosevelt, believing the decision a mistake, said, "I'm sorry to hear that." Stubbing his cigarette out in the ashtray on his desk, he wagered, "I'll bet that the Supreme Court will never let him be deported." Smiling at Biddle, President Roosevelt then offered, "and the decision is a long way off."[9]

Given the events, the fairest interpretation of President Roosevelt's comments is that he saw the decision as meritless, felt politically unable to veto Biddle and get in the middle of a political fracas (during a war and in an election year), and was therefore counting on the Supreme Court—which he had famously tried to pack—to fix the error. In this political vacuum, Biddle, supported by Schofield's efforts, was able to take a case not properly before him and issue a decision.[10]

After meeting the president, Biddle issued his decision, which echoed Schofield's plea. In so doing, however, Biddle did more than just reinstate Judge Sears' decision. Rather, in an attempt to strengthen the deportation determination beyond just the Lundeberg-O'Neil testimony, Biddle proceeded to find credible and valuable the testimony of witnesses that even Judge Sears had rejected.[11] Accordingly, when Attorney General Biddle reinstated the deportation decision in 1942, Bridges was now literally at the end of the line within the executive branch. Absent rapid help from the judicial branch, he would be on a boat back to Australia, forever removed from the country he had lived in for almost the previous quarter century and for nearly his entire adult life.

Bridges Appeals to the Judicial Branch

Stunned, Carol King went to Washington to learn how long the defense team had to begin habeas corpus proceedings in the judicial branch; she was told that within thirty to ninety days Bridges would be picked up and delivered to Australia. But the government actually issued a telegraphic warrant to San Francisco INS officials to arrest and remove Bridges immediately, before his lawyers could file a federal court habeas corpus appeal.[12] Learning of the apparent treachery, Bridges' lawyers rapidly filed a habeas corpus petition in the San Francisco federal court to stop any imminent deportation and overturn the deportation decision. They succeeded in at least precluding a physical deportation pending a federal court assessment of Bridges' case, buying some breathing room to fight the deportation decision within the judicial branch's courts.

By the time the case moved from the executive branch to the judicial branch, procedure took root, and the government clung to numerous legal doctrines that call for judicial branch deference to the executive in its handling of matters within its purview and expertise. Clouding the case in these doctrines that demand deference to the executive and deference to the first fact-finder Judge Sears, the federal district court judge in San Francisco agreed with the government prosecutors and, in February 1943, dismissed Harry Bridges' appeal. The federal judge found Lundeberg's and O'Neil's testimonies perfectly appropriate and concluded Harry Bridges had received a fair hearing.[13]

When he lost the habeas corpus petition before the federal trial judge, Harry Bridges appealed to the Ninth Circuit Court of Appeals, the federal appellate court that decided appeals emanating from several western states, including California. After more briefs and a full argument, the Ninth Circuit, in June 1944, agreed in a split 3-2 decision with the federal trial judge. Echoing the same concerns for deference to the executive's handling of immigration affairs, the three judges in the majority concluded that Harry Bridges had received a fair hearing in its totality. Stunningly, even while the three judges entered that conclusion, they indicated that they were not sure the truth of Harry Bridges' Communist Party ties had in fact come out at trial, concluding they "lacked the pleasurable satisfaction that…the truth has been revealed." That is, even though the judges believed the evidence may well have failed to show Bridges was a communist, they still affirmed Biddle's and Judge Sears' conclusion that the evidence was sufficient. As a result, the majority sidestepped a careful review of O'Neil's and Lundeberg's testimonies and resorted to legal artifices—institutionalized deference to the original factual findings, respect for the co-equal branch of government—to avoid a genuine, close inspection.[14]

Judge Healy, of the Ninth Circuit, wrote a lengthy, impassioned dissent for himself and another judge. He was particularly upset at the use of O'Neil's recanted, contradictory hearsay statements, and rejected the idea that the disconnect could be bridged with legal doctrine. "No amount of philosophizing can serve to make a silk purse out of this obvious sow's ear," he wrote. Judge Healy examined the entire record, and concluded that it was patent to "any candid person who takes the trouble to examine the record" that the government woefully failed to prove its case. Judge Healy also addressed the denial of Bridges' due process rights: "I desire particularly to point out what seems to me to be the fact, namely, that the crucial finding in the case was arrived at in reliance upon incompetent evidence—evidence, moreover, received and considered in violation of a regulation of the department designed to ensure fair hearings and to safeguard the rights of aliens."[15]

Fundamentally, Judge Healy saw the entire proceeding as devoid of the basic tenets of due process generally demanded in all American courts, and ultimately the trial before Judge Sears was an empty procedure more akin to the type of lawless proceeding sought originally by the unconstitutional H.R. 9766 bill of attainder: "Rather than deport the alien on evidence which would be condemned and proscribed without hesitation by any American court it would seem a more forthright procedure to do what was proposed in the first place, deport him by legislative resolution 'notwithstanding the provisions of any other law.'"[16] But Judge Healy's dissent did not carry the force of law.

Thus, by September 1944, two federal courts and six federal judges had now looked at Bridges' case, and four of the six federal judges had concluded that Bridges should be deported. At the same time, within the executive, two members had found Bridges deportable (Sears and Biddle), and five had found Bridges not deportable (the BIA members). At this point, of the thirteen minds that had assessed the question, the matter was split 7-6 in Bridges' favor. However, like the Electoral College voting process, total votes are not the whole picture, and Bridges was to be deported because the last word in the executive was Biddle's, and the last word in the federal courts, at that point, belonged to the Ninth Circuit.

Bridges had one last chance, and that rested with an appeal of the Ninth Circuit's decision to the United States Supreme Court. Bridges' problem, though, was that by law the Supreme Court was required to take very few appeals. Almost the entirety of the Supreme Court's docket is made up of cases it chooses to hear, and it hears only a small number of cases every year.[17] For example, in 2013, there were over 350,000 federal trial court cases, over 57,000 circuit courts of appeal decisions, and over 250,000 completed immigration cases.[18] Yet the Supreme Court took only seventy-two appeals for full briefing and argument, one of which was an immigration case.[19] Getting the Supreme Court to take an appeal is the lawyer's version of being struck by lightning.

Bridges' Last Chance Before the Supreme Court

Lightning struck. The Supreme Court agreed to hear the case and immediately set argument for April 2 and 3, 1945. Because Justice Jackson had been the attorney general who initiated the second deportation trial (and appointed Judge Sears), he was conflicted and had to recuse himself. This created a curious risk for Bridges. With Justice Jackson recused, there were now eight justices to decide his case. If they split 4-4, Supreme Court rules require that the lower court decision stand. Adding to the ominous atmosphere, the Supreme Court in 1945 was at its peak in terms of the liberal-conservative conflict occasioned by President Roosevelt's court-packing efforts of the mid-1930s.[20]

Over two days in April 1945, lawyers for Bridges and the government battled with the justices and each other over the case. Bridges' fundamental argument was that he was denied due process when he was ordered deported on the basis of, one, Lundeberg's testimony where Lundeberg was a sworn enemy and had made prior statements to the FBI that Bridges was not a Communist Party member, and, two, O'Neil's unsworn statements to the FBI

(Harry Bridges is a communist), which were the opposite of what he swore to at Bridges' trial (Harry Bridges is not a communist).

In a response of cruel irony, the government argued to the court that Harry Bridges' due process appeal should be denied because he had been afforded "more due process of law than perhaps any of the numerous ones who have been deported in the past" in light of the myriad trials he had been subjected to!

Justice Reed immediately called the government on the disingenuous assertion, noting that while Bridges had been subjected to a quantitatively large number of hearings, such a feat was not necessarily an indication he had been afforded genuine, qualitative due process.[21] Indeed, the reality is that as the number of hearings increased, there was a corresponding decrease in the quality of due process afforded Harry Bridges. As the contentious argument ended, the court took the case under submission and issued no decision that day.

Behind closed doors, the eight Supreme Court Justices were in hot disagreement over Harry Bridges' fate. As reflected in Justice Frank Murphy's notes, contemporaneously recorded as the justices debated the case, Chief Justice Stone began, arguing that the court's "function here is a narrow one...was there evidence to support it [Judge Sears' decision]. If so, our duty ends." Like the lower federal courts' conclusions, this sentiment encapsulates deference to the executive in its handling of immigration cases. In analyzing the question, Stone expressly concluded: "There is no limit in right of Congress to expel a man. [Bridges'] presence here is contrary to will of Congress."[22] In other words, the question for him was not whether Harry Bridges received a fair trial. It was the sterile legal question of whether there was any evidence to justify Sears' decision. If so, the court should look no further.[23]

The narrow view of Chief Justice Stone drew an immediate quip from Justice Black, who asked: "Suppose it said a member of the Democratic or Republican party?" Chief Justice Stone did not respond, but Justice Black's surgical question went to the heart of what Congress was doing: legislating deportations on ideological grounds.

Justice Black saw the case as requiring the opposite conclusion, indicating that he doubted any court would allow a conviction on the evidentiary record of Lundeberg and O'Neil. The case was so weak that if no normal court would sustain it, Justice Black was troubled as to why the Supreme Court would allow the executive to get away with such a result simply because it is the executive. Indeed, Justice Black struck at the heart of the matter and argued that in reality "he is deported because he is a labor leader."

Justice Reed seemed to agree: "My feeling is he has not had a fair hearing when you sum it all up."[24]

Justice Frankfurter then spoke, and, as an immigrant himself, he spoke from his heart: "I have a special appreciation, having come in as an alien. I speak from a depth of conviction about this country and its future...I consider this action of the attorney general amiss and foolish." Justice Frankfurter was born in Austria and immigrated to New York in his early teenage years, attended Harvard Law School, and was appointed to the Supreme Court by President Roosevelt in 1939.

But his concern was that if the Supreme Court reversed to save Harry Bridges, then Congress would react even more harshly with more restrictive immigration laws. "You will be doing a great injustice to [the] future because members of Congress will say we will let no one in," he asserted. "It will be a great injustice to immigrants to this shore," he pled. Thus, while he was leaning to deference to the executive and Congress, saying, "We are concerned with power of Congress to deal with aliens," he also felt in his heart that "Biddle is a damn fool in this action."[25]

Justice Black interjected that it was private industry that had started the enterprise, but Justice Frankfurter remained focused on his concerns for how a decision would impact future legislation and future cases, stating that he had not "reached the point that is an outrage."[26]

Within the Supreme Court, the Bridges case was highly divisive on ideological grounds, a division on the fracture lines about the role of the federal courts, the role of Congress in controlling aliens, and about the concept of what exactly constituted a fair hearing. Justice Black strongly saw the case as an outrage requiring reversal, and Justice Reed seemed to agree. The chief justice on the other hand seemed fairly sure that Bridges had to be deported. Most moving in Justice Murphy's notes, the immigrant Justice Frankfurter was deeply torn and struggling. And the others were a mystery. In short, the matter was now in the hands of the eight divided justices.

As April bled into May and May into June, still no word had come. Every year by mid-June, the Supreme Court recesses, and June 18, 1945, was the last day of the court's term.[27] Bridges' case had still not yet been decided, and so on this last day of the term, everyone knew that word would now come. As lawyers anxiously waited in the courtroom, finally the Supreme Court took the bench and announced the results.

As the court began to explain the decision, it was clear that Bridges had won! As the Supreme Court read its decision, it voided Judge Sears' and Attorney General Biddle's deportation order. Bridges won 5-3, one mere vote away from a 4-4 tie that would have resulted in his expulsion from America. The three dissenting justices who believed Judge Sears' decision should be affirmed were Chief Justice Stone, Justice Roberts, and the lone Supreme Court immigrant, Justice Frankfurter.

Justice Murphy joined the majority opinion, saving Harry Bridges, but also wrote his own concurrence, an opinion he read from the bench, the words at once pointed, moving, and aspirational for how the nation could and should do better: "The record in this case will stand forever as a monument to man's intolerance of man. Seldom if ever in the history of this nation has there been such a concentrated and relentless crusade to deport an individual because he dared to exercise the freedom that belongs to him as a human being and that is guaranteed to him by the Constitution."[28]

Justice Murphy expressly recognized the undaunted public and private enterprise that took root to undermine Bridges, a dark footing that led to serial constitutional violations: "Wiretapping, searches and seizures without warrants, and other forms of invasion of the right of privacy have been widely employed in this deportation drive."[29]

Justice Frank Murphy, United States Supreme Court, February 1940. He read from the bench his moving words about the "crusade" against Harry Bridges depicting "man's intolerance of man." Library of Congress Prints and Photographs Division, Harris & Ewing Collection, LC-H22-D-8346.

The broken process that trapped Bridges, Justice Murphy noted, entirely subverted American notions of due process: "It is not surprising that the background and intensity of this effort to deport one individual should result in a singular lack of due process of law...When the immutable freedoms guaranteed by the Bill of Rights have been so openly and concededly ignored, the full wrath of constitutional condemnation descends upon the action taken by the government. And only by expressing that wrath can we give form and substance to the great, the indispensable democratic freedoms to which this nation is dedicated."[30]

Biddle sat in court that day to hear the decision issued, and Justice Murphy glared at Biddle while issuing his wrath of constitutional condemnation against the government's misconduct.[31]

President Roosevelt's 1942 comments to Biddle proved prescient, but by now Roosevelt had died, and so never lived to see his prediction validated.

Citizenship at Last?

Five days after the Supreme Court issued its decision, Bridges applied again for citizenship. Jubilant, on September 17, 1945, Bridges, with his lawyer Gladstein and a gaggle of friends, attended a citizenship hearing before Judge Thomas Foley in the San Francisco Superior Court. Bridges also brought two union officials and friends, Henry Schmidt and Paul Schnur, to act as official witnesses and attest to his character. But Schnur, an obvious non-native English speaker, left his citizenship papers at home and could not prove his citizenship status as was required to attest for Bridges. Gladstein quickly cast around the other attendees and found J.R. (Bob) Robertson, a union official and former prize fighter from Texas with a drawl to match. Robertson thus was asked to step in and vouch for Harry Bridges because no clerk would question Robertson's legitimacy as an American. Robertson agreed, unaware that his simple act of kindness on this celebratory day would have profound, fateful consequences.[32]

One of the questions posed to Bridges by Judge Foley was whether he was now, or ever had, belonged to the Communist Party of the United States. Bridges responded, "I have not; I do not." Schmidt and Robertson likewise affirmed under penalty of perjury that Bridges was not a Communist Party member.[33]

Bumpy, like all of Bridges' interactions with the legal system, the government lawyers suddenly produced an affidavit of Bridges' ex-wife, Agnes Bridges, who had recently divorced him in December 1944. In this affidavit, Agnes claimed Harry was a Communist Party member. Bridges denied her allegations, and his lawyer Gladstein offered evidence that in the divorce proceeding she had actually stated the opposite under oath, rendering this newly procured affidavit dubious. Given the circumstances, Judge Foley refused to accept Agnes' affidavit as valid evidence, the government lawyer made no further objections, and so Judge Foley granted Bridges' citizenship petition.[34]

Elated, Bridges was at last an American citizen. "It was the first time I have seen Harry so flustered, nervous, and excited. There were real tears in his eyes as he took the oath," described one witness.[35]

A Rocky Road to Citizenship, But Not the End of the Road

Ultimately, the Knowles-Keegan-Doyle 1930s axis from the first trial had given birth to a concerted governmental effort in the 1940s for the second trial—a trial aided by rival unionists and other conflicted private witnesses, no doubt—but chiefly organized by the attorney general's selection of Judge Sears and subsequent reinstatement of Judge Sears' decision, coupled with intense FBI investigatory efforts and Del Guercio's pressure on witnesses as well as the background HUAC hearings focused on painting Bridges as a national threat. The implementation of the macro-government agenda is ultimately seen at the exact point where the proverbial rubber hits the road: the government lawyers, the witnesses used from O'Neil to Lundeberg to Cannalonga, and the use of the law to advance a position in a court. When the first legal environment freed Harry Bridges from deportation, powerful forces in D.C. created a new legal environment with greater executive control through the Department of Justice and FBI, and asserted greater political control over the proceedings to shade the likely outcome. The judge was chosen for political reasons to appease legislative branch members. And the judge in turn showed no compunction about denying Bridges' lawyers more than six weeks to prepare and then believing an admitted perjurer's alleged hearsay testimony. When uncontroverted wiretap evidence was offered, the judge used legal doctrines to avoid addressing the import of the executive's tactics. Then at trial the evidence supported the inference that Prosecutor Del Guercio threatened and cajoled Lundeberg, getting him to tell a tale he never once offered before. Del Guercio even accused Bridges' lawyer of being a communist, all to poison the well with Judge Sears and hang Bridges by virtue of his chosen lawyer.

In the end, despite amending immigration laws twice to ensnare Harry Bridges, despite the vast resources of the federal government and FBI, despite selecting the trial judge and controlling the verdict by reaching out and reversing the BIA, and despite securing federal court solicitude couched in terms of deference to the executive fact-finding role, Harry Bridges still prevailed. For the second time, Bridges, now citizen Bridges no less, believed that he was free to move on with his life.

And Bridges did just that, continuing to lead the union in racially progressive ways. As recounted by Cleophas Williams, who later would be the first African-American elected president of the ILWU Local 10 in San Francisco, Harry Bridges persisted with a program of equality as he spoke to union members in the mid-1940s at union meetings: "Harry Bridges talked at most meetings... He said that if things reached a point where only two men were left on the waterfront, if he had anything to say about it, one would be a black man...No vacillating at all. After that, the hounds were really at his tail."[36]

But while Harry Bridges continued his progressive agenda, the attorney general, the INS, and the FBI, bolstered by HUAC and Congress, had not given up on deporting him. Unchastened by Justice Murphy's stinging words and the Supreme Court's reversal, these government agencies were now ready to raise the stakes, and this time move the trial from the executive branch immigration courts to the more punitive judicial branch criminal courts, courts where governmental leverage over Bridges could be massively increased, with criminal indictment power over Bridges' friends, Schmidt and Robertson.

CHAPTER 6

Rearming: A Third Act

"The law has yet another hold on you."

SHAKESPEARE, *MERCHANT OF VENICE* (1596)

T he United States Code is the official name of the compendium of all enacted federal laws. Written in small font, the Code fills hundreds of volumes of burgundy books covering every topic under the sun, running along many dozens and dozens of linear feet of law library shelves. In 1946, Section 746(a) of Title 8 of the Federal Code—a law buried amidst the hundreds of Code books—stated as follows: "It is hereby made a felony for any alien or other person, whether an applicant for naturalization or citizenship, or otherwise, and whether an employee of the Government of the United States or not, ...(1) Knowingly to make a false statement under oath, either orally or in writing, in any case, proceeding, relating to, or under, or by virtue of any law of the United States relating to naturalization or citizenship."[1]

More FBI Investigations and the Grand Jury

Armed with that law, the Department of Justice set to work with the FBI to find a new set of witnesses to prepare a *criminal* prosecution against Harry Bridges for violating Section 746(a). Specifically, this time the government decided it would try to charge Bridges with lying during his naturalization hearing. That is, although Bridges had won, and the Supreme Court had concluded that there was no evidence he was a Communist Party member for purposes of an INS deportation case, now the government saw a creative strategy of charging perjury under the federal criminal laws related to his denials of any Communist Party affiliation made at the very naturalization ceremony the Supreme Court gave him because he was not a Communist Party member. If it seems circular, it is: Bridges proved he was not a Communist Party member and therefore was allowed to naturalize. But to naturalize, he had to swear an oath that he was not a Communist Party member. That act of swearing triggered the arcane Section 746(a), and so Harry Bridges was caught in the grip of the law's circularity. More concerning to Bridges, a federal criminal prosecution allowed the government not only to strip away his American citizenship, but also to throw him in federal prison first.

By the summer of 1948, the federal government had conducted further witness interviews and compiled a large new roster of a third and entirely new set of witnesses. Recently declassified documents show that government immigration agents compiled a confidential memorandum summarizing the evidence the government prosecutors could submit to mount a federal case against Bridges for ostensibly violating Section 746(a). This confidential memorandum lists several witnesses—almost all of whom were former Communist Party members—who would now testify that Bridges had attended official party meetings with them. Despite three full years of investigation, this secret memorandum did not recommend a federal criminal prosecution, and instead recommended prosecutors pursue a civil claim of denaturalization.[2] A civil claim could not lead to imprisonment, however.

At the same time, other government agents began casting around to find other bases to void Bridges' citizenship. For example, in now-declassified documents from the government's archives, there is a 1948 memorandum from an INS commissioner to a regional INS office that contained reference to governmental investigations into Bridges' alleged extramarital affairs. Apparently, one woman indicated to government investigators that she had regular sexual relations with Bridges. The INS commissioner thus instructed the regional agent to "have this witness again questioned in detail with the object in mind of determining whether she may be used as witness to establish that Bridges had committed frequent acts of adultery during the period for which he was required to prove good moral character" for his citizenship.[3] These inquiries into Bridges' sexual relations had begun years earlier by INS lawyer Bonham, as discussed earlier.[4] But now, government lawyers and agents were discussing whether to seek his deportation for being an alleged adulterer. Ultimately, the government lawyers did not pursue adultery as a basis to deport, but no stone was left unturned in the pursuit of Bridges' removal from American life.

More sinister evidence became available to the FBI when witnesses told of a conspiracy to murder Bridges. Specifically, a witness named Robert Bell came to the FBI and provided a sworn affidavit that he had been propositioned by a group to assassinate Harry Bridges. Bell testified that he had been shown a .38 caliber revolver—police-issued, no less—that he was to use to murder Bridges. Bell refused. But upon receipt of Bell's evidence, the FBI reported that "the information furnished did not appear to indicate a violation of the laws within the investigative jurisdiction of the Bureau," and thus no action could be taken.[5] An assassination plot of a national labor figure was not within the FBI's "jurisdiction," but rumors of adultery remained squarely within investigative purview. The FBI's files provided to this author do not contain any evidence that the FBI ever bothered to alert either state police officials of the murder plot, over which state officials presumably had "jurisdiction" within the FBI's worldview, or even Harry Bridges himself.

In the pursuit of Bridges, government lawyers in the late 1940s even tracked down Stanley Doyle from the first trial to see if they could resuscitate him and find a way to use him as a witness to try to get before the jury the "Harry Dorgan" Communist Party Membership Card (which government officials had concluded was a forgery, as discussed in Chapter 3). Despite a decade passing, Doyle had not lost one iota of his venom for Bridges. Now calling Bridges an "alien murdering communist," Doyle had equal scorn both for Secretary Perkins, whom he called "a conspiratorial female ex-cabinet member," and Dean Landis, for issuing his 1939 decision. However, when asked by the federal government to testify, Doyle again refused, his unwillingness again signaling the dubious value of his assertion that the "Harry Dorgan" Communist Party Membership Card that he had procured was legitimate.[6] For the second time, Doyle would not make an appearance. The clear import: the card was a fake, and Doyle could not testify to its authenticity.

Ultimately, the broader political landscape fueled the government's cause, from Senator Joseph McCarthy's infamous anti-communist investigations to HUAC's ongoing efforts to root out communists. In 1947, J. Edgar Hoover, lauded and respected nationally, appeared before HUAC. "The Communist Party of the United States is a fifth column if there ever was one. It is far better organized than were the Nazis in occupied countries prior to their capitulation…It reveals a condition akin to disease that spreads like an epidemic and like an epidemic a quarantine is necessary to keep it from infecting the nation," Hoover testified.[7] The broader social context, thus, meant that the time was not ideal for Harry Bridges to face yet another trial.

Bridges' ILWU union was itself another casualty of the hostile environment, because around this time the CIO expelled it and other left-leaning unions from its protective umbrella. The ILWU, with Bridges at its helm, soldiered on as an independent union, but saw the expulsion as a cynical effort by the CIO to curry favor with those running the national anti-communist investigations.[8]

Eventually, in 1949, and despite the then-secret 1948 INS memorandum that had already concluded that no basis for a criminal prosecution existed, the Department of Justice nonetheless convened a secret grand jury in San Francisco. Prosecutors wanted to press criminal perjury charges against Harry Bridges, and to charge his two friends, Henry Schmidt and J.R. Robertson, with aiding and abetting Bridges, and a joint conspiracy to defraud the United States government into issuing citizenship papers to Bridges. On May 25, 1949, after hearing weeks of evidence, the grand jury returned an indictment against Bridges for perjury in his naturalization ceremony, and against Bridges, Schmidt, and Robertson for conspiracy and aiding and abetting Bridges' effort to fraudulently secure his citizenship. The same day the Department of Justice filed a criminal prosecution seeking prison sentences for all and denaturalization for Bridges, it also filed a civil lawsuit seeking denaturalization.[9]

At the same time, Bridges' lawyers were also now in the government's crosshairs. As now-declassified records demonstrate, the Department of Justice had undertaken further investigations into the lawyers' backgrounds. The Department of Justice asked the FBI to uncover information on Gladstein and Grossman, and to "report as to the nature of any derogatory information contained in any file."[10] If the FBI reports could help tarnish Bridges' lawyers, then Bridges would go down with them in the court of public opinion. The government lay in wait with this strategy, eager to unfold the scorched-earth approach before the jury, hoping to tarnish Bridges by reference to his lawyers' alleged politics.[11]

While these government investigations continued throughout the mid-1940s, Harry had met and fallen in love with Nancy Berdecio, recently divorced from her first husband, the famed Bolivian painter Roberto Berdecio. By chance, Nancy's professional background was in the law as a legal secretary and stenographer—Harry Bridges just couldn't escape tangling with those in the law it seemed! Harry and Nancy married in 1946, and by the close of the decade had two children, Julie and Robert Bridges.[12]

By 1949, Bridges was now almost fifty years old, his youthfulness from the first investigations in the mid-1930s and the first trial in 1938 having given way to a receding hairline and the beginnings of a wrinkled brow. Still trim, Bridges was certainly no longer the uncomfortable longshoreman stepping forward into the limelight with his worker's cap in hand, and instead looked every bit the union statesman comfortably wearing the popular double-breasted suits of the time, and still an engaging public speaker.

The Third Trial

As trial began in November 1949, Gladstein found himself imprisoned for six months for contempt of court in a high-profile case where he had defended alleged communists on the East Coast. Although Bridges could have sought an extension of the trial date to allow Gladstein to serve his sentence and return, the consensus was that Gladstein's presence, as a lawyer who defended alleged communists, could hurt Bridges.[13] Although a lawyer's clients in one action should have no bearing whatsoever on a lawyer's different client in a second action, Bridges' concern had precedent. As discussed earlier, Prosecutor Del Guercio, in the second trial, repeatedly tried to impugn Bridges' character, based upon his lawyers' alleged beliefs; and Special Prosecutor Doyle, in the first trial, had attacked Gladstein as a "commie." Thus, Bridges and his San Francisco lawyers, Gladstein and Grossman, certainly would have assumed similar tactics would be employed again, and so Bridges was forced to hire new counsel.

This time the defense recruited Vincent Hallinan, a highly regarded, aggressive, and colorful San Francisco attorney. Irish-Catholic by background, Hallinan looked like a classic movie star: a square jaw, large face, hawkishly smart eyes, thick, curling eyebrows, and a remarkably thick bundle of brown hair, even at age fifty. A college national boxing champion, Hallinan's aggressive, street-fighter court demeanor matched his rugged, tough appearance.[14] Bridges' co-defendants, Schmidt and Robertson, hired Hallinan's law partner, James MacInnis, who looked like a fifteen-year-younger version of Hallinan.

Vince Hallinan (left) and James MacInnis (right), defense lawyers for Bridges, Schmidt, and Robertson. Copyright San Francisco History Center, San Francisco Public Library.

Judge Harris

The criminal and civil cases were assigned to Judge George Harris of the federal court in San Francisco. Judge Harris stayed the civil case until the criminal case concluded.[15]

From the beginning, Judge Harris and Hallinan did not get along. Apparently, some years before, Hallinan found himself in a legal dispute with a man named Eugene Aureguy over $10,000 that Aureguy believed Hallinan owed. Aureguy and Hallinan were apparently sworn, bitter enemies, but Judge Harris was a friend of Aureguy. At the time of the dispute, Judge Harris was a state court judge and, Hallinan contended, took Hallinan one day into his private judicial chambers and pressured Hallinan to pay Aureguy the $10,000. Hallinan refused, and at the subsequent trial Aureguy called Judge Harris as a witness, and Judge Harris testified on Aureguy's behalf and against Hallinan. The trial ended in Hallinan's favor, with no money owing.[16]

The defense believed this history rendered Judge Harris biased, and so asked him to recuse and disqualify himself to avoid any appearance of impropriety.[17] Generally, this kind of a perceived conflict of interest would cause a judge to recuse himself, because the law demands that judges must avoid not only actual biases and conflicts but also situations that others could reasonably think cause bias, even if in fact the judge lacks a bias.[18] The theory behind such a strict rule is that judges should be neutral so as to provide legitimacy to their decisions, and if there is even a reasonable question as to their neutrality—if the average man on the street would have doubts about the judge's impartiality—then the law's legitimacy is protected by the judge stepping aside.[19] However, Judge Harris refused to let go of the case, intent on staying centrally involved in the heady events of the time. He even ordered that the motion to disqualify and all its unsavory contents itself be stricken from the federal court records.[20]

United States District Judge George Harris. He was nominated to the federal bench by President Truman in 1946. Courtesy of the United States District Court for the Northern District of California.

Opening Statements...and the Fireworks Begin

Although criminal cases are usually prosecuted by the local United States Attorneys who live locally and work in the federal courts of their city, the government secured a private, special prosecutor to prosecute the criminal jury trial, Joseph "Jiggs" Donohue. Appointed with official prosecutorial powers, Donohue was a prominent, politically connected Washington, D.C., attorney.

Possessing a small pale gray mustache, Donohue had stark black eyebrows set against an otherwise chalky white face adorned

with big brown eyes, one of which drooped. Above his large forehead, what was left of his extremely thin, graying hair was slicked
back tight. As he stood at the podium to address the jury, he wore a
bulky double-breasted suit with a heavily starched shirt and necktie
tight as a noose.

Donohue began with the government's version of the evidence, explaining that he would prove that Bridges, Schmidt, and
Robertson engaged in a conspiracy to knowingly mislead the court
into issuing citizenship papers. "The government will produce here
witnesses whose testimony will show and establish to a moral certainty and beyond all reasonable doubt that the defendants...were
members of the Communist Party of the United States," he started.[21] Targeting Bridges in particular, he continued: "We shall prove
that on that date [when he swore his citizenship oath] and many
years preceding that day, he was an active, energetic, dues-paying
member of the Communist Party of the United States." The government prosecutors insisted that Bridges had been a member since
1934, concealed his membership, and used the fake name of "Harry
Dorgan." To prove this, the government would call witnesses who
would testify that Bridges had been a long-standing member, had
attended meetings, and had played a prominent role in the Communist Party.[22]

Hallinan then began his opening statement. As he began explaining that this was the third trial, Prosecutor Donohue jumped
up and objected that Hallinan should not be allowed to discuss the
prior cases and also asserted that Hallinan's tone was too argumen-
tative. Judge Harris agreed.[23]

So Hallinan proceeded to explain to the jury that a conspiracy existed, but it went the other way: "Now we have been told
that counsel is going to prove there was a conspiracy. And there
was. There was a conspiracy and a criminal conspiracy." But, Hallinan thundered on, "the conspiracy that will be demonstrated
here to a moral certainty and beyond any reasonable doubt is not a

conspiracy of these poor men to help one of them attain citizenship." Rather, "we will show the jury that the witnesses who take the
stand, one and all…are engaged in a mean and criminal and fraud-
ulent and inhumane conspiracy to destroy one man."[24]

Special Prosecutor Joseph "Jiggs" Donohue, who came from Washington, D.C., to prosecute Harry
Bridges. Courtesy of ILWU, San Francisco.

To prove the counter-conspiracy, Hallinan asserted that he had to go back to the roots of the problem, to 1934. As he started explaining to the jury the history of the labor union and Bridges' activities, again Donohue objected, arguing that the jury should not hear about Bridges' history in the union. And again Judge Harris agreed: "I cannot feel at this juncture how this historical narrative, however interesting it may be to all of us, would tend to prove or disprove any of the material allegations in this indictment."[25] Judge Harris's conclusion was remarkable if not stunning: the government was allowed to argue that Bridges' history since 1934 showed he was a secret Communist Party member engaged in a conspiracy to hide his membership, but Bridges was not allowed to argue that the full history in fact showed he had been framed as one by a counter-conspiracy.

Defiant, Hallinan refused to bend to the apparent shackling of his defense. Instead, he continued with an explanation of Bridges' role in the union, the historical Shape Up practice that Bridges abolished, the prior trials, and the witnesses who had lied about his membership. Curiously, Donohue did not object to any of this. But after a short while, Judge Harris ordered a recess and had the jury leave the courtroom. Judge Harris then stated that he had noticed that Donohue had not objected. This is itself odd, in that a lawyer may object or not. The court generally shows no paternalism to the lawyers in this regard, and if a lawyer chooses not to object, the court, as umpire, allows the case to proceed. After all, it is not the umpire's job to make sure the pitcher chooses the right pitch to throw.[26]

Donohue, with Judge Harris's obvious prodding, then instantly objected to Hallinan's discourse. Closing the loop, Judge Harris agreed.

Perplexed, Hallinan argued for symmetry: "the government is entitled to show there was a conspiracy to commit the one perjury," but he [Hallinan] "could not show there was a conspiracy to commit the other perjury…there exists a conspiracy of witnesses to take the witness stand and swear to a falsehood, namely that Harry Bridges was or is a member of the Communist Party."[27] Hallinan explained that the evidence would show a conspiracy to frame Bridges by a massive number of witnesses, arguing he had every right to try that case to the jury.[28]

Raising his eyebrows, Judge Harris showed skepticism at Hallinan's theory: "If such a conspiracy exists…it is one of the most fantastic defenses that I have had presented to me. To say that 125 witnesses have conspired over a period of many, many years is somewhat fantastic."[29] Hallinan then explained that it was not fantastic, because the Supreme Court had already said as much when it reversed Judge Sears' conclusion. Angered, Judge Harris finally showed his cards and decreed: "I am not bound by the assertion, by the pronouncements, nor by the opinion of any member or members of the Supreme Court."[30] At that claim, a lawyer can do little but wait for the trial to end and appeal. Hallinan could only retort in subtle sarcasm: "Your Honor finds fantastic what the Supreme Court found to be fact."[31]

Fundamentally, the problem Judge Harris created was that he refused to accept the idea that Hallinan could prove a conspiracy. This put the cart before the horse, because he had not heard the evidence yet. More importantly, though, it was for the jury to decide whether Hallinan's conspiracy theory made sense. And because Judge Harris refused to believe such a conspiracy did exist— despite not knowing what the evidence would show and despite the fact that he had no problem entertaining the assumption that the government could prove that its claimed conspiracy existed—he refused to let Hallinan discuss the topic before the jury.[32] With that, the day ended.

As the second day of trial began, Hallinan continued his opening statement. As he began describing the lack of credibility in the government witnesses, Donohue again objected. Angered, Judge

Harris told the jury that Hallinan's references to the witnesses was "speculative"—although Judge Harris never said as much to the jury about Prosecutor Donohue's assertions of what the government witnesses would say.[33] For roughly an hour, as Hallinan gave his opening statement, Donohue launched a constant barrage of objections, compounded by Judge Harris's comments that Hallinan's opening statement was improper. As one reads the transcript today, Hallinan barely got a word in to the jury without constant discourse; the transcript reads like anything but an opening statement, which generally elicits few, if any, objections, as lawyers are allowed to outline their vision of the case. Instead, the transcript reads like a bitter verbal debate with Hallinan the recipient of constant judicial and governmental anger. Frustrated, Hallinan at one point asked for five minutes of uninterrupted time to explain what the witnesses would say. But he achieved no more than a few seconds before the government again resumed its objections.[34]

In his opening, Hallinan eventually turned to Lundeberg, the discredited witness from the second trial, who would not be able to support the claim against Bridges, Hallinan believed. Hallinan explained that Lundeberg was a man of violence and harbored animosity towards Bridges. Judge Harris again refused to let Hallinan make such claims. "These excoriations and vituperative manner bearing upon Mr. Lundeberg and others has no place at the present time," Judge Harris ordered.[35] Similarly, when Hallinan characterized the other government witnesses as being provably dishonest, Judge Harris outright rejected his theory in front of the jury.[36] Judge Harris even assaulted Hallinan's competency, stating in front of the jury, "You are going far afield from any opening statement that I have ever heard in this court or any other court."[37]

Remarkably, at times when even Donohue did not object, Judge Harris objected for him. "I think in the absence of the prosecution noting an objection, the court will intrude itself," Judge Harris offered.[38] Hallinan again pled that he must be permitted to tell the jury what was coming, but Judge Harris refused, ordering that he could not "assassinate in advance every witness who might take this stand."[39] Judge Harris essentially denied Bridges' lawyer the opportunity to question the veracity of the government's witnesses, as if to do so was an unlawful "assassination" attempt.

By the close of the second day of trial, Hallinan had been repeatedly denied the ability to tell his story of what the evidence would show in terms of a counter-conspiracy. Hallinan was visibly frustrated at the tiny box Judge Harris and Prosecutor Donohue had corralled him into. After all, the government believed Bridges, Schmidt, and Robertson had conspired to defraud the United States into issuing citizenship papers, and Donohue outlined for the jury its conspiracy theory and the evidence behind its theory. Hallinan believed that a counter-conspiracy existed: one to frame Bridges as a Communist Party member. Hallinan wanted to tell the story of the prior trials and the government's perjured, discredited witnesses as proof that this was part of a long-running saga with very different roots from the ones Donohue claimed. However, at each step, Donohue had objected, and Judge Harris had agreed with Donohue, essentially cleansing the story as it unfolded before the jury as if the prior fifteen years had never happened. By the time Hallinan finished, only the most obtuse juror would not understand that Judge Harris respected the government lawyers, but thought little of Bridges' defense.

As rough a time as Hallinan had experienced, it was about to get a lot worse.

Contempt!

As the third day of trial began, Donohue called his first witness, INS lawyer Lloyd Garner, who explained that he had investigated Bridges' citizenship application; held a citizenship hearing with Bridges, Schmidt, and Robertson; and attended Bridges' final

naturalization hearing. One issue that came up was the infamous
Agnes Bridges affidavit. That was the affidavit produced at the citizenship hearing before Judge Foley, where Bridges' ex-wife, during
a bitter divorce battle, stated that Bridges was a Communist Party
member, but which affidavit was not accepted into evidence at the
hearing and had been withdrawn by Agnes in a subsequent sworn
declaration. Here, again, Donohue was unable to enter it into evidence, although Judge Harris's clerk marked it for identification as
Government Exhibit 5.[40]

Because it was marked for identification, but not admitted,
the jury was never supposed to see the alleged declaration. Judge
Harris ordered his clerk to hold it. Hallinan, perhaps suspicious,
objected that the clerk should not hold it, but Judge Harris disagreed, explaining that the responsibility to control the documents
is a "grave one in a case like this."[41] Thus, the Agnes Bridges declaration was taken by Judge Harris's clerk. This seemingly innocuous
event would become a matter of some controversy later.

Hallinan began his cross-examination by developing the
defense theory that Garner was part of the large government
conspiracy manipulating the legal system to imprison Bridges. But
Judge Harris refused to let him take that tack, mocking the defense
theory as he sarcastically quipped: "This chain of co-conspirators
that is gained and augmented in force and number until now it
reached the proportions of 125 people, all of them, all of them are
out of step with Harry Bridges." The tension rose as Hallinan responded in kind to Judge Harris: "I say that you have no right to
make your mind up as to whether a conspiracy of these witnesses exists or does not exist; that is something direct to the jury."[42] Almost
every question Hallinan asked drew objections from the government lawyers, who in short order charged Hallinan with contempt
in front of the jury.

Hallinan objected that such a charge was improper to make
before the jury and asked that the jury be informed to ignore it,

because charges of contempt were reserved for resolution between the lawyers and the judge outside the presence of the jury, whose only job was to adjudicate the defendant's guilt, not wade into the propriety or lack thereof of lawyers' behavior. Judge Harris refused and instead positively echoed the government lawyer's charge: "The statement made by counsel may well be within the realm of his province to make. I shall not instruct the jury to disregard it...your persistent conduct ... may well eventuate in the situation that counsel refers to."[43] With that public shaming of Hallinan in front of the jury, the day ended.

The next day, as the lawyers waited in the courtroom while the jury waited in the jury room, Judge Harris took the bench. Reading from a lengthy prepared statement, Judge Harris suddenly declared Hallinan in criminal contempt. He identified scores of alleged contemptuous remarks by Hallinan from the prior three days, reading from his statement that he had stayed up until 3 a.m. that morning preparing. Judge Harris spoke for about two hours, quoting from the days' events, and charged Hallinan with "incompetent and inflammatory" behavior. He charged Hallinan with besmirching and belittling behavior towards the government's witness, Garner, who Judge Harris concluded was a decent, "mild-mannered deputy" and "administrative officer of the United States." Hallinan tried to speak, but was initially denied the opportunity. When Judge Harris was done with his lengthy tirade, he ordered Hallinan immediately jailed for six months.[44] Hallinan never had notice or an opportunity to prepare a written defense against the written charge, the findings, the verdict, or the sentence.

Pandemonium broke out. Two United States Marshals grabbed Hallinan's arms to drag him from the court, while at the same time Hallinan was objecting that Judge Harris was biased.[45] Holding his ground at the lectern, Hallinan stated that he would make an affidavit that day swearing under penalty of perjury that Judge Harris had previously stated his ill will towards Hallinan and that he was out to get him.[46] Judge Harris denied the charge, but Hallinan insisted that he be allowed to swear it under oath so that Judge Harris could swear the opposite, if he dared. Judge Harris sternly retorted, "You will not file the affidavit." Hallinan, however, said that he would, and Judge Harris angrily ordered, "You will not file any affidavit before me, Mr. Vincent Hallinan."[47]

The government lawyers then joined the fray and launched a second front against Hallinan. Prosecutor Donohue rose to defend Judge Harris and accused Hallinan of being a "mad dog." Hallinan started yelling that Donohue had no right to participate in a contempt charge as this was between Judge Harris and Hallinan, but Donohue refused to stay quiet and walked to the lectern where Hallinan stood. Hallinan asked him to leave, but Donohue refused, provoking Hallinan, who remarked that in his younger days the temptation—to punch Donohue—would have been too great to resist.[48] But Hallinan, restrained by United States Marshals perhaps more than age, resisted such temptation that day.

Judge Harris then ordered the marshals to take Hallinan away for six months and disbar him from the court.[49] In all the chaos, Judge Harris seemed to forget that Bridges was on trial and needed a lawyer to defend him. Hallinan tried to explain the predicament, but the government lawyers interrupted to demand that Hallinan not even speak since, technically, due to Judge Harris's disbarment, he was now no longer a lawyer before the court.[50] Yet, suddenly, it seemed to dawn on Judge Harris that Harry Bridges needed a lawyer.

Confused as to how to proceed, Judge Harris asked, "Is Mr. Richard Gladstein available?"

Hallinan wryly retorted, "Mr. Richard Gladstein has a fate somewhat similar to the one you have just bestowed on me," referring of course to the fact that Gladstein was jailed for contempt in a case where he had defended accused communists.[51] It seemed that all of Bridges' lawyers found themselves jailed for contempt.

Judge Harris wanted to force Bridges to find a new lawyer. Yet he did not speak to Bridges, and instead asked the *government* lawyers their opinion on the matter. The government lawyers, not surprisingly, in turn praised Judge Harris's wise judgment and temperament, and argued that the integrity of the court system was more important than any one case, and that Hallinan had to be jettisoned instantly, even if Bridges was left without his chosen counsel.[52]

With venom, the government prosecutor went for the kill: "Mr. Hallinan—I will not refer to him as counsel—I will not prostitute the word by using it in relation to this matter. He has desecrated this temple of justice...Your Honor, this is a temple of justice. He is trying to make this a bawdy house."[53]

The brothel charge was too much for the restrained Hallinan, who asserted, "What a shabby fraud, Your Honor...to have counsel make a statement like that about a man who is helpless to do anything about it."[54]

The government lawyers then proposed that MacInnis should represent Bridges as well as Schmidt and Robertson, or that the trial be delayed two weeks so that Bridges could find a new lawyer. MacInnis refused, arguing that Judge Harris had shown great bias against Bridges and Hallinan, and in favor of the government's case and its lawyers.[55]

Hallinan in turn asked to have the bailiffs unhand him, to which Judge Harris responded with sarcastic glee: "They are very, very gentle people, Mr. Hallinan. You will become accustomed to them after a while."[56]

Wanting immediately to imprison Hallinan, Judge Harris finally turned to Bridges: "Now, do you have anything to say, sir?"

"I might have, Your Honor, but what good would it do?" Bridges cautiously, honestly offered. "I have selected counsel that I want, but he is not available anymore," he continued. "What I would like is to have the trial wait until he is available, and that is quite a long time, it seems here." Intelligently praying on public opinion about the trial, Bridges then declared, "If things go wrong, I will never, never think that it was a square deal."[57]

After the day's extreme rancor, Judge Harris curiously began talking about himself in glowing first person terms. "I suppose I am a rather peculiar sort of fellow. I can't harbor malice. I can't harbor the subject matter that Mr. Hallinan poured into this court today," he mused.[58] Judge Harris's words conjured Shakespeare's "the lady doth protest too much, methinks." Judge Harris then retreated to his chambers, his Shakespearian protests reverberating in the courtroom.[59]

Judge Harris eventually returned to the bench and begrudgingly granted Hallinan a stay, ruling that he could remain until the end of the trial, at which point he would be imprisoned. The die was effectively cast, however, and the trial proceeded in a legal environment as unfriendly to Bridges and his legal team as the broader socio-political environment.[60]

From left to right, Harry Bridges, Henry Schmidt, and J.R. Robertson, all co-defendants in the criminal trial in San Francisco federal court. April 1950. Copyright San Francisco History Center, San Francisco Public Library.

The Government's Main Witnesses Are Caught Lying

The government started its case with two central witnesses, each of whom were former Communist Party members, and each of whom testified that Harry Bridges had attended an upper-echelon Communist Party Politburo meeting. The first, Manning Johnson, testified that he had been a high-ranking Communist Party member but had subsequently left the party. However, while a member, Johnson testified, he had attended a New York meeting of senior Communist Party members on June 27, 1936, and that Bridges not only attended but also was elected to a high-ranking position that afternoon, where he complimented the Communist Party on how well it operated.[61] Sitting down, Donohue no doubt felt good about his case.

Harry Bridges, however, was scratching his head and searching his memory.[62]

Hallinan quickly set to work and demonstrated that Johnson was in fact a professional government witness. Admitting he had testified in around twenty cases, the government essentially had him as a witness on demand, serially testifying in cases of alleged communists all over the country, with the government paying his expenses. Then, Hallinan established that the government had interviewed Johnson ahead of the first trial, and despite the now-dynamite testimony he offered in 1950, the government had chosen not even to call him as a witness in 1939. The implication Hallinan contended: Johnson never made the claims in 1939, but now he was making the claims because he was on the government payroll as a professional witness. Hallinan also managed to get Johnson to admit, begrudgingly, that he was a closet racist: Johnson left the Communist Party because it advocated a Negro Republic in the Deep South.[63] By the time Hallinan was finished, fair questions hung over Johnson, but he had testified, seemingly damningly, that Bridges attended a secret high-level meeting on June 27, 1936.

Donohue next put Paul Crouch on the witness stand. Like Johnson, Crouch was a former Communist Party member who had now turned and become a professional, serial witness for the government in various anti-communist prosecutions around the country.[64] Crouch corroborated Johnson's testimony about Bridges' presence at the Communist Party election meeting on June 27, 1936, a meeting Crouch had also attended.[65] As Donohue handed Crouch to Hallinan for cross-examination, Donohue must have been supremely confident. Two witnesses had placed Bridges at the same, specific Communist Party event where he allegedly took an oath as a high-ranking party member. That was about as good as it could get for Donohue.

Hallinan, however, did not appear overly concerned and began his cross-examination slowly, going back to June 27, 1936. Crouch confirmed he was certainly present at the New York Politburo election meeting with Bridges. As Hallinan drew the details out, Crouch confirmed it was in New York City, even recalling the stifling New York heat. At Hallinan's prodding, Crouch remembered that the Politburo election meeting occurred in the afternoon or evening of June 27, and Bridges attended and was elected.[66]

Reaching a crescendo, Hallinan pulled out a stack of papers and showed Judge Harris that on the night of June 27, 1936, Bridges had attended a labor meeting in Stockton, California, a public event that even the press had attended. As Hallinan slowly produced newspaper article after article showing that the press quoted Bridges' remarks that night, Johnson's and Crouch's credibility was imploding.

Sketch of the trial by famed American illustrator Howard Brodie. Vince Hallinan is at the podium asking a witness a question. Judge Harris is on his bench, the jury is on the left, and the defendants are seated at the defense table on the right with Harry Bridges in the middle. Copyright Howard Brodie Estate.

Believing he had finally turned the tables, Hallinan demanded that Judge Harris hold Johnson and Crouch in contempt of court for clear perjury. Normally, Donohue, as an acting United States Attorney, would call a grand jury to indict the witnesses for perjury, but, as Hallinan remarked, how could anyone believe Donohue would indict them when Johnson and Crouch were Donohue's own "bloodhounds."[67] Hallinan even begged Judge Harris for symmetry and equality in judicial handling of the matter: "I am to be both imprisoned and disbarred. Here these men come in here and commit abject, flagrant, arrant perjury, bold-faced, smiling, a grin on his face as he narrates the thing; the other man, a…foul Hyena of Hell comes in here…How long are they going to get away with it?"[68]

But Judge Harris refused to hold them in contempt. Whereas Judge Harris and Prosecutor Donohue argued that the dignity of the court required disbarring and imprisoning Hallinan for contempt for his overzealous lawyering (and stripping the accused of his chosen counsel), the dignity of the court did not require even charging with contempt the government's witnesses despite their demonstrable lies. Instead, Judge Harris told Hallinan that it was not the judge's role to charge the witness, and Hallinan should just argue to the jury who was telling the truth. Given the clear proof that Bridges was not in New York on the very specific day when the professional witnesses placed him there, Hallinan was no doubt distressed that Judge Harris blunted his obvious victory, yet also hopeful the jury would now at last see through the government's case.[69]

Donohue then moved to another alleged former communist, called Lawrence Ross. Donohue first had Ross testify to his solid American credentials, an illustrious academic background as a University of Kentucky graduate with deep American roots in a Kentucky farming family.[70] As Ross was talking, Hallinan's investigators raced from the courtroom to begin research into Ross's background.[71]

Like Crouch and Johnson, Ross testified that he got drawn into the Communist Party, but grew disillusioned with the party and eventually left, at which point he took up professional witnessing against communists in the United States government's anti-communist prosecutions of the 1940s. Looking to avoid a repeat of the Crouch-Johnson June 1936 fiasco, Ross testified that, while he had attended the 1936 convention, he had not seen Bridges present.[72] But he did testify that he had been at other Communist Party meetings where Bridges had attended and spoke—on dates he could not specifically remember (thereby depriving Hallinan the ability to prove that the highly public figure Bridges was elsewhere on the day in question).[73]

As cross-examination was under way, Hallinan's investigator returned and handed him a telegram. There is nothing better for a lawyer cross-examining a witness than to corner the witness and show that the witness just lied under oath. If a witness perjures himself in supporting the government's case, exposing the lie not only destroys the witness's credibility, but destroys the government's credibility in the entire prosecution. This is the heart of reasonable doubt. Having already managed to break Crouch and Johnson on the June 1936 New York party meeting issue, Hallinan must have looked at the telegram with utter delight. Hallinan was ready for a cross-examination that trial lawyers dream about.[74]

As he reviewed the telegram, Hallinan immediately shifted his questioning, asking Ross to restate and reconfirm where he was born, his name, and what university he had attended. Ross reconfirmed his name, his 1903 Kentucky birth, his father's status as a farmer, and his attendance at the University of Kentucky.[75] Hallinan was laying a trap.

"Do you remember anybody in your class at that school?" Hallinan demanded.

"I'm afraid I do not," Ross oddly offered.

"Can you remember one person who was a college classmate of yours at that school?" Hallinan again probed.

"No, sir," Ross nervously answered.

"You didn't go there at all did you?" Hallinan demanded.

But Ross insisted that he had gone to the University of Kentucky. Hallinan then asked if Ross had ever used a different name, and Ross denied it.[76]

The trap set, Hallinan was ready to spring it. The telegram he held came from the University of Kentucky itself, and showed that Ross had never attended, and, what is more, that Ross was not born in Kentucky and was instead a Polish immigrant, perhaps here illegally himself! Donohue, sensing the disaster that was about to unfold, started complaining that Judge Harris should dismiss Ross because his wife and son needed him, and the cross-examination now had ventured into irrelevant matters. Ross joined and begged to return home because of family demands. Judge Harris was about to let him go, so Hallinan had to share some of his evidence of Ross's lies to convince Judge Harris to keep Ross on the stand. Judge Harris ordered Ross to return the next trial day.[77]

Ross and Donohue had the evening to prepare, well aware of the high likelihood that the lies had been discovered. The next day on the stand, Ross quickly admitted his lies in an effort at self-confession to blunt his prior day's lies. His real name was Rosenstein, he was born in Poland, and he came to the United States in 1910 at age seven. He attended high school in the Bronx, New York, and it was not even clear if he had ever set foot in Kentucky. Nor was his father a farmer, the very symbol of American honesty and greatness. In short, Ross/Rosenstein's entire identity was a lie, one he concocted in a plan to Americanize himself. Trapped, he then had to admit that in other communist deportation proceedings across the country he had lied under oath about his background and his American qualifications.[78] But even in confessing his lies, he sought to minimize them, claiming a mere "evasion of the truth" in an attempt at "Americanization."[79] Finally, he admitted that he had the day before desperately tried to leave the trial because he knew from the questions that his lie had been uncovered. He thus was perfectly content to ride off into the sunset and leave his lies buried forever, notwithstanding the dire fate of three men on trial.[80]

Hallinan and MacInnis were both livid and demanded that Ross/Rosenstein be held for contempt and sent before the grand jury, and that Donohue be sanctioned for his efforts to escort Ross/Rosenstein out of state to shield him from the devastating cross-examination that was to unfold. Donohue rejected the charge, and Judge Harris seemed uninterested in Ross/Rosenstein's blatant lies. The acrimony escalated. Hallinan complained that he had been trying to prove a conspiracy all along, had been denied the right to argue it, but here there had been three witnesses in a row caught lying, and even Donohue had tried to aid the perjuring Ross/Rosenstein to escape scrutiny. How could this not be the very conspiracy he promised to show?

With his typically colorful, aggressive flair, Hallinan attacked Donohue: "I have not seen inferior merits or inferior qualities better rewarded since Caligula made a consul of his horse and Charles II knighted a beefsteak…And I say now in closing that anything I have said about Mr. Donohue, any implications or any inferences that I have made as to his dishonesty and his corruption, I double and redouble!"[81]

But Judge Harris could not be swayed and refused to make a contempt finding, instead sanitizing Donohue's efforts to shield Ross/Rosenstein by instructing the jurors to erase from their minds all of Hallinan's complaints about Donohue.[82] Ross/Rosenstein meanwhile was released, neither charged nor cited.

Bridges Lets an Old Friend Off Easily

Donohue's last major witness was George Wilson, a CIO labor man. He joined the Communist Party in 1941 and left in 1945, and he clearly did not want to be a government witness. A long-term friend of Bridges, Wilson testified with palpable physical and emotional distress. As one observer reported, "He sat there with his mouth open and his tongue hanging out and his chest heaving as if he was gasping for air. His head was rolling from side to side and he was slobbering as he tried to answer questions. This man was in terrible distress. It was a pity to look at a man distressed by what he was doing."[83] The press reported similarly: "It was like an acute physical sickness; it caused him to fidget and move his hands aimlessly about and run his tongue around the inside of his mouth and swallow his words and give vent to odd contortions of the legs and shoulders."[84]

Wilson knew he was betraying a friend and did not want to testify, but he had allegedly been pressured by prosecutors who had leverage over him. Apparently Wilson had once signed an affidavit saying he was not a communist, a lie since he was one, and now faced the pressure of a prosecution and prison sentence for perjury himself, witnesses reported.[85] His testimony lasted no more than fifteen minutes, and as he finished testifying, Donohue squarely asked him whether he had attended official Communist Party meetings with Schmidt and Robertson—who were citizens, so that alone was not illegal for them—and Wilson said he had. But Donohue—a skilled lawyer—posed more vague questions when it got to Bridges. Donohue asked if Wilson had attended several meetings with Bridges, and Wilson testified about a meeting at the Governor Hotel where various labor officials were present along with Bridges. They discussed labor issues, yet he did not squarely say Harry Bridges was a Communist Party member or that the Governor Hotel meeting was an official Communist Party meeting. Wilson eventually did declare that the Governor Hotel meeting involved a bunch of communists discussing labor issues.[86]

Wilson's final comment was bad, but, given the elliptical nature of how it eventually came out, was also seemingly weak. On cross-examination, Hallinan got Wilson to agree that the meeting was a discussion about California state CIO labor policy. The distinction was important because a labor meeting that may have had some communists present stood in great contrast to an official Communist Party meeting. After only a few questions, Judge Harris ordered an atypically early recess, owing to the stuttering Wilson, who was clearly having physical and emotional problems on the stand.[87]

At the break, Bridges, Hallinan, and the legal team discussed strategy. Licking his lips, Hallinan wanted to break Wilson with a devastating cross-examination. But Bridges had always liked Wilson and was moved by seeing him in terrible physical distress. "George's wife called me last night and said, 'George is in terrible, terrible condition. He is absolutely out of his mind with misery at what's happening.' She said, 'Don't be too hard on him. I don't know what to do,'" Bridges explained in the impromptu strategy meeting. Bridges added that Wilson's wife had offered, "'He's got a weak heart and if you go after him too hard, it might be too much for him.'" Bridges then concluded, "After all, he's an old friend. There wasn't anything vicious in his testimony. He testified only because they had him on the spot and he had to."

Hallinan the trial lawyer still wanted to pounce and destroy Wilson, opening up the fact that Wilson was pressured to lie and exaggerate to escape the Sword of Damocles hanging over him. Bridges instead decided to let Wilson go easily, and so as they resumed, Hallinan asked only one more question and rested. In all, Wilson didn't spend more than twenty minutes on the witness stand in a near six-month trial, but letting Wilson off would prove fateful.[88]

A Catholic Priest Enters the Firing Line

As the defense began their case, the defense called Father Meinecke, its first character witness. Father Meinecke was a Catholic priest in his 60s who lost one of his legs in surgery and testified that it made him a more, not less, charitable man.[89]

Father Meinecke personally knew Bridges, and Hallinan wanted Father Meinecke to offer reputation evidence about Bridges, specifically that Bridges was an honest man and was not a Communist Party member. This material would help the jury understand that Bridges was a decent man, and Father Meinecke was an honorable character witness to help reassure the jury that Bridges was not a communist. To be sure, that he was a Catholic priest could carry significant weight in front of the jury. Father Meinecke thus testified that he had known Bridges since the mid-1930s, when Bridges sought Father Meinecke's help to get his daughter into a local Catholic school. The two became friends of sorts and spent hours discussing local political waterfront issues. Father Meinecke was himself involved in local waterfront politics, and also an avid anti-communist, and so testified that he had inquired deeply of Bridges to discern Bridges' character. His conclusion was that Bridges was not a communist, and Bridges' reputation was one of utmost honesty and decency. Hallinan was done with his questions within twenty minutes or so.[90]

Donohue then cross-examined Father Meinecke, and instantly tried to claim the mantle of religious righteousness by raising Bridges' divorce with Father Meinecke and implying Bridges was out of favor with the Church.[91] Father Meinecke rejected the charge. Donohue then sought to establish that Father Meinecke did not truly know the inner heart of Bridges. He asked the questions one would expect but did not score any significant points in cross-examination. Despite his age, Father Meinecke was feisty and fast.

When Donohue asked if he was moved to a new parish where there were no trade unions—implying the Father was himself a biased militant trade unionist and punished by the Church for it—Father Meinecke rejected the charge, and in hilarious dead-pan, offered Donohue forgiveness for Donohue's implied slur.[92] Donohue tucked his tail between his legs and sat down after no more than thirty minutes, certainly aware that he failed to break Father Meinecke.[93]

Matters now turned. Normally, at that point, the witness would be excused and the defense would call its next witness. But Judge Harris refused to excuse Father Meinecke even though Donohue had completed his cross-examination. Instead, Judge Harris claimed he had one question of the Father, but proceeded to lead a scathing multi-question cross-examination himself in a bid to demonstrate that Father Meinecke was old and had a bad memory. Judge Harris slyly asked typical cross-examination questions that opposing lawyers would ask, things such as how often he spoke to Hallinan, how long he prepared for his testimony, and then who had refreshed his memory in anticipation of his testimony, implying the Father had a failed memory and so was coached. Judge Harris then outright impugned Father Meinecke's memory: "Do you have difficulty, Father, with your memory or recollection under ordinary conditions?"[94] By the time Judge Harris was done, any reasonable juror—in awe of the federal judge who sat literally higher than them on his bench—would believe that the federal judge knew something significant and had proved it. Indeed, Judge Harris all but discredited Father Meinecke as a potentially bumbling priest with a failed memory.

This was remarkable because Donohue and the government prosecutors had every opportunity to attack Father Meinecke on these grounds and chose not to. A judge rarely if ever takes it upon himself to come to the aid of the government to help destroy a witness, because the government has able lawyers who know how to try their case. Yet Judge Harris did just that with Father Meinecke.

This is another fingerprint of judicial impropriety that hangs in the trial record and demonstrates a judge who too vigorously put his thumb on the delicate scales of justice.

The defense lawyers were aghast. Hallinan, already facing a jail term, objected but did not take the charge, this time leaving it to his law partner, MacInnis. Livid, MacInnis complained that Judge Harris had transcended the bounds of judging and had become a partisan advocate. MacInnis asked the judge to admonish the jury to ignore the judge's questions. Judge Harris rejected the charge and even stated that MacInnis had invited him to ask Father Meinecke questions. This was not true; MacInnis had earlier objected to a specific government question that had nothing to do with Father Meinecke's age or memory and told Judge Harris to confirm that specific issue with Father Meinecke. The cold record shows MacInnis never offered Father Meinecke to Judge Harris as some sort of feeding-frenzy witness. Judge Harris's obvious dissembling is itself another instance of judicial impropriety.

"There is no impropriety in my questioning," Judge Harris instructed the jury.

"I say there is," MacInnis rapidly retorted. "I have never heard anything like that. You ought to be ashamed of yourself," he boldly added.[95]

Donohue suddenly asserted that he now wanted more time with Father Meinecke, even though he had already rested his cross-examination.[96] Judge Harris gave it to him, and so Father Meinecke was ordered to return the next day to face Donohue again.

The next day, Donohue picked up where Judge Harris had left off in a perfect tag-team formation. Donohue grilled Father Meinecke about the intricacies of American foreign policy during World War II and the Communist Party's position. Donohue grandstanded that because communists opposed World War II, if Bridges had ever said anything that opposed the war, then he must be a Communist Party member. Pushing Father Meinecke on ancient and irrelevant political issues around World War II, Dono-hue sought to demonstrate that Father Meinecke lacked deep intel-lect or recall of old events. No slouch, Father Meinecke did his best to answer the arcane questions that anyone would have a hard time answering, holding firm to his belief that one could be a militant trade unionist without being a communist.[97]

Father Meinecke should have been on the witness stand for an hour. But because Judge Harris had interjected himself deeply into the direction of the testimony, Father Meinecke spent two days on the stand. By the time Father Meinecke was off the stand, Judge Harris had mightily damaged his credibility, and Donohue had then gladly taken the hand-off and continued the assault. What had been a quick witness and a character building opportunity to help Bridg-es, instead now devolved into an example of judicial intervention to aid the government and its legion of lawyers.

But it wasn't over. After Father Meinecke left, Judge Harris turned to MacInnis and held him in criminal contempt for his chal-lenges to the judge's supremacy. He sentenced MacInnis to three months in prison at the end of the case. Hallinan now had a cell-mate.

The Defendants

Bridges, Schmidt, and Robertson all denied any grand con-spiracy. Bridges, for the third time now, spent days testifying on the stand about his past in Australia, the labor struggles of the 1920s, his political views, and his labor union fights in the 1930s that brought him to prominence. Critically, he testified at length about the dem-ocratic nature of his union and the undemocratic character of the earlier Blue Book union controlled by the employers.[98] This was one of the central ironies to the entire Bridges deportation saga: the em-ployers' Blue Book union operated much like a country behind the Iron Curtain—no voice for the workers, no voting, no transparency, corruption at the top. Bridges' democratic union was transparent and democratic: every worker had one vote with no racial, religious, or political discrimination. And Bridges was decried the communist by the employers.

Bridges also confirmed that he was in Stockton, not New York, on the night he was allegedly inducted into the Communist Party, categorically denying the charge of Crouch.[99]

Bridges then proved ongoing FBI wiretapping and surveillance with teletype message evidence. Bridges' union office, like many companies of the time, had a teletype machine that would be turned on and connected to an operator. When turned on, a person could type a message to a recipient who would receive it at their office, after the message went through relay stations. The recipient could reply in real time, all the while an operator from the teletype company (such as Western Union) managed the process. People could do the equivalent of modern-day telephonic conference calls or group Skype communications, by connecting multiple offices at the same time, and all could send messages to one another. The message would come out of the machine at the other end on a long ticker tape. And, as Bridges explained to the jury, sometimes he would receive a ticker tape message that began with transcribed operator notes stating "hold, the FBI is not on the line" before the actual message then followed.[100] The accidental slip by the operator transcribing every word uttered on the line proved FBI monitoring of communications.

Bridges also discussed his personal financial situation: earning a salary of $540 a month, less than some workers in the union because the union policy was that officers never earned more than the highest paid laborer; living in a $14,000 home mortgaged for twenty years; and driving a ten-year-old De Soto.[101]

By now Bridges was a skilled witness. Whereas in the first two trials, the government lawyers had tried with some success to limit his testimony, now Bridges spoke for extended periods in response to questions, deftly talking at length yet all the while responding to the specific question. Donohue became visibly frustrated as Bridges would spend several minutes answering questions, weaving in and out of the union history to make his point. At one point, Donohue thought he had Bridges when Bridges admitted that his union had some communists in it: "I know the membership of our union generally…but the handful of communists in our union, they couldn't do much about our union one way or the other in so far as deciding its policy. The best they could do, and everybody in the union knows it, they stand up on the floor, communists as well as other people, and they propose a certain proposition…If they haven't got a good proposition, they won't get any support no matter who they are. And that goes for me, too."[102] Bridges believed his union democratic, allowing every member, regardless of politics, his right to speak and air an opinion. Donohue saw the same evidence as communist coddling, indicia of Bridges' secret membership.[103]

As Donohue pressed, Bridges again reiterated his position as a labor leader focused on basic working conditions: "What bothers our workers today is that they want to be able to work; they haven't got enough work. There isn't enough jobs. The unemployed are growing. The people aren't working enough. They are beginning to go hungry. They are getting insecure. Payments are becoming due on their house, the automobile, the radio, and they've got to give them up. Day after day we get more and more complaints, and believe me, the question of communism is not a real problem, not as far as our union is concerned. The question of the workers getting enough to make a living and getting a little security, that is the real problem."[104] How the jury would interpret Bridges' lengthy testimony was anyone's guess at that point.

Harry Bridges testifies in the federal criminal prosecution, February 7, 1950. Copyright San Francisco History Center, San Francisco Public Library.

Finally, as to poor J.R. Robertson, he had never even attended the naturalization hearing to be a witness, and instead was yanked in at the last second when the main witness was not accepted. Stuck in a trial fighting for his freedom, Robertson reported that he spent his trial days often staring at the court ceiling where he could make out a swastika symbol in its design. Given the facts, it was inconceivable that Robertson could have been part of a conspiracy, which by definition requires pre-planning. Apparently, even Donohue eventually realized that Robertson could not have been part of a conspiracy, and offered to dismiss him. However, Robertson, although a nervous wreck in the trial, in a show of solidarity nonetheless chose to stand or fall with his fellow defendants.[105]

Closing Arguments

From the moment Donohue took the podium to deliver his closing argument, his fangs were out, noting for the jury that Bridges' lawyers had regularly represented communists around the country.[106] The implication was clear: if they represented other communists, then Bridges must be one too. Playing heavily to the jury's passions, he then started by discussing a near-irrelevant defense witness, Jean Marie Murray. The only thing of interest Murray had said occurred when she was asked to swear an oath to tell the truth "so help her God." She agreed to tell the truth but could not agree to swear an oath to God because she believed only in "justice on earth." In closing, Donohue attacked her as a "God-denying, America-hating" woman and used her refusal to swear an oath to imply Bridges was part of some godless enterprise.[107] This picked up on the theme Donohue had explored when he tried to get Father Meinecke to agree Bridges was not a good Catholic because he was divorced. Overall, Donohue pandered to the jury's perceived religious sensibilities and prejudices, and the fact that he chose to start his closing argument on this point demonstrates how strongly he believed he could sway the jury by focusing on these broader subtext issues. In all, Donohue spoke for a day, pushing the jury to follow the testimony of Johnson, Crouch, Ross/Rosenstein, and Wilson.

Vince Hallinan, the veteran trial lawyer, arguing the case to the jury. Courtesy of ILWU, San Francisco.

Hallinan confronted a mighty task. Judge Harris had from the first days of the trial circumscribed Hallinan's defense theory of a government conspiracy, had taken it upon himself to attack Bridges' character witnesses, and had found Hallinan in criminal contempt, something even the jury now knew. Hallinan nonetheless made a multi-day impassioned plea to the jury. He reminded them that the government's witnesses were caught lying on the stand about Bridges' attendance at the New York Communist Party event. He lampooned Ross/Rosenstein, who was caught lying about his background. He argued that all of these witnesses were professional, paid government witnesses, traveling the nation to testify in communist deportation trials. If he had a jury of citizens concerned about government overreach, Harry Bridges had a winning argument. But if the jury was more concerned about the threat of communists on American shores, Bridges faced great personal risk. And in the middle of it all, Judge Harris's comments and courtroom behavior lingered like an elephant in the corner of the courtroom.

After the many days of closing arguments, the six-month trial finally ended on March 31, 1950, the longest federal court trial in San Francisco history at that time.[108] On that last day, it has been reported, FBI agents were stationed outside the homes of the jurors, and the press was told the FBI agents were needed to protect the jurors, intimating to all that the jurors faced some sort of reprisal risk if they convicted Bridges.[109] In the courtroom, Judge Harris in turn instructed the jury on the law, and the jury was excused to begin deliberations.

The Jury Returns

After four days of deliberations, on April 4, 1950, the jury announced it had a verdict. Reporters, family, and spectators packed the courtroom. As the jury shuffled in, one reporter, shocked by the fated, grim appearance of the jury, lost his composure and exclaimed out loud, "Oh Jesus, look at them." Before the jury even took their seats in the jury box, Schmidt's daughter began wailing.[110]

The verdict was read. Bridges, Schmidt, and Robertson were convicted of perjury and conspiracy on all counts. As Hallinan later recalled, Judge Harris beamed with delight as the verdict was read.[111] Bridges stood tall and, having been through fifteen years of such "trials," appeared hardly shocked that the system had reached this end. Schmidt was equally relaxed. Hallinan on the other hand was completely shocked, his face frozen. Like many a trial lawyer facing long odds, Hallinan had really thought that his skills would win the day and overcome any obstacle. He simply could not believe that he had failed to pull the proverbial rabbit out of the hat and establish at least reasonable doubt.[112] And poor Robertson, who was asked the day of Bridges' hearing simply to attest to Bridges' good standing because Bridges' main witness could not attest, had now also been convicted of conspiracy to commit fraud on the United States and was staring at years in federal prison. The experience was indeed Kafkaesque.

Judge Harris congratulated the jury, and in a moment of zeal betrayed his rejection of his role as a neutral arbiter when he excitedly exclaimed to the jury, "I desire you and each of you to know… that you have evidenced an intelligent appreciation of the facts in the light of the legal principles applicable. You have finally found the golden truth shimmering in the fiery crucibles of this trial."[113] The statement is nothing short of bizarre for a judge who is supposed to be neutral. Judges simply don't, or shouldn't, provide grand congratulations to juries on the avowed correctness of their verdicts.

In short order, Judge Harris swiftly sentenced Bridges to five years in prison and revoked his citizenship papers, meaning that after his five years in federal prison he would be returned to Australia. Schmidt and Robertson were sentenced to three years.[114] The United States Marshals immediately descended on the three and began to handcuff them, but the lawyers intervened and secured a continuance of the existing bail order through the appeals process.[115] Not for the first time, Harry Bridges' fate rested in the hands of the higher federal courts.

Beaming at the verdict, Judge Harris turned to Hallinan and resentenced him to six months in federal prison, and MacInnis to three months.[116]

CHAPTER 7

Prison for Speech

"If there is any fixed star in our constitutional constellation, it is that no official, high or petty, can prescribe what shall be orthodox in politics, nationalism, religion, or other matters of opinion or force citizens to confess by word or act their faith therein."

UNITED STATES SUPREME COURT IN *WEST VIRGINIA V. BARNETTE* (1943)

I t is axiomatic to our society that the citizenry have the right to engage in open, robust discussion about political issues and candidates. This value is crystalized in the First Amendment's free speech guarantee. Political speech in particular sits at the core of the First Amendment. As the Supreme Court has held: "Whatever differences may exist about interpretations of the First Amendment, there is practically universal agreement that a major purpose of that Amendment was to protect the free discussion of governmental affairs. This of course includes discussions of candidates, structures and forms of government, the manner in which government is operated or should be operated, and all such matters relating to political processes."[1] Sometimes, however, whether the courts breathe life into these platitudes depends upon the speaker and the speaker's message, an unfortunate reality that Harry Bridges was about to learn the hard way.

War!

Just as the appeal process began, communist North Korean troops invaded South Korea, on June 25, 1950, sending shock waves through America. As mobilization for the Korean War began, Bridges' union was confronted by the looming war, and the union had to decide its position on the war, because wars can affect all manner of union business, such as wage freezes, strike restrictions, and the like. Bridges spoke to the ILWU on June 28, 1950, and he argued that the union should formally demand that the United Nations intervene to secure a cease-fire to avoid an atomic world war.[2]

Bridges declared: "I am opposed to war, always have been, and will do my best to continue to be opposed to war...I just think that wars are terrible things; that they should be prevented, if possible, and once they break out they should be settled as quickly as possible and in the best and most peaceful manner." Bridges argued that as far as Korea was concerned, he did not know who was the true aggressor, and he feared the war spreading throughout Indo-China, with repercussions on American soil: "Before we start putting ourselves on the war wagon of that type, let us take a look-see and see what the impact is going to be on our union, our union conditions, and on the lives and whole future of the American people..."[3]

The union rejected his position and voted to support President Truman. Bridges, however, had spoken against the looming Korean War.

Apoplectic at Bridges' anti-war speech, Prosecutor Donohue raced back to Judge Harris with a motion to rescind Bridges' bail. Normally, bail is revoked when a person poses a flight risk. But Donohue's motion was not about flight risk. Instead, Donohue's motion focused on Bridges' anti-war beliefs, where Bridges also wrote an editorial arguing that public support for American involvement to protect South Korean democracy from communists was a fallacious theory to justify war because South Korea was no more democratic that China or Turkey. Bridges' commentary had set Donohue off. Prosecutor Donohue asked Judge Harris to revoke Bridges' bail because of his "course of conduct and activities dangerous and detrimental to the public welfare and inimical to the safety and national security of the United States."[4] Hysterical, Donohue believed Harry Bridges was Public Enemy Number One: "It is almost incredible, if Your Honor pleases, that this great country of ours can survive [if Bridges is] permitted [his] liberty to publish this kind of filth in criticism of the country…He is our enemy."[5]

Hallinan for obvious reasons did not attend the bail revocation hearing to defend Bridges. Instead, Bridges attended with Norman Leonard, a partner in the law firm with Gladstein and Grossman.

At the hearing, Leonard, tall and often seen wearing a bow tie to accompany his owl-shaped reading glasses, asked Donohue a critical question, emblematic of the entire bail revocation proceeding:

"For the record, so I may understand the government's position, do I understand that in the course of this inquiry, or whatever he may call it, the rules of evidence and the rules of law are not applicable?"

"Of course they are not," Donohue asserted.

Startled at the government's gleeful abandonment of the rule of law, Leonard fumed at the show-like nature of the proceeding: "Now, then, is the court going to determine the legal question or the factual question without proceeding in the normal, thousand-year-old, time-tested method in Anglo-American jurisprudence, for determining those matters? Then we might just as well not be in a court."[6]

Leonard tried to save Bridges by putting him on the stand to explain his speech and explain why he was not a threat. On the stand, Bridges stated: "I think now more than ever it is my duty, and I do not consider it disloyal to intensify the fight to prevent this war in Korea from spreading and developing into a third world war...I don't want to see another world war. I don't want to see the United States of America in another world war. I think I have got a patriotic American duty to do what little I can to stop it."

Bridges was also worried about the practical impact of a large-scale war on the union: "Well, at times of war, why, hysteria can develop and it can be detrimental and harmful to a union...I think the impact upon our economy will be too great. I know what happened to prices already..."[7]

Bridges' testimony was not enough, and Leonard's dark assessment of a contorted legal proceeding proved correct when, at the end of the hearing, Judge Harris immediately revoked Bridges' bail and sent him to prison.[8] As Judge Harris imprisoned Bridges because he spoke his anti-war beliefs, the First Amendment and its guarantee of free speech—uniquely important to political speech about major political issues such as the propriety of a national war—simply disappeared from Judge Harris's equation. The eloquent First Amendment platitudes issued by the Supreme Court in its *West Virginia v. Barnette* decision quoted at the chapter's outset, words issued only a few years before Judge Harris's decision, offered no refuge to Harry Bridges and failed to rein in Judge Harris. The absurd irony to the entire show, nearly comic but for the serious consequences and underscoring the real speech-repressive purpose of the bail revocation proceeding: if in fact Bridges fled the country, he would have fulfilled the exact objective that the government had relentlessly pursued for the prior fifteen years.[9]

Bridges took a rapid appeal of the bail revocation order to the Ninth Circuit Court of Appeals in San Francisco. Nineteen days later, a three-judge panel decided the bail issue on an emergency basis. Two of the judges expressed revulsion at Judge Harris's prostration to the executive: "The whole matter appears finally to boil down to the contention that Bridges is a proven communist in that he was found guilty of perjury for swearing the contrary in his naturalization proceeding; and that the subsequent development of the Korean crisis renders him per se a menace to the public security, hence the district court was right in revoking his bail and ordering him confined," the Ninth Circuit ruled.

The Ninth Circuit judges continued: "The conclusion, if we may say, is as startling as it is novel. The power of waging war is lodged by the Constitution in the Congress and the executive branch of the government. In the three great wars in which this country has engaged in the past ninety years, the executive arm has found ways and means of dealing for itself with suspected subversives and those thought foes of the national security. President Lincoln was not slow to take such measures on his own responsibility whenever he thought that course expedient, however little the courts of his day might like his methods. The examples freshest in the memory of the present generation are the setting up by the executive during the second world war of military rule and the suspension of the writ of habeas corpus in the Territory of Hawaii, plus the enforced removal pursuant to presidential proclamation of the entire Japanese population from the Pacific Coast. But here, in this case, a procedure admittedly without precedent in the history of the Republic has been inaugurated, namely, to make the courts the effective instruments of executive expediency."[10]

In no uncertain terms, the Ninth Circuit judges likened Judge Harris's decision to the historical prostitution of judges to the Crown, one of the most basic ills the American Constitution sought to eradicate with its separation of powers: "There was a period in

English history when high judges prostituted themselves to the role of mere instruments for carrying into effect the arbitrary will of the Crown; and the memory of that experience took deep lodgment in the hearts of the English-speaking peoples. It was in part owing to those unhappy experiences that in our constitutional system the judiciary was set up as an equal branch of the government, independent both of the executive and the legislative arms. The conception of the founders was of an unfettered judiciary standing, wherever necessary, between the individual and the exercise by the state of arbitrary power."[11]

It is hard to write a more stinging indictment of judicial abdication and abandonment of basic precepts. Yet even then, ominously, one of the Ninth Circuit judges dissented, insisting that Bridges remain in prison because Bridges dissented against the Korean War policy: "He has deliberately forfeited such claim to be admitted to bail, and his brazen conduct is opposed to the welfare of our government in this period of crisis and emergency."[12]

After three weeks in prison, Bridges was released, all hopes to avoid a lengthy prison term and deportation now pinned on the appeal of the convictions.

Hallinan and MacInnis, on the other hand, were not so lucky and served their contempt sentences at the McNeil Island Penitentiary in freezing Puget Sound.[13]

Jury Misconduct?

Meanwhile, Bridges' investigators had interviewed the jurors. In these long-archived documents, never previously published, the juror interviews show that they faced tremendous social pressure to convict. For example, one juror reported to others during the trial that her friends had told her to "take care" of that Bridges. Another admitted that he believed it was "impossible to get an unprejudiced, fair-minded jury in a case of this sort." The juror interviews also show that some jurors believed others were convinced from the beginning to convict Bridges, and some jurors insisted on discussing the evidence in small groups during the trial, even though such talk was not permitted amongst jurors during the trial. One juror even reported that the government's witnesses, except Wilson, were all paid perjurers, but still he voted to convict.

Breathing life into the adage that "no good deed shall go unpunished," multiple jurors confirmed that Wilson's testimony was the central basis for convicting Bridges. Wilson of course was saved from Hallinan's scathing cross-examination because of Bridges' compassion due to Wilson's health issues. "If George Wilson lied, I have helped to convict an innocent man," one juror reported. The same juror believed "Bridges to be one of the most persecuted men in history," but he still voted with the group to convict.[14]

In the end, only one juror had held out to acquit—a Chinese immigrant—but he experienced such pressure that he suffered bouts of diarrhea and vomiting, and so eventually capitulated and voted to convict.[15]

And what of the infamous Agnes Bridges affidavit? It was of course never formally admitted at trial, and Agnes Bridges was never called as a witness to attest to her allegations. Under the law's eyes, the document was not even evidence, because it was unauthenticated hearsay and was simply inadmissible. Indeed, Donohue had never tried to admit the document, nor call Agnes Bridges to the stand, which itself renders curious the entire act of giving it to Judge Harris and the clerk.[16] As Hallinan later recalled, after the affidavit was locked in the court's drawer during the trial, he forgot about it. But years later, after all of the trials, Hallinan reported that he learned from one of the jurors that Agnes Bridges' affidavit magically found its way from the locked drawer to the jury room. All the jurors read it, as the juror allegedly told Hallinan, and the affidavit formed a large basis of the jury's decision to convict.[17]

The sunlight of history can now wash over that document, one that should never have been presented to the court, and which should never have been seen by the jury, as Hallinan reported occurred. In recently declassified documents, a government confidential memorandum dated September 1948—before Bridges was indicted and before the affidavit was given to Judge Harris—identifies Agnes Bridges' alleged testimony, but also specifically declares that when the government agents approached her about the affidavit, she *denied* its truth: "The subject was confronted with the contents of the affidavit and denied the truth of the allegations set forth therein concerning his membership in the Communist Party and possession of a communist membership book."[18] Thus, with the passage of time and the declassification of secret documents, we can see that government prosecutors knew that Agnes Bridges specifically recanted her alleged affidavit (given while in bitter divorce proceedings against Bridges), yet nonetheless the government prosecutors offered it to the court in Bridges' trial, an offering that seemingly made its way to the jury room. These small turns of the law's wheels, as they all add together, were each fragments of the larger trial, yet as they are joined together, they form a mosaic whose comprised whole depicts a crusade.

Appeals

Bridges, as with his second deportation case, now had to appeal the jury's criminal verdict to the Ninth Circuit Court of Appeals again. As with his first trip there after the second deportation case, the Ninth Circuit again held against him and against Schmidt and Robertson. In Bridges' first trip to this court, after Judge Sears' decision, he had lost 3-2, at least garnering two dissenting votes. This time no judge took his side, even though the Ninth Circuit obliquely seemed to concede that Judge Harris's treatment of Father Meinecke was improper.[19]

The ILWU members in turn protested the Ninth Circuit decision by taking a one-day strike as a sign of solidarity with their embattled leader.[20]

For the second time, Bridges' last chance at avoiding deportation—as well as now a five-year prison sentence—depended upon convincing the Supreme Court to exercise its rarely invoked discretion to review cases. By now it was 1953, and Senator McCarthy had given his famous "I have in my hand" speech, Julius and Ethel Rosenberg had received the death sentence, and the Hollywood blacklisting of communists was well underway.[21] The Red Scare of the early 1950s provided an ominous backdrop to Harry Bridges' second attempt to get the Supreme Court to throw off the government's deportation efforts.

But lightning struck again as the Supreme Court agreed to review his criminal deportation case.

Back to the Supreme Court

In Bridges' first Supreme Court case, in 1945, one of the justices had recused himself. This time two did, leaving Bridges' fate in the hands of the seven remaining justices.

At oral argument, Justice Black, who supported Bridges in the first case, remained perplexed at the lengthening crusade, asking the government lawyer, "If you can try a man for something and get him up and let him testify and then indict him for perjury, and let him be acquitted, and then try him again, and then let him testify, and then try him again for perjury, what is the limit?" The government's appellate lawyer starkly responded that there was no limit to the number of prosecutions. The circular, byzantine trap could last forever, leaving Bridges in the grip of the law's absurdity.

Justice Frankfurter, the lone immigrant justice on the court, had disagreed with the 1945 Supreme Court opinion that saved Harry Bridges, and had voted to deport Bridges then. But Justice

Frankfurter now seemed to have a different attitude about the Bridges deportation saga. After pressing the government's lawyer about denaturalization proceedings and the government's prior prosecutions, Justice Frankfurter finally stated, "Your arguments should not embarrass you, but the cases should."[22]

If getting the Supreme Court to hear his case twice was rare, winning twice is a veritable black swan. Harry Bridges was just such a swan. On May 4, 1953, the Supreme Court issued its decision, and for the second time in the long-running deportation trials found in Harry Bridges' favor in a 4-3 decision that reversed the convictions and reinstated Bridges' citizenship. A testament to the executive's improper, relentless crusade, now, for the second time in eight years, the Supreme Court unwound the government's deportation prosecutions and again rebuffed the executive's deportation campaign.

Eight years after the first Supreme Court decision, Justice Frankfurter, the lone immigrant justice, now changed sides, and his was the deciding vote that saved Harry Bridges.

As written, the decision was a technical, legalistic document that lacked the powerful prose of Justice Murphy's 1945 opinion, or of the Ninth Circuit judges who condemned Judge Harris for his supination on the bail revocation issue. The Supreme Court concluded that when Bridges testified at his naturalization hearing in August 1945, the government had three years to pursue a criminal claim under the governing statute of limitations. It chose to wait over four years to indict Bridges. The suit accordingly was time-barred on technical legal grounds. In short, in its zeal to deport Harry Bridges, the executive had pursued a criminal case that was barred by the governing statute of limitations, an escapade that unnecessarily cost the taxpayers and the defendants dearly, in both financial and human terms.[23] Accordingly, all the convictions were reversed and Bridges' citizenship reinstated.

Justice Felix Frankfurter of the United States Supreme Court. He voted against Harry Bridges in the first appeal to the Supreme Court but voted for Harry Bridges in the second appeal. Library of Congress Prints and Photographs Division, Harris & Ewing Collection, LC-USZ62-36966.

When news reached the three defendants, all of whom were in a union conference with other union officials, each reacted differently. Schmidt calmly puffed his pipe. Robertson, the strapping former Texan prize fighter, literally fainted. And Bridges, now firmly believing the trials were behind him, sat silently, tears rolling down his cheek.[24]

And the Crusade Continues

Supreme Court Justice Murphy carefully selected the word "crusade" when, in 1945, he described the government's deportation efforts. Justice Murphy's "crusade" label had proved prescient beyond even his imagination. Since he penned that word, a third deportation trial had unfolded, coupled with the federal criminal prosecution and prison sentence, all with a new, and third, cast of characters testifying. Witnesses now swore under oath Bridges was at a secret New York Communist Party meeting, when in fact evidence proved he was in California the day of the alleged meeting. Other witnesses were professional, anti-communist witnesses, and Ross/Rosenstein repeatedly perjured himself under oath, claiming experience and backgrounds that were entirely fabricated to give himself deep "American" credentials in the trial against the alleged nefarious foreigner.

At the same time, Harry Bridges had experienced the wrath of Judge Harris, whose thumbs heavily rested on the scales of justice and decisively impacted the jury's perception of the case. From the curtailment of Bridges' counter-conspiracy defense theory, to the refusal to recuse himself despite an appearance of bias against Hallinan, to the criminal contempt charges against Hallinan and MacInnis, to the improper attacks on Father Meinecke's credibility, Judge Harris had tipped justice's delicate scales against Bridges in front of the jury, a group that, as history now shows, felt pressure to convict.[25] And despite it all, when the dust settled after a second trip to the United States Supreme Court, Harry Bridges had won, now for the third time.

But sometimes the facts, and even the law, don't matter when the judgment of otherwise rational people becomes obscured by the haze of fanaticism engendered by a crusade. That's the nature of a wrathful crusade, because it proceeds both steadfast in the belief that the end justifies any means, and oblivious to the legal, moral, or social dictates of right and wrong. Not capitulating, the government lawyers and executive officials now exploited one last legal technicality. Because the Supreme Court's decision rested on statute of limitations grounds, it had not technically condemned the jury's factual verdict itself; and because the government's civil lawsuit did not face the same statute of limitations, the government believed it could take another bite at the apple and again seek a factual finding that Bridges was a member of the Communist Party. Thus, during the height of America's Red Scare, the government, despite having thrice lost, now wagered for a fourth and final battle to deport Harry Bridges.

CHAPTER 8

The Final Campaign

"There is a point beyond which even justice becomes unjust."

SOPHOCLES, *ELECTRA* (410 BCE)

W hen the Supreme Court reversed the criminal convictions in 1953, the government prosecutors had one last trick up their sleeve: a federal court civil denaturalization lawsuit, an action not barred by the statute of limitations. This civil lawsuit was filed when the criminal indictment was filed in 1949, but at that time, Judge Harris stayed the civil case until the conclusion of the criminal case. Now that the criminal case was over, the civil case's stay order could be lifted and the civil denaturalization proceeding could proceed. The civil case required the government to prove again that Bridges lied when he swore his oath of citizenship.

Many actions can be charged as criminal violations as well as civil violations—all without triggering the Constitution's prohibition against double jeopardy—giving the government incredible leverage over the accused.[1] A criminal charge requires the government to prove the case "beyond a reasonable doubt" and can lead to prison for the defendant if convicted. A civil charge is subject to lower standards of proof known as "preponderance of the evidence" or "clear and convincing evidence" standards. Under those significantly lower standards, a fact-finder decides for whichever side has the greater weight of the evidence. Thus, the government now needed to prove Bridges' Communist Party membership only by the lower, "clear and convincing" standard, an easier yardstick to meet than the criminal "beyond a reasonable doubt" standard. This was the final card the government had to play. As one of the government prosecutors explained, still "the government then held out under oath that it had clear, convincing, and unequivocal evidence that Mr. Bridges had committed perjury."[2]

Because the case was a civil one, the specter of prison was off the table, but denaturalization and deportation remained decidedly on the table as the avowed goal. The government thus prepared to play its final hand.

The Final Showdown's Stage Is Set

By the time the government's civil case was ready to proceed, 1953 had passed to 1954, and 1954 to 1955. The times were beginning to change, and the Red Scare of the 1940s and early 1950s had peaked and, although still potent, was starting to lose some public support and steam. By 1955, in one of Senator McCarthy's Senate hearings into alleged communist activities, army representative Joseph Welch challenged Senator McCarthy with his impassioned, now-famed rhetorical plea—"Have you no sense of decency, sir, at long last? Have you left no sense of decency?"—one that caused the entire Senate gallery to erupt in applause.[3] Likewise, journalist Edward Murrow had famously broadcast a television show challenging the legitimacy of Senator McCarthy's tactics and quoted Cassius's statement as ascribed by Shakespeare: "The fault, dear Brutus, is not in our stars, but in ourselves."[4] These fingerprints of the beginning of a changing atmosphere at least bode slightly better for Bridges than the atmosphere of his prior trials.

Having lost three times already, the government—one may think—would have shown up at the fourth trial expecting to lose and simply trying to put on a case to appease certain political elements. Not so. The government arrived for a fight it intended to win. Stunningly, and as each trial before proceeded, the government again managed to rustle up an entirely new set of witnesses, none of whom had testified in either the first or second trial, and only a couple of whom were repeat players from the third trial. Even though it professed to believe wholeheartedly in Crouch, Johnson, Ross/Rosenstein, and Wilson, from the third trial, the government warehoused these witnesses in favor of a new roster. The government, it seemed, could rustle up witnesses the way a Texas oil well delivered oil.

The civil trial was set for June 1955, in the same federal court in San Francisco as the criminal trial. This time, a jury would not decide the case, because the issue of denaturalization did not belong before a jury under the Seventh Amendment of the United States Constitution. Rather, this time only the judge would decide it. Bridges' problem, of course, was Judge Harris. It goes without saying that, given the criminal trial before Judge Harris, if Judge Harris presided over the civil case, Bridges would lose and be deported.

But in a remarkable twist, Judge Harris did not secure assignment of the civil trial, despite his handling of the criminal trial and initial handling of the civil suit when he stayed it. Rather, the chief judge of the San Francisco federal court now assigned the civil trial to Judge Louis Goodman. The archived court records and

docket sheets do not identify why this assignment occurred, but it is safe to assume
that the acerbic environment
and the problems that had
plagued Judge Harris in the
criminal trial were enough
to raise skeptical eyes in all
quarters as to his ability to
maintain an unbiased courtroom. Judge Harris certainly
harbored deep feelings about
the criminal trial even decades later when he discussed
it with interviewers for his
memoirs. In those interviews,
he regularly was curt and
asked the interviewer to move
along as the discussion circled
around the heady issues that
Hallinan had provoked him
with decades earlier.[5]

United States District Judge Louis Goodman. He
was nominated to the federal bench by President
Roosevelt in 1942. Courtesy of the United States
District Court for the Northern District of California.

Two decades had now passed since the government's deportation investigations began in 1934-35, and Bridges was now in his
mid-fifties. Recently divorced from Nancy, his face had grown long
and leathered, his wrinkles had deepened, and his hairline had reced-
ed, exposing a large forehead creased with brow lines, like seagulls
aloft above the horizon. Time had relentlessly marched forward, and
the changes in Bridges' appearance since his early days in the Great
Strike and the first trial were obvious.

Bridges had made some strategic changes, too. This time,
he secured a new trial lawyer, Telford Taylor. A brigadier general in the United States Army, Taylor became renowned after his

prosecution of Nazi war criminals at the Nuremberg War Trials at the end of World War II, the most important international prosecution in history. An international statesman of the law, after the Nuremberg Trials, Taylor had returned to the United States and was in private practice by the 1950s. With a widow's peak and thick eyebrows, Taylor looked every part the distinguished gentleman. As a lawyer of international repute, Taylor's presence radiated the highest of stakes and caliber.

Taylor was also willing to battle the political forces that pushed the anti-communist agenda, and by 1955 had long been a leading critic of HUAC's and Senator McCarthy's pursuits of communists. In 1953, Taylor, at personal risk, had publicly criticized McCarthy's tactics in a speech at West Point, arguing that Senator McCarthy was "a most dangerous threat" and a "dangerous adventurer." He charged that Senator McCarthy's tactics in his anti-communist hearings were "calculated to create panic."[6] He also accused President Eisenhower of cowering in fear to the congressional communist investigations.[7] In another speech to the New York Young Democratic Club, he crystallized the issue of a broken system: "Witnesses have been intimidated to the point where the people don't know what charges are brought against them and what accusations are meaningless."[8]

By 1955, Taylor had published a book, entitled *Grand Inquest*, challenging the tactics of HUAC, Congressman Dies, and Senator McCarthy in particular. Taylor's public stance of course worried his prestigious New York law firm's partners, as the ramifications of openly defending alleged or actual communists and of challenging the entrenched governmental power structure were profound.[9] But in his writings and his defense of those persecuted on ideological grounds, Taylor's central thesis posited that the law must reign supreme over political expediencies. He wrote: "Freedom as we know it can exist only under the law. That is why nothing is more dangerous to our traditions...than that high officials...should openly display their contempt for the law. Nothing, that is, unless it be the failure of other officials and of the citizenry to insist upon the law's vindication."[10] Taylor's theme would form the backbone not only of his writings, but also his defense of Harry Bridges.

For Bridges, securing Taylor as his lawyer was not risk-free. Taylor was a known, outspoken critic of the government's anti-communism tactics, and so Taylor was also necessarily a lightning rod in that political environment. But Taylor was also bold and adamant, and Bridges no doubt pinned his hopes on the fact that Taylor's gravitas from his Nuremberg days would help lift the equally bold Bridges above the dangerous political environment.

Harry Bridges and attorney Telford Taylor discussing the case. Copyright San Francisco History Center, San Francisco Public Library.

In time, the two men formed a strong working relationship with daily strategy sessions. In one, as Taylor and his legal team discussed adopting a legal strategy that contended that the serial trials denied Bridges due process, Bridges quickly retorted with sardonic wit, "Hell, I don't deny that I've had due process. I've had all the due process I want."[11]

Taylor later remarked that Bridges was one of the brightest clients he had ever represented.[12]

Opening Statements—Everyone Tries a New Approach

Time and experience had altered all the parties' approach to the issues. The Department of Justice, for its part, had learned from the debacle of the Crouch-Johnson testimony about the alleged New York June 1936 meeting, and so prepared to parade witnesses who avoided that subject. The government lawyers also by and large abandoned the use of professional witnesses—the serial anti-communist witnesses who traveled around the country giving testimony in deportation cases—although even then it could not give up such witnesses entirely. The Department of Justice had also abandoned resorting to politically connected Washingtonians like Donohue, and instead used the local San Francisco United States Attorney, who normally tried all San Francisco federal cases, a man named Lynn J. Gillard.

Bridges' legal defense team also settled on a new tack. Rather than defend with their own colorful offense against the government—in an attempt to prove the government had been waging a twenty-year conspiracy/crusade, as in the third trial—the legal defense approached the government's case more clinically. Taylor used the massive passage of time against the government's case in more subtle ways, both to undermine the credibility of witnesses who, in 1955, were discussing matters that allegedly occurred in 1933-34, and to highlight that American democracy had survived the alleged communist Harry Bridges.

At the same time, Taylor focused on historical events through a different prism—not the conspiracy prism that Hallinan advanced in the third trial—taking a new, creative tack that asserted that in the combustible situation of the 1930s, where revolution hung in the air, the formation of strong unions gave people a fighting chance and actually averted a communist revolution. Taylor argued: "Mass unemployment, bread lines, idle factories, and deserted stores—these were the great dangers of 1933 and at times the breakdown of the economic system seemed imminent. And one result of this widespread poverty, unemployment, and unrest was a nation-wide revival of aggressive trade unionism and a wave of strikes for better wages and working conditions..."[13] Thus, rather than being a pawn in the revolutionary movement of the Communist Party, Bridges actually acted to its detriment by forming strong unions, thereby giving people better wages, safe conditions, and the absence of any need to subscribe to a communist revolution.

"The longshoremen of the Pacific Coast needed no communists to tell them that the Shape Up was a plague spot of corruption and favoritism; that casual, spasmodic work made a mockery of job security; that the black list was stifling their efforts to speak with one voice through a union of their own. The charge that waterfront labor was the mouthpiece or tool of the communist is an insult to the men and to human intelligence alike," Taylor explained.[14]

Taylor's approach cleverly painted Bridges out of the Communist Party, and avoided the need to delve too deeply into a government conspiracy. A shrewd approach, it avoided asking a federal judge to conclude things that he would generally be highly resistant to conclude or publicly articulate (the existence of conspiracies), yet it still offered a path to victory by focusing on Bridges' labor achievements as hardly matters of communist success, but instead as matters of basic American pride.

At the same time, Taylor employed a strategy to dull the impact of Bridges' own admissions that he had accepted help from the Communist Party to achieve his labor aims. Taylor contextualized the issue by reminding Judge Goodman that in World War II America had accepted help from the Soviet Union. That act alone certainly could not a communist make, Taylor dangled to Judge Goodman.

The Schomaker-Saunders Axis

The government again called many witnesses, but as with all prior trials, its case hinged on a few key witnesses who professed first-hand knowledge.

The government's principal witness was a recycled one, John Schomaker, who had also testified as a minor witness at the third trial. A near spitting image of Clark Gable, Schomaker had escaped the June 1936 fiasco of the third trial and was not a professional anti-communist witness, so he escaped the same vicious defense assaults that plagued the other witnesses in the trial before Judge Harris. Thus, the government decided to reuse him.

Schomaker claimed that in late 1933, as Bridges was coming to prominence on the waterfront, Schomaker, a Communist Party member, had approached Harry Bridges in a restaurant to get him to join the party. But Bridges refused, believing the Communist Party too "far-fetched" and with too many future aims not of practical significance to workers' needs in the moment. Within the month, however, Schomaker claimed Bridges joined because the Communist Party's program—hours, wages, workers' rights—suddenly appealed to him. Schomaker then claimed that after Bridges joined, he took the name "Harry Dorgan," paid his dues to Schomaker, attended party meetings, and Schomaker delivered the now-infamous "Harry Dorgan" Communist Party Membership Book to Bridges.[15]

Taylor began his cross-examination with the calm of a statesman, not the aggressive bravado of Hallinan's street-fighter style.

Taylor took Schomaker back to 1933 and had him identify all the Communist Party meetings, who attended, who said what, and where the meetings occurred. Schomaker complied with Taylor's calm, disarming style, giving excruciating detail about both Communist Party meetings on the waterfront that predated Bridges and also recruitment meetings that Bridges allegedly attended.[16] As Taylor moved along, he asked Schomaker how he flipped Bridges, who in late 1933 apparently refused to join the Communist Party, but then in early 1934 suddenly and willingly joined. Schomaker explained that he and other party officials had settled on a great Communist Party program that they sold to Bridges in a series of indoctrination meetings—wages, hours, working conditions, and the right to unionize. And Schomaker confirmed that Bridges was moved to join by that.[17] When Taylor asked how Bridges responded to the offering, Schomaker even professed to remember Bridges' physical reaction over two decades earlier:

"Did Bridges indicate that those proposals were sufficient?" Taylor asked.

"Yes, he indicated by his—well, I'd say the way he'd cock his head and cock his eye a little bit that he agreed," Schomaker offered.[18]

By the time Taylor was done, Schomaker had not been visibly pressured—no heated, visibly dramatic exchanges—and he probably left the witness stand feeling that he gave a great performance. However, Taylor believed he had dynamite, and, like a squirrel with a nut, quietly saved it for later.

The government's other major witness was a seaman named David Saunders, also a former Communist Party member. Saunders offered a vividly recalled story about how one day, a few weeks after the June 1936 New York Communist Party Convention, he went to Harry Bridges' offices to collect party dues. As he entered Bridges' office, Saunders asked, "How about paying some dues?" Bridges then "pulled out $3.00, slapped it on the desk, and gave it to me.

And I said, 'O.K., I will turn it over.' Said thanks and beat it." Saunders even remembered the money was in the form of silver dollars, not bills.[19]

This time Gladstein cross-examined Saunders and dove right into Saunders' claims. Saunders emphatically stated that Bridges' offices where Saunders collected the $3.00 in July-August 1936, shortly after the now infamous New York Communist Party Convention (that Saunders attended), were in the Balboa Building on 593 Market Street.

"Is it fair to say, Mr. Saunders, that time you have testified going up to see Mr. Bridges in his office was either July or August of 1936?" Gladstein asked.

"I think it would be safe to say sometime during that period," Saunders answered.

"Certainly couldn't be in July or June of 1937, could it, sir?" Gladstein probed.

"No," Saunders confirmed.

"Well, then, if I understand you correctly, the only time in your life you went up to Mr. Bridges' office in the Balboa Building was on this one occasion in July or August of 1936, am I right about that?" Gladstein demanded.

"That's correct." Saunders thus guaranteed these events occurred in 1936, not 1937.[20]

In short order, Saunders further admitted that he was not a dues collector for the party, never went to Bridges before or after the alleged $3.00 incident, gave no receipt-stamps to Bridges, which as it turned out by other evidence, was in fact customary for the Communist Party in the 1930s, and never again collected dues from Bridges.[21] The story sounded fishy and fabricated because it did not add up. The specificity of the 593 Market Street address in 1936 did not seem to faze Saunders, who did not apparently realize the significance of his claim. Again, Taylor and Gladstein elected a strategy of silence, opting to spring the trap later.

But as Gladstein continued to cross-examine Saunders about his honesty, Saunders became testy in response to Gladstein's more aggressive cross-examination style. Saunders admitted that the Coast Guard revoked his license to go to sea (owing apparently to his Communist Party activities) and he wished to get it back but was rejected. This occurred in the late 1940s, and he was trying to get it back by 1950-51 because he was struggling financially, barely surviving, and his career as a seaman was critical to him. Saunders thus traveled to Washington to talk to the federal board in charge of his license.

"In essence, isn't it true that you told them you had been a Communist Party member, that you left the Communist Party, that you no longer agreed with it, that you wanted to be cleared, and so on?" Gladstein asked.

"That is correct," Saunders stated.

"Their decision was adverse?" Gladstein pressed.

"I think Washington rejected it," Saunders admitted.[22]

But, oddly, Saunders later got his license back. And Gladstein now tied Saunders' professional witnessing work to his reacquisition of his seaman's license.

"How long did you stay away from following the sea?" Gladstein asked.

"I don't think I got back to the sea again until about 1952, shortly after the Smith trial." The Smith Act trial was a trial in Los Angeles where Saunders testified for the government in a communist deportation case. Saunders had now fallen into Gladstein's trap and essentially admitted that the government suddenly reinstated his seaman's license when he began testifying against communists. Gladstein ended his examination with Saunders fuming at the attacks on his character, the air heavy with the implicit quid pro quo between Saunders, as a former party member testifying for government prosecutors, and the government suddenly restoring his sea license by machinations of the legal process in Washington.[23]

Bridges Testifies and Taylor Closes

This trial was the fourth formal time Bridges had testified at trial on the exact same set of issues, the fourth time in nearly twenty years. No doubt exhausted at the sheer number of times he had been asked the same sets of questions, Bridges again took the stand to explain his union days, his activities, and his political beliefs.

As to the specific charges of Schomaker-Saunders, Bridges categorically denied any such meetings, joining the party, or paying any dues. Bridges also confirmed a crucial detail that was the predicate for Saunders' testimony, notably that he never occupied the Balboa Building in 1936 when Saunders categorically swore he collected $3.00 from Bridges! Instead, he occupied it in 1937.

Careful analysis reveals Bridges' testimony in the civil trial lacked the extended oratory of his testimony in the earlier trials—he did not have the same kind of extemporaneous narratives he offered in the first and third trials—but it wisely captured his sentiment and the broader context of the trial: Bridges was a progressive labor leader, he built a union, he was leftist in his beliefs and accepted help from communists but was not a formal member of the party, the serial trials had gone on forever and, while consequential, were now more an annoyance and a sign of the everlasting animus towards his union. In short, American democracy in 1955 had survived Harry Bridges, notwithstanding two decades of hysteria to the contrary.

Bridges' testimony and sentiment tracked Taylor's message, one of reason and middle-of-the-road politics in response to over-aggressive, hysterical crusading. Sometimes the best litigation strategy is to be narrow and understated, plying a trade that may even seem boring to outside observers (those accustomed to the televised courtroom dramatics of *Perry Mason* and *L.A. Law*), but such calmness can be disarming to the opponent and only highlights the undue, incredible hysteria of the other side.

As Taylor began his closing argument, he took apart the witnesses and the sheer incredible nature of their testimony. In cross-examination, Taylor had secured Schomaker's absolute confirmation of the alleged communist events Bridges attended, and with calm questioning Taylor got Schomaker to give specific dates, specific locations, and specific people who attended, including word-for-word what they said—all twenty years earlier. As Taylor lulled Schomaker into offering such precise descriptions of the events, Schomaker failed to realize that the rope he was creating to hang Bridges in fact was to hang himself. Now Taylor unmasked his strategy, raising the question of how it was possible for anyone to have such remarkable recall two decades later about such minute details.[24] After all, how could Schomaker really remember that Bridges cocked his head slightly and moved his eyes in a particular way during a conversation, the type of staggering minutiae that no one could accurately remember two decades after the fact. The sheer intricacy of the detail proved the story was a lie, especially when Schomaker could not remember with comparable detail more recent events.

Taylor then hung Schomaker with his testimony again. Schomaker had testified that Bridges rejected the party in late 1933, but then in early 1934 was swayed to join because of the Communist Party's program. Taylor argued: "Your Honor, this notion that the Communist Party delivered a program which contained anything that would appeal to Bridges as new and original or anything that he had not been familiar with and pushing for months, even years, before these fictitious meetings are said to have occurred, is complete nonsense. Every element in this program had been a part of the old ILA [union]."[25] In short, why would Bridges find amazing a so-called Communist Party 1934 "program" that advocated that which Bridges had already been working for in 1933 anyway? "Every element of this imaginative class struggle program as described by Schomaker—six-hour day, thirty-hour week, Coast-wide contract, union hiring hall, resort to strike if necessary—is to be found in these proceedings of the [old union]," Taylor stated.[26] And, as Taylor explained, the Communist Party in 1934 rejected the idea of acceding to President Roosevelt's urgent request not to strike and to arbitrate, yet it was Bridges who agreed with the president to postpone the strike, the antithesis of what the Communist Party wanted.[27] Schomaker's testimony collapsed in upon itself.

Taylor also attacked Saunders' strange story: he was not a dues collector, but on one occasion collected dues and vividly recalled Bridges slapping down three silver dollar coins. His recall was fantastic and dramatic, but there was one small problem: Bridges never occupied the building on Market Street in 1936 where Saunders swore he visited Bridges! Saunders was also a corrupt and captive witness of the government, trading testimony for benefits, Taylor aggressively argued: "This record establishes him as a man who had lost a means of livelihood as a merchant seaman because of action taken by the Coast Guard screening him from the waterfront for a period of three years… There is nothing accidental about the date when Mr. Saunders was cleared by the Coast Guard and when he first sailed again as a seaman. That date, that clearance, that freedom to pursue employment, occurred only after he had become a government witness…"[28] The charge was serious: Saunders, like witnesses in the third trial, exchanged his integrity for financial reward from the government. Saunders became a professional, serial anti-communist witness helping government prosecutions and magically found his seafaring ban lifted by the government.

Taylor undoubtedly possessed a certain gravitas owing to his time as a Nuremberg prosecutor, where he witnessed the horrors of the Nazi state in his prosecution of Nazi war criminals. That experience gave him the unique credibility to opine on the manner in which a legal system can aid the law's collapse when it caters to powerful executive demands. "I myself had some opportunity to see in Germany the remains of a society in which the judges failed the courts, a society in which judges wrote opinions and became glued to the path of least resistance," Taylor described.[29] Taylor's words at once pled for due process: for following the law, not the passions of the moment or artificial legal doctrines. In short, he argued that the law's dignity had been lost in this twenty-year crusade that had witnessed the American legal system turned upside down as the executive ran amuck.

"And I will conclude by saying to Your Honor that a judgment for [Harry Bridges] in this case will not in the deepest sense be a judgment against the government, or a judgment for Mr. Bridges or a judgment for or against anybody touched by this controversy. *It will be a judgment that the law abides here and that's all the justification it will need.*"[30]

After dozens of witnesses and almost six weeks of evidence, the trial finally ended on July 21, 1955.

Judge Goodman Rules

At 10:00 a.m. on July 29, 1955, Judge Goodman's courtroom was packed. As Judge Goodman appeared and took the bench, he held a written statement of his decision. Perched on his bench a few feet above the courtroom's participants and spectators, Judge Goodman looked at the lawyers and Harry Bridges. As he started reading, observers were unsure how to interpret Judge Goodman's body language and where his words were leading.

"The government has proved by clear and convincing evidence that the Communist Party is an organization that, at the times here involved, advised, advocated, and taught the overthrow by force and violence the government of the United States," Judge Goodman began.[31] One of Bridges' friends thought it was positive and started nodding affirmatively to Bridges, but Bridges softly shook his head negatively, believing the news bad.[32] "But," Judge Goodman continued, "whether it has so proved that Bridges was in fact a member of the party is a far different question."[33] With that, he let much steam out of the cooker, and the pressure began to subside for Bridges, his lawyers, and Bridges' supporters, as all observers realized Judge Goodman was siding with Bridges and at last drawing the curtain closed on the lengthy deportation trials.

As he continued reading, Judge Goodman castigated the government's witnesses one by one, essentially agreeing with all of Taylor's carefully framed arguments built upon the methodical cross-examinations. "There are grave improbabilities in Schomaker's story. It is not at all convincing...Saunders' testimony is inherently flimsy; it has discrepancies. It is unacceptable...The inherent infirmity of the government's case lies in its own evidence," Judge Goodman declared.[34]

Judge Goodman dissected all the testimony in great detail. He simply did not believe Schomaker's assertion about how he allegedly recruited Bridges into the Communist Party. Judge Goodman explained that Schomaker's story of how Bridges was a well-known labor figure who rejected the party initially, but who then suddenly changed his mind, simply made no sense when the alleged hook that got Bridges was a program that was identical to the exact labor program Bridges was already advocating on the waterfront: wages, hours, conditions, unions, and the like. Likewise, the fact that Schomaker had staggering recall of the indoctrination meetings a full twenty years later—whose house the meetings were held in, who the attendees were, what exactly was said—yet at the same time lacked any such recall of other similar events more recent in time, was too much for Judge Goodman, who accepted Taylor's defense theory. In short, Judge Goodman believed the government's witness Schomaker outright lied under oath.[35]

Judge Goodman also believed Saunders lied to the court. The idea that the Communist Party would send Saunders to demand dues from its most important member was "peculiar, to say the least," for Judge Goodman. Equally odd, Saunders was himself a high-ranking party member from the waterfront, but he could offer no testimony at all about any of Bridges' alleged Communist Party activities on the waterfront other than the alleged $3.00 incident. Critical, however, Judge Goodman found that Saunders' 1936 meeting at Bridges' office could never have happened because Bridges did not occupy the Market Street building in 1936. In short, Saunders had concocted a complex narrative to hang Bridges, but had gotten his dates wrong. Taylor's methodical attention to detail—a trial lawyer's bread and butter—had worked.

Judge Goodman even implicitly condemned Judge Harris's conclusions in the third trial and Judge Sears' conclusions in the second trial: "Only a weak yielding to extra-judicial clamor," referring to the broader socio-political atmosphere that so heavily infected those prior jurists' decision-making, "would excuse acceptance of the testimony of witnesses in this case as proof of the allegations of the complaint."[36] Judge Goodman, as a federal judge in the judicial branch, stood firm against the executive branch, his comments echoing Taylor's artful plea for the law to stand above the heated vicissitudes of the day's politics.

Harry Bridges (left) and his attorneys Norman Leonard (center) and Telford Taylor (right). Courtesy of ILWU, San Francisco.

As Judge Goodman read his decision, both Harry Bridges and his union men in attendance started crying. And when Judge Goodman finished, the courtroom erupted in roars of yelling and cheering, back-slapping, and euphoric whoops of joy.[37] As the courtroom buzzed, Judge Goodman returned to his chambers, leaving Bridges and his lawyers, Taylor, Leonard, Grossman, and Gladstein, at the end of the longest deportation saga in American history, finally able to walk out of a Bridges deportation trial knowing they would not need to return to court together ever again. Ashen at Judge Goodman's remarks, the government officials lingered in the corner of the courtroom, defeated yet still defiant.

Twenty years a deportee, Harry Bridges was finally and forever an American citizen.

HUAC's Last Stand as the Curtains Close on the Cast of Characters

"What's past is prologue."

WILLIAM SHAKESPEARE, *THE TEMPEST*, ACT 2, SCENE 1 (1610)

Fighting for the Right to Marry

Normally when an adult man and adult woman go to a county clerk to get a marriage license, it is a pretty routine legal experience. But nothing in Harry Bridges' life with the law proceeded routinely, as he found when, on December 9, 1958, he arrived at the county clerk's office in Reno, Nevada, to marry Noriko Sawada. An American of Japanese ancestry, Noriko had spent the World War II years interned in one of the domestic concentration camps used to imprison Japanese-Americans.

As they arrived at the Reno clerk's office, they handed the marriage application to the county clerk. The clerk looked at them, turned to Noriko and asked, "What's your nationality?"

"American," Noriko firmly offered. "I was born here."

"That's right. She's the American. I'm the foreigner," Bridges quipped in his Australian accent.

"Are you black, white, brown, red, or yellow?" the clerk demanded of Noriko.

Forced to answer, Noriko offered, "Under those categories, I must be yellow."

"It's not where you were born. It's blood that counts," the clerk ordered. The clerk then denied Harry and Noriko a marriage license because the couple were interracial.

Given Harry Bridges' odyssey through the court system over the prior twenty years, the clerk's comments registered a cruel irony. Having spent twenty years in deportation battles precisely because the absence of U.S. birth was dispositive—thereby enabling and permitting ideological deportation proceedings—now, when it came to marriage, the fact that Noriko's birthplace was in the United States was suddenly irrelevant in the law's eyes. Harry Bridges could not win either way.

At the time, Nevada, like many states, had laws on its books that prohibited interracial marriages, known as anti-miscegenation laws. These laws enforced racial segregation by regulating marriage and personal relationships, in the same way that Nazi Germany's Nuremberg laws and South Africa's apartheid laws did. On the American continent, the anti-miscegenation laws traced all the way back to the early days of the Colonies.

Bridges called a local Reno lawyer for help and secured a court hearing for the following day to address the denial of their marriage license. Fearing further reprisals, he and Noriko took separate rooms in a hotel so as not to violate Nevada's prurient-centric laws. The next day, Bridges' lawyer appeared before a local judge, District

Judge Wines. The matter was an instant *cause célèbre*, and the press were in the court, having been apprised of the existence of yet another trial involving Harry Bridges.

At the hearing, Bridges' lawyer argued that the Nevada law was unconstitutional: "All men are created free and equal. These two seek that inalienable right to happiness." Then the Reno district attorney took the podium and argued that the laws were perfectly acceptable because "marriage is more than just a contract in which two people can agree. The state has an interest in marriage and its offspring so it can maintain control over society."

Judge Wines called a short recess to reflect. By now, the courtroom was packed with spectators and the press, all waiting anxiously to hear the judge's decision. A while later, Judge Wines returned to the bench. "I see no evil which would justify the state interfering with the freedom of an individual to marry," Judge Wines explained, thereby immediately declaring Nevada's law unconstitutional. As Judge Wines finished speaking, applause broke out and people descended upon Harry and Noriko to congratulate them. Harry and Noriko, with reporters in tow, immediately walked over to the clerk's office and refiled marriage application papers. Now with a marriage license in hand, and still trailed by a crowd, Harry and Noriko crossed the street to a justice of the peace and were married in a private ceremony.[1]

Like every one of Bridges' legal battles, appeals followed. This time, the district attorney took an appeal seeking to undo the marriage. But the Nevada legislature intervened, and, given the public scrutiny to the issue that the Bridgeses' marriage had provoked, formally repealed Nevada's anti-miscegenation law. In one fell swoop, and at Harry and Noriko Bridges' urging, Nevada's restrictive marriage laws collapsed, allowing people of different races to marry freely.

What Harry and Noriko Bridges achieved in 1958 for people of mixed races seeking to marry in Nevada was a feat that would take the United States Supreme Court another decade to provide to the rest of America.[2]

Bridges Battles HUAC One Last Time

The law and Harry Bridges just plain collided. Even after twenty years of litigation, multiple trials, two victorious trips to the Supreme Court with full vindication, and litigation over his right to marry, citizen Bridges still faced unique federal scrutiny. In 1957, Harry Bridges applied for and secured his U.S. passport so that he could travel to Europe, the Soviet Union, and North Africa to meet with foreign labor leaders. The passport form had Communist Party affiliation questions on it, the same ones that he had answered on his citizenship application, the same ones that had landed him in his last two federal court trials, with the short stint in federal prison. The passport form asked, "Are you now a member of the Communist Party?" and "Have you ever been a member of the Communist Party?" This time he simply refused to answer the questions, and left that part of the form blank. The passport issued from the government bureaucracy, and Harry Bridges traveled abroad.

Upon Bridges' return, however, he was again summoned by congressional subpoena to appear before HUAC for a hearing set for April 1959. This time, HUAC was holding hearings into the need to amend U.S. passport laws to prohibit certain Americans deemed politically dangerous from traveling abroad. When HUAC called Harry Bridges to testify under oath, it was ostensibly to discuss legal passport issues as they related to Americans traveling abroad and meeting with foreign communists. Harry Bridges dutifully complied with the subpoena and traveled to Washington, D.C., to attend the hearings and answer questions.

Immediately after he swore under penalty of perjury to tell the truth, the HUAC inquiry turned to the same ground covered in myriad investigations and trials that had engulfed his life since the 1930s. Literally a few questions into the hearing, Bridges was asked if he had ever gone by the name "Harry Dorgan." Bridges responded like the weathered, experienced legal combatant that time had made him: "Just a minute, I would like to ask a question... My understanding is that my appearance here is in connection with passport legislation, and I am just wondering, and I have reasons to inquire, what is the relevancy of that question towards passport legislation?"[3]

Defiantly, Bridges pressed: "I wonder what I am doing here, Mr. Chairman. You are proposing to pass legislation to prevent tainted people from going overseas. It seems to me that I am about your worst subject. If I can't get a passport after two trips to the Supreme Court and a half a dozen hearings giving me a clean bill of health, what chance is there for the average citizen? What am I doing here?" As the inquiring congressman pressed further, Bridges candidly responded, "The name Dorgan came up...has crept up a couple of times in more than twenty years of litigation against me, five or more court hearings, and two trips to the U.S. Supreme Court. Now if answering this question opens up again over twenty years of litigation that has been settled by the courts..." Rightly fearful that, in what was supposed to be a "passport security" hearing, the government was really laying the foundation for another perjury or deportation case against him, Bridges simply refused to answer.[4]

As such, Harry Bridges invoked his Fifth Amendment right under the United States Constitution to say nothing. The Fifth Amendment expressly includes the right not to answer questions if the answers may be used against the speaker, stating that no person "shall be compelled in any criminal case to be a witness against himself."[5] Inserted in the Bill of Rights at the Republic's founding to protect the citizenry against government efforts to compel people to speak in a manner that the government may then use against them, its historical roots drew from the Puritans' experience when refusing to cooperate with interrogators in England. This right against self-incrimination in the modern age gave birth to the famed Miranda rights from the Supreme Court's 1966 *Miranda v. Arizona* decision that required police to provide certain notice of legal rights to criminal suspects at arrest.[6]

Bridges had learned the hard way that answering questions and telling the truth means little when the government intends to prosecute someone, and so in 1959 he refused to answer and refused to be trapped in twenty more years of litigation. He feared that if he answered the question in the negative, the government would start a new campaign against him claiming that he had perjured himself. Twenty years could easily become thirty or forty.

"I had over 20 years of litigation where the courts had found despite many, many charges and accusations, you see, to the contrary...I took the Fifth Amendment here today for the first time in my life. If I had taken it over 20 years ago, I would have saved my union a lot of money and expense, and I would have saved myself a lot of trouble. And I know why, because there has been more than one attempt to frame me on the same issue, and now I am getting older and wiser," Bridges explained.[7]

"You understand I have had five decisions in my favor on that question, don't you? You understand that I just for the first time have taken [the Fifth Amendment], not because I am guilty, but because I am in a better position than anybody else to answer that question and say no. I am in a better position because I have got court decisions saying I am not," he added.

Frustrated, HUAC members wasted Harry Bridges' day with endless questions about what he did on his trip, who he met, and what they discussed. In the midst of these inquiries about his time abroad, the questions always circled back to whether Bridges was a Communist Party member. Although Bridges' lawyer sat next to him, the lawyer barely uttered a word. Instead, Bridges was essentially a deft lawyer himself—having learned the long and difficult way—fully aware of the nuanced nature of leading questions and the nature of appropriate legal objections to improper questions.

Unable to trap Bridges, finally the inquisitors turned their attention to whether Bridges would offer others to the HUAC altar. Refusing, Harry Bridges responded with a dagger to HUAC's heart: "But so many people get dragged in here and smeared and slandered, and the courts have said that about this committee, [people] who are not in the same position to fight as I am, innocent people that have been destroyed...I am not going to help this committee in that sense."[8] Bridges, thus, angrily and publicly challenged the legitimacy of the entire HUAC enterprise, itself an act that he well knew was potentially fraught with peril. In so doing, Bridges refused to bow to HUAC, refused to help HUAC destroy other innocent lives, and stood his ground asserting his rights under the American Constitution.

Ultimately, a full quarter of a century after he led the Great Strike of 1934, Bridges defiantly told his inquisitor, "You are off the beam, Congressman."[9]

****

After the April 1959 HUAC passport hearings, no new deportation or criminal prosecutions were ever initiated against Harry Bridges, although the IRS made its appearance on the scene to demand that Bridges pay taxes on the defense funds raised by the ILWU to save him. In time, HUAC would become synonymous with extreme governmental intolerance for, and abuse of, basic civil rights due to the famed communist witch hunts of the 1940s and 1950s, and so by the 1960s, HUAC changed its name to the House Committee on Internal Security, distancing itself from its own past, before eventually being dismantled entirely in 1975.[10]

As for the trials' myriad witnesses, Earl King and Ernest Ramsay were eventually released from San Quentin in 1941 when the governmental excesses in their prosecutions came to light and California's governor pardoned them.[11]

Harper Knowles, the ringleader-architect from the first trial who headed the American Legion's Subversive Activities Commission, by the early 1940s, had taken his anti-radical expertise and founded a private dossier, anti-communist blacklist service called the Western Research Foundation, which continued to provide government agencies with information on perceived radicals and subversives.[12]

After the first trial, Captain Keegan claimed that Dean Landis's decision was a "white-wash," and then evidence later came to light that Captain Keegan had long been taking bribes in the local employer-union wars in Portland, Oregon.[13]

Stanley Doyle, the special prosecutor for Oregon, who had run undercover operatives within Bridges' union, procured the alleged "Dorgan" Communist Party Membership Card (that the INS concluded was a fake), and maintained secret communications channels to the United States Senate, but who abjectly refused to expose himself to questions in the first Bridges trial, left the West Coast after his role in the Bridges saga and settled in Montana. He opened a law practice, and in 1961 was appointed as a justice to the Montana Supreme Court. He served as a justice of the Montana Supreme Court until 1967 and died in 1975.

Witness Harry Lundeberg, from the second trial, ran the rival Sailors' Union of the Pacific and died in 1957 at the age of fifty-six.

Most of the other witnesses disappeared into the oblivion of history, including Laurence Milner, Aaron Sapiro, and John Leech from the first trial; James O'Neil and Maurice Cannalonga from the second trial; Manning Johnson, Paul Crouch, and Lawrence Ross/Rosenstein from the third trial; and John Schomaker and David Saunders from the fourth trial.

As for the government prosecutors, Prosecutor Thomas Shoemaker, from the first trial, was promoted to deputy commissioner of the INS. Raphael Bonham, from the first trial, remained in the Pacific Northwest Division of the INS. Prosecutor Albert Del Guercio, from the second trial, became district director of the INS in Los Angeles, where he aggressively prosecuted other communist deportation cases, including the famous case of the Chinese Caltech physicist Tsien Hsue-Shen. Special Prosecutor Joseph Donohue, from the third trial, landed on his feet when he was appointed commissioner/mayor of Washington, D.C. He later entered private practice in the early 1970s, and, in great irony given his vitriolic assault on Bridges, defended one of the Watergate defendants charged with perjury.[14]

Harry Bridges' lawyers represented many others in the ongoing communist deportation cases of the 1930s and other important civil liberties cases of the mid-twentieth century. Carol King was a founding member of the National Lawyers Guild, a pro bono legal organization that survives today, still helping those in need. She litigated dozens of communist deportation trials, cases where famed journalist I.F. Stone colorfully reported "she bested David-and-Goliath odds." She died in 1952 at the age of fifty-six.[15]

The rambunctious, colorful Vincent Hallinan served his six-month contempt sentence, giving boxing lessons to inmates and proudly noting that he served time but saved Bridges from prison. He then ran for president on the Progressive ticket in 1950, was convicted of tax evasion in another politicized prosecution, and in his later years defended student protesters in the tumultuous 1960s.[16]

Richard Gladstein, Aubrey Grossman, and Norman Leonard, all of whom defended Bridges through the trials, litigated other labor rights and civil rights causes, as well as defending many alleged communists in the Red Scare, and built a preeminent labor and employment law firm in San Francisco in the mid-twentieth century. The law firm, Leonard Carder LLP, still exists today, still represents the ILWU, and, in a curious arc across time, Harry Bridges' granddaughter, Nicole Bridges, works at the firm.[17]

Telford Taylor continued to challenge publicly Senator Joseph McCarthy and the communist witch hunts of the 1950s. In what was perhaps his most vexing, trying case, he represented American citizen Junius Scales, who was the only American citizen imprisoned solely for membership in the Communist Party. President John F. Kennedy commuted Scales' sentence in 1962, vindicating Taylor's position. In later years, Taylor was a famed professor of law at Columbia University and publicly criticized the Vietnam War. Due to the wide-ranging respect bestowed upon him, the National Basketball Association asked him to be a special master to decide its internal sports disputes.[18]

Secretary of Labor Frances Perkins held her position until 1945, the longest tenure in history for a Secretary of Labor, later taught at Cornell University and died in 1965 at the age of eighty-five. In 1980, the United States Department of Labor's headquarters in Washington, D.C., was named the Frances Perkins Building.

Dean James Landis, who in 1939 had been widely expected to be the next Supreme Court justice, was publicly vilified after ruling for Harry Bridges in the first trial, became *persona non grata* in Washington, D.C., and was unable to secure any judicial appointment. Forever out of favor because he refused to deport Harry Bridges, he eventually left Harvard and, after personal misfortunes, in 1961, was found dead in his swimming pool at the age of sixty-five.[19]

In contrast, after deciding against Bridges in the second trial, Judge Charles Sears was appointed chairman of the Western New York Enemy Alien Hearing Board, where he presided over the internment and deportation of people of Japanese, Italian, or German ancestry during World War II.[20]

Judge George Harris, the beneficiary of life tenure reserved for federal judges, remained on the federal bench after the third trial, until his death in 1983.

Judge Louis Goodman, of the fourth trial, became chief judge of the Northern District of California overseeing the growth of the

Northern District of California, which court today is considered one of the most robust federal courts in the nation for handling patent disputes. He served as chief judge until his death in 1961.

Supreme Court Justice Frank Murphy, who had joined the Supreme Court in 1940 at the age of fifty, remained on the Supreme Court until 1949 when he unexpectedly died at the age of fifty-nine. As well as his powerful words in the Harry Bridges case, he authored in 1944 an impassioned, vehement dissent in another notorious case called *Korematsu v. United States*, a case where, in the fear-laden environment of World War II, the majority of the Supreme Court permitted the forced internment of Japanese-Americans. In 2011, the Department of Justice filed an official notice conceding that the *Korematsu* case was wrong, vindicating at last Justice Murphy's 1944 dissent.[21]

Supreme Court Justice Felix Frankfurter, who struggled with the first Bridges appeal but eventually sided with Bridges in the second appeal, remained on the Supreme Court until 1962, when he had a stroke and retired. He died in 1965 at the age of eighty-three, the last foreign-born Supreme Court justice in American history.

Evelle Younger, the FBI (and OSS) agent whose name was discovered on paperwork in the adjoining hotel room used to spy on Harry Bridges, later became the California attorney general and ran for governor in the late 1970s on the Republican Party ticket. Harry Bridges indicated publicly that bygones should be bygones, and Evelle Younger sent him a pair of inscribed drinking glasses in gratitude.[22]

The ILWU grew to be one of the strongest unions, blanketing the entire West Coast of the United States, including Hawaii. A model across the world, it was one of the first unions to insist on racial integration and has remained alive and strong for decades, boasting over 42,000 members in 2015.

And Harry Bridges led the ILWU until 1977, when, at the age of seventy-six he retired, only to take up the cause of advocating for

elderly rights and nuclear disarmament as an official of the World
Peace Council. Some years after his trials, the United States government invited the once-so-dangerous Harry Bridges to Washington
to address labor issues with government officials. "The praise I got
really belonged to the members of this union," he humbly offered,
"and the attacks on me were all directed at them."[23] He died in
1990, still married to Noriko. On the centennial of his birth on
July 28, 2001, California Governor Gray Davis declared the breezy
summer day Harry Bridges Day.

But on that spring day in 1959, when Harry Bridges left the
HUAC passport hearings in Washington, D.C., he certainly left as
an American in the greatest aspirational sense of the word. An immigrant from Australia, he brought his Australian political and cul-
tural values about human rights for workers and racial and political
equality in unions to America, integrating them into a union and
insisting on their acceptance in America. Standing tall, he defended
himself against the powerful forces that worked to deport him for
twenty years, and never allowed the prosecutions to derail him from
his efforts to help achieve and advance the cause of his union and his
economic, social, and political beliefs. He rejected bribes and risked
assassination. Imprisoned for his belief that a new war across the
world was wrong, he refused to silence his voice in return for personal security from his persecutors. He refused to offer fellow union
members, friends, or others to the HUAC altar despite the frenzied
times of the Red Scare, during which it is well documented that
many citizens, so as to curry personal security and favor, made such
offerings. At great personal risk for decades, he challenged those in
power who abused their power.

While Harry Bridges was not born an American, he certainly
died one.

POLICY

Where the Legal System Failed for Twenty Years

"[T]here is, even now, something of ill-omen amongst us. I mean the increasing disregard for law which pervades the country; the growing disposition to substitute the wild and furious passions, in lieu of the sober judgment of the courts; and the worse than savage mobs, for the executive ministers of justice."

ABRAHAM LINCOLN, 1838, COMMENTING UPON THE OUTBREAK OF MOB VIOLENCE ACROSS AMERICA[1]

"Justice is incidental to law and order."

J. EDGAR HOOVER, FBI DIRECTOR (1935-1972)[2]

Twenty years. Four trials. Four prosecutors. Biased judges. Impeachment proceedings. FBI wiretaps. Two trips to the Supreme Court. Tens of thousands of pages of trial transcripts. Over two hundred witnesses. Hundreds of exhibits. Bribes, threats, and intimidation. Perjury. Even murder plots. A testament to man's intolerance of man. A crusade.

How Exactly Did This Happen?

The key question that the Bridges deportation trials present is one that goes to the heart of persecution-by-prosecution, the heart of the use and abuse of the legal system by those with power against those who challenge the status quo. The specific, critical question is how exactly can such a relentless crusade be institutionalized? How does the pursuit of justice within the confines of due process morph into a relentless crusade blind to due process? The answer is in the small, often imperceptible, turns of the law's wheels, turns that occur when decisions are made by the constituents of the legal system. The answer is seen when the legal system's inhabitants allow themselves to drift from the magnetic north of due process, as echoed in the concerns voiced by Abraham Lincoln in the quote above, and instead veer to the ideas expressed in Hoover's quote. It is seen when the constituents of the legal system trade the sober supplication of the law for the satiating elixir of politics.

The Executive

The law bending to a crusade is first seen in the complete control the executive possesses over immigration deportation proceedings. The executive chooses who it deports, and then controls the proceedings that govern deportation trials. The executive chooses the judges and prosecutors, leaving the deportee to find his or her own lawyer. The executive exercises this incredible power in a highly politicized area of law and social policy, where immigration is both divisive and a useful vehicle for political divisiveness. This was evidenced by Bonham's comfort in violating protocol and up-ending his superiors by leaking documents (and even investigating Bridges for adultery), and in the rhetoric of the congressional House members in their floor discussions about deporting Bridges. The executive exercises this power in an area of law and in a court system with limited oversight from the judicial branch. And so Attorney General Jackson appointed his friend Judge Sears, promising senators that Judge Sears would not perform like Dean Landis. In turn, Attorney General Biddle, on his own initiative, reversed the BIA and reinstated Judge Sears' decision. Biddle the prosecutor also acted as the judge, turning the concept of separation of powers on its head and trapping Harry Bridges in the vice of the law.

The executive in turn sought help from its investigative arm, the FBI, which sought permission from the executive to wiretap, a request Attorney General Biddle granted, closing a loop of self-fulfilling circularity. Then when the FBI illegally wiretapped, and Bridges proved it, the executive's lawyers took over and justified the excesses, convincing the already-favorable and hand-picked Judge Sears to look the other way. Meanwhile, as history now shows, executive officials in the FBI signed affidavits that appeared to be false and secreted them away for decades. And when assassination evidence was provided to the FBI, it concluded that a murder plot lay outside its jurisdiction, while at the same time government investigators zealously pursued inquiries into Bridges' sex life. This course of conduct shows that the FBI itself was politicized in the pursuit of Bridges, so insistent that he was guilty and should be deported that it turned a blind eye to assassination evidence to try to shade legal proceedings.

The Prosecutors

The executive prosecutors are a subset of executive branch legal constituents who participated in a persecution-by-prosecution campaign, as seen by their decisions about what evidence to use, the witnesses they put on the stand, what those witnesses would say, and how those witnesses were pressured pre-trial. The erosion of due process is seen when prosecutors seek to win, more than to do justice, despite the oath that governs federal prosecutors to "prosecute on behalf of Justice or Lady Justice."[3]

In the first trial, Prosecutor Shoemaker refused a bill of particulars, a small detail in the grand arc of the case, but it was a position that was at odds with basic fairness and due process, and was adopted for political reasons. That decision did not cause Bridges harm in the specific case (Bridges ultimately won before Dean Landis after all), but the decision is emblematic of the ease with which persecution-by-prosecution can take root. When those charged with ensuring the process works fairly and properly lose even the slightest sense of what is fair and right, and bend the rules or cut corners, the legal environment becomes suddenly malleable and open to further small turns and tweaks that send due process out of kilter in a series of small, often imperceptible, turns. This environment then easily bred other acts, such as when Prosecutor Shoemaker, in the first trial, knowing full well the "Harry Dorgan" card was fake, nonetheless tried to get it into the case.

The case of prosecutors not hewing to justice and instead fighting to win at all costs was amplified in the second trial. There, Prosecutor Del Guercio, taking advantage of the hostile anti-Bridges environment (and the broader anti-communist environment that was witnessing other ideological prosecutions and deportations) that gave birth to the new immigration laws aimed at Bridges, tried to elicit testimony proving Bridges' citizen lawyers were members of the Communist Party. This fact, even if true, was completely irrelevant, but Del Guercio's contentions helped toxify the environment into a guilt-by-association one. Then, when Del Guercio argued that the government had no relevant records about witness Lundeberg, when all the while the government had material that showed Lundeberg's bias towards Bridges, the fingerprints of persecution-by-prosecution further appear. Similarly, it is seen by Del Guercio's acidic, caustic attacks on Bridges, when Del Guercio, for example, insisted that one who used the word "solidarity" must be a communist. Del Guercio's actions were not designed to elicit the truth of the questions at hand, to discern true justice, but instead to grandstand in his tenure presiding over a proceeding more akin to a witch hunt.

Overzealous prosecution is seen in the third trial when Prosecutor Donohue pushed the judge to hold Bridges' lawyer in contempt and execute a jail sentence immediately so as to rid Bridges of his chosen counsel mid-trial, a move that would give Donohue a great advantage before the jury and disadvantage Bridges both by denying him the lawyer of his choice and poisoning the jury. Knocking fairness and due process further out of kilter then occurred when Donohue argued that family demands should excuse Ross/Rosenstein from further testimony right before his lies were to be exposed. Rabidly assaulting Bridges' lawyer—calling him a "mad dog" and contending that Hallinan turned Judge Harris's temple of justice into a brothel—are other examples of a prosecutor making his arguments, but the arguments are twisting the truth for tactical advantage, in the process losing alignment to the justice polestar. Even Donohue's resort in his closing argument to playing upon the religious sympathies of the jury—by castigating Bridges for being divorced, as if it rendered him a fallen Catholic, to reference to a minor witness (Ms. Murray) as a godless un-American because she swore an oath to justice rather than God—demonstrated a ruthless spinning of facts to distort the search for the truth rather than aid it. Donohue angled to win at all costs, and in the process his decisions demonstrated that he strayed from the concept of ensuring the achievement of justice.

As prosecutors put witnesses on a stand and argue about evidence and the law, all in a sterile courtroom environment, there is a cloak of sanctity that appends to the proceedings, a divorce from reality that blesses the process and each individual decision, assertion, or argument as presumptively legitimate. And each little decision is but one of thousands of decisions that make up a trial, each wrong one buried amidst the myriad, discretionary decisions lawyers make, each one justified by a desire to win that shrouded the blind nature of justice that Lady Justice demands.

Private Defense Lawyers

Given the unlimited resources of the federal government, Bridges' ultimate victories hinged heavily on private defense lawyers willing and able to take his case. Indeed, the private lawyers are a bright spot in the entire saga, from the first investigations and trials in the 1930s through the last trial in 1955.

The lawyers' fearless representation of Bridges came at real personal cost. All had to represent a person who was condemned in governmental corridors and in the powerful private economic arena. The heavy anti-communist air made it difficult for them to take the cause, which in turn fueled public and private anger towards them. King, Gladstein, Grossman, and Leonard all found themselves on government and FBI watch lists, part of federal investigative efforts to challenge their authenticity as Americans and paint them as a danger to American democracy, which they all experienced when their personal beliefs were repeatedly challenged in the trials, even though they were not on trial. Hallinan and MacInnis of course paid the heaviest price as they were imprisoned for their advocacy efforts, an imprisonment that was unfair given the improper environment created by Prosecutor Donohue and Judge Harris. And Taylor, at great personal risk, publicly challenged the governmental architects of the Bridges crusade, HUAC and Congressman Dies in particular, a challenge that found him on the receiving end of Senator McCarthy's famed subpoena power and Senator McCarthy's public assertions that Taylor himself was a disloyal American.[4]

Yet all the while they were also mothers and fathers trying to survive in their local communities and economies. Their personal courage to stand against the winds of the times in defense of people like Harry Bridges was a fundamental predicate to the eventual achievement of justice in the court system.

The Judges, Ill and Good

The institutionalization of persecution-by-prosecution in the immigration proceedings is seen in the judges appointed. When balanced fairness was the prism used by Secretary Perkins, the highly respected and learned Dean Landis was appointed. But in the charged political environment that had already amended the immigration laws specifically to target Harry Bridges, Judge Sears was appointed by the attorney general—the man in charge of the prosecution—because Sears was a friend to the attorney general. Regardless of how qualified Judge Sears was as a trial judge, that small tweak in the law's working further damaged the legal environment's legitimacy. In turn, Judge Sears heard dozens of government witnesses, found many of them to be liars, yet trusted two who were admitted liars and spent no more than a couple hours on the witness stand out of ten weeks of trial. His opinion thus ultimately reads as one written to justify a conclusion already reached before any evidence was heard.

Similarly, when in the height of the Red Scare in the 1950s, Bridges appeared before Judge Harris in his third trial, that judge crossed the typical boundaries of judicial neutrality and demonstrated a palpable bias against Bridges and his lawyers from the very first minutes before the jury. First, when Judge Harris was pressed on his appearance of a bias, he refused to cede control over the trial, even though judges in such circumstances should disqualify themselves. His decisions—condemning Bridges' lawyer in front of the jury, castigating Bridges' legal theory in front of the jury, concluding that the government's witness was an honorable one that Hallinan should not unfairly attack, and, conversely, attacking Bridges' character witness, Father Meinecke, when even the aggressive prosecutor chose not to—in many ways began and ended the affair. His final excited utterance to the jury—that it had found the ultimate truth—betrayed his abdication of pure neutrality. A federal judge, dressed in his black robe sitting above the jury, is the closest a formally secular country has to a government-sanctioned priest and can easily influence the trial atmosphere for the jurors.

The federal judiciary's bending to the time's demands, rather than holding to the magnetic north of due process, went beyond Judge Harris, however. It is seen when the Ninth Circuit judges upheld Bridges' conviction even though the judges believed the evidence did not really justify his conviction, all because of a slavish adherence to formal legal doctrines that permitted the judges to bury their heads like ostriches in an exercise of deference to the executive, a policy that made little sense given the politicized nature of the proceedings. If ever there was, and is, a need for judicial oversight, it is to curb the executive's political excesses that bubble to the surface in its self-controlled and politicized court system.

There is also a story of judicial branch redemption in the Harry Bridges deportation trials, namely the United States Supreme Court and the decisive role it played in the positive resolution to the second trial. While the executive immigration courts were ultimately beholden to the executive in Bridges' second and third trials, and the lower federal courts (the federal district courts and the Ninth Circuit Court of Appeals), in the third trial, approved the deportation and conviction decisions because of their desire to defer to the executive, ultimately the United States Supreme Court, as head of the judicial branch, stood firm against executive power and checked the mistakes of the lower courts. Twice. These checks and balances saved Harry Bridges. However, Bridges was also struck by lightning twice, as it borders on the impossible to get the Supreme Court to take a case. Had he not been so lucky to secure Supreme Court review in both cases (something he would likely not have secured in this day and age), he would have been imprisoned and deported because the lower federal courts instantly fell into line with the political atmosphere of the day. Of course, in the fourth trial, Judge Goodman stood firm too, refused to be swayed by the day's heated political atmosphere, and held firm to the dignity of the law, echoing the artful arguments of Bridges' lawyer Telford Taylor.

The Law's Persecution of Dissent

Aside from the prosecutors, the executive branch policymakers, and the judges, the law's caving to support a crusade is also seen in the use, and manipulation, of the law by private actors and legislators to justify a result in a moment of fear. It is seen by the pressure brought to bear upon the Department of Labor by private industry (through Knowles and the American Legion) and state government (Captain Keegan and Special Prosecutor Doyle of Oregon), an effort in turn joined by those in Congress who used the threat of impeachment to pressure the Department of Labor and its lawyers into an acrimonious deportation battle, despite the fact that the Department of Labor had conducted an investigation and did not believe that Bridges was a communist. In turn, HUAC members gladly let Knowles read a private "indictment" into the federal record. Thus, even when the Secretary Perkins impeachment process failed, HUAC had won: Secretary Perkins was scorned with a censure statement, and all government prosecutors knew that prosecuting Harry

Bridges to the end was fine, but letting up on Harry Bridges would be met with personal scorn and intimidation. In turn, Prosecutors Shoemaker and Bonham denied a standard bill of particulars, and Bonham engaged in witness misconduct as evidenced by Canadian barrister Garfield King's testimony.

When Bridges, having earned his citizenship because he prevailed at trial showing he was not a Communist Party member, swears in as a citizen, the law's buried provisions emerged to allow Bridges' swearing-in statements (which the Supreme Court authorized Bridges to make) to be used as a basis to institute what essentially was an identical proceeding. Given the law's vicissitudes, this action was deemed new and not subject to any double jeopardy principles.[5] The law's absurd circularity was exploited to trap and imprison Harry Bridges, something it took Justice Black in the Supreme Court to finally identify as a central problem.

As the Law Turns

The arc of the story thus traces the ease by which persecution-by-prosecution and abdication of due process can take root in the myriad small decisions of the system's constituents, and the corresponding difficulty and costs the system—and most importantly the individual, Harry Bridges—bore simply to reorient due process. These small turns of the law's wheels by the individual constituents of the legal system are what make persecution-by-prosecution in immigration cases truly terrifying, because it is in the law's minutiae that lawyers and judges, politicians and jurors, executive officials and FBI investigators made their individual decisions and ultimately performed in a series of ideological deportation trials where due process repeatedly gave way to a crusade divorced from basics tenets of normative American justice.

And it is in this legal minutiae that anyone can be trapped. Harry Bridges, with a well-funded union and a large public presence, still spent twenty years fighting for his American life in the law's trenches, barely managing to wait out Thomas Paine's prophetic admonition that with enough time eventually reason catches up. That being so, what chance does the average person have in a system whose odds are so stacked?

Ultimately, the Bridges saga exposed the fault line between Lincoln's words and Hoover's words. The concept of justice encapsulated in Hoover's quote at the outset—where achievement of justice is incidental to the greater social good of maintaining a version of law and order—permitted the very due process devolutions that befell Bridges, because the greater social goal was to maintain a particularly perceived political state of society. Lincoln's words, on the other hand, pull for the preeminence of the steady hand of the law, intentionally and cautiously detached from the heady political winds of the moment. Eventually, Lincoln's vision prevailed insofar as Harry Bridges was concerned, but the battle left many casualties and victims.

Today, the same battles over what exemplifies the correct conception of American justice continue, battles that play out in myriad court cases across the country in our modern world, with its own social and political fears unique to this time's struggles with aggressive police responses, deep government surveillance, terrorism, and immigration and prosecutorial overreach, the actors in such dramas being today's lawyers and judges, politicians and jurors, executive officials and investigators, all actors in the ever-unfolding and evolving fight for justice and due process.

ACKNOWLEDGMENTS

I have to thank my wife, Janeen, who reviewed myriad drafts and regularly forced me to explain matters more succinctly and clearly, and who traveled with me and helped in the complex research efforts needed to sift and secure the massive volumes of materials. Pauline, my mum, who reviewed all drafts in amazing detail and always had invaluable and critical insights and suggestions. Every one of your comments and questions, tough as they were, pushed me to try harder. Fred, my father, whose support and passion for these matters is a cornerstone. Mark, my brother, for reviewing and offering both his sage legal and practical advice and commentary.

Beyond family, so many contributed in so many important ways to this book finally coming together. Based on myriad archived materials spanning multiple trials and decades reposed in myriad libraries and personal archives across the country, it simply would not have been possible absent the help of so many generous people who gave their time freely to help me with the many different facets that this story comprises, from labor history to legislative history to legal court history to the nuanced autobiographical histories of lawyers of the mid-twentieth century.

In that vein, I need to thank Harvey Schwartz, one of the preeminent labor historians of our time with respect to the San Francisco strikes and the ILWU, who spent significant time reviewing my manuscripts, offering suggestions and critiques, and offering fantastic anecdotes from his firsthand knowledge about many of the book's most significant players. Harvey's spirit of generosity in terms of his time and intellectual acumen weaves throughout the entire book, from the largest of issues to the smallest of details.

Robin Walker, the ILWU librarian and archivist in San Francisco, who reviewed drafts and generously shared her time and deep historical knowledge about the ILWU and Harry Bridges.

Professor Robert Cherny (Retired) of San Francisco State University, who has written extensively on Harry Bridges and shared many insights with me as well as his writings on Harry Bridges.

Sally Bird, Calidris Literary Agency, the first agent to believe in this story about an Australian expat who made his way to America!

And, of course, Robbie Bridges, Harry's son, for your suggestions and firsthand insight into your father and his times.

Many others have reviewed the manuscript and provided important suggestions, commentary, and/or research support, and I am immensely grateful for your valuable time and energies brought to bear on this project: Reza Bavar, Jonathan Bush, Erwin Chemerinsky, Dottie DeHart, Ann Fagan-Ginger, Susan Hill, Lorne Lahodny, Ashley Lamb, Fred Lane, Marie Louie, Leonard Morales, Maurice Possley, Catherine Powell, Ian Ruskin, John Tehranian, Stephen Welch, Michele Welsing, Nate Westbrook, and Laura Wytsma.

Finally, of course, as a lawyer I feel a debt of gratitude to the hard-fighting lawyers who fearlessly represented Harry Bridges. On the front lines demanding due process for their clients no matter the environment and no matter the personal cost, they shone a bright light for future generations of lawyers.

ENDNOTES

Chapter 1

1   *United States v. Harry Bridges*, Case No. 32117-H, Harry Bridges Testimony at 5162 (Feb. 7, 1950) (hereafter for all witness testimony in the various court cases, "Bridges [Witness] Test. at [page number] (date)").

2   Charles P. Larrowe, *Harry Bridges: The Rise and Fall of Radical Labor in the U.S.* (Lawrence Hill & Co. Publishers 1972), at 3 (hereafter "Larrowe").

3   Bruce Minton & John Stewart, *Men Who Lead Labor* (Modern Age Books 1937), at 175; ILWU Local 19 of Seattle, Washington, *Harry Bridges: A Biography* http://www.ilwu19.com/history/biography.htm (last accessed May 8, 2014).

4   Larrowe at 4.

5   Irving Bernstein, *The Turbulent Years: A History of the American Worker, 1933-1941* (Houghton Mifflin Books 1969), at 252; Minton & Stewart at 175.

6   Minton & Stewart at 176; ILWU Local 19 of Seattle, Washington, *Harry Bridges: A Biography* http://www.ilwu19.com/history/biography.htm (last accessed May 8, 2014); Bridges Test. at 5151 (Feb. 7, 1950).

7   ILWU Local 19 of Seattle, Washington, *Harry Bridges: A Biography*, located at http://www.ilwu19.com/history/biography.htm (last accessed May 8, 2014); Bridges Test. at 5697-99 (May 29, 1941).

8   Larrowe at 4-5; Bridges Test. at 5157-59 (Feb. 7, 1950).

9   Bridges Test. at 5731 (May 29, 1941); Larrowe at 4-5; Bernstein at 253; Bridges Test. at 5167 (Feb. 7, 1950).

10 Bernstein at 253; Dean James Landis Decision, *In the Matter of Harry Bridges* (Dec. 28, 1939), at 122 (hereafter "Landis Decision"); Larrowe at 6.

11 Bridges Test. at 5175-95 (Feb. 7, 1950); Larrowe at 8.

12 Larrowe at 8.

13 Henry Mayhew, *London Labour and the London Poor* (1861), quoted in Bernstein at 254.

14 Bridges Test. at 3064 (Aug. 4, 1939); Bridges Test. at 5174-76 (Feb. 7, 1950); *see also* Howard Kimeldorf, *Reds or Rackets? The Making of Radical and Conservative Unions on the Waterfront* (University of California Press 1988), at 82.

15 Bridges Test. at 5176 (Feb. 7, 1950); Minton & Stewart at 176-79.

16 Bernstein at 253; Minton & Stewart at 176-79; David Selvin, *A Terrible Anger: The 1934 Waterfront and General Strikes in San Francisco* (Wayne State University Press 1996), at 45-47. One hold-out was Tacoma, Washington, where the ILA survived with two locals, Locals 38-3 and 38-30, the only to survive on the West Coast. Selvin at 52.

17   Harvey Schwartz, *Solidarity Stories: An Oral History of the ILWU* (University of Washington Press 2009), at 12; Bridges Test. at 5176-5195 (Feb. 7, 1950); "Oral History of Harry Bridges," International Longshore and Warehouse Union, Edited by Harvey Schwartz (July 27, 2004), located at http://www.ilwu.org/oral-history-of-harry-bridges (last accessed Dec. 1, 2014) (hereafter "Oral History of Harry Bridges").

18   Schwartz at 11; Harvey Schwartz, "Harry Bridges and the Scholars: Looking at History's Verdict," *California History: The Magazine of the California Historical Society,* Vol. LIX (Spring 1980), at 67 (hereafter "Schwartz, 'Harry Bridges and the Scholars'"); Bridges Test. at 3061 (Aug. 24, 1939); Bridges Test. at 5173-75 (Feb. 7, 1950); Larrowe at 9.

19   Bridges Test. at 5188 (Feb. 7, 1950); Larrowe at 11; Bernstein at 256; Selvin at 45-46.

20   Larrowe at 11; Bernstein at 257; Harry Bridges Letter to Hon. Marcantonio, June 1, 1940, reprinted in Cong. Rec. Senate at 12386 (June 13, 1940).

21   Larrowe at 14-16. The number "38" was the ILA Pacific Coast District number and "79" was the local number within the Pacific Coast District.

22   *Harry Bridges-A Man and His Union,* Produced by Berry Minott and John Knoop (1992; MW Productions), DVD (quoting video interview of Sidney Roger).

23   Reminiscences of Frances Perkins, "An Oral History" (Columbia University 1955), Vol.6, Pt.2 at 321 (hereafter "Perkins Oral History"); "National Affairs," *Time Magazine,* July 19, 1937, at 13; "Bridges Reaches Crisis in His Labor Leadership," *New York Times,* July 16, 1939.

24   Bridges Test. at 5208-12 (Feb. 7, 1950); Bridges Test. at 2593-98 (1939); Kimeldorf at 87-88; Larrowe at 14-16.

25   Larrowe at 16-19; Bridges Test. at 5230-33 (Feb. 7, 1950).

26   Bridges Test. at 5230-33 (Feb. 7, 1950); Landis Decision at 101.

27   Harvey Schwartz, "Harry Bridges: A Centennial Retrospective," (Harry Bridges Institute 2001), at 11 (hereafter, "Schwartz, 'Harry Bridges: A Centennial Retrospective'").

28   Bridges Test. at 5208-12, 5230-35 (Feb. 7, 1950); Landis Decision at 101.

29   Larrowe at 16-19.

30   Larrowe at 18-19.

31   Larrowe at 19-20.

32   Larrowe at 20; Kimeldorf at 82-88.

33   Bridges Test. at 5217-21 (Feb. 7, 1950); Larrowe at 21.

34   Perkins Oral History Vol.6, Pt.2 at 326.

35   Larrowe at 20-21.

36   Larrowe at 22-25; Bernstein at 261; Bridges Test. at 5233 (Feb. 7, 1950).

37   Bernstein at 257-59. In one anecdote, Joseph Kennedy lit into Harry Bridges, and Harry Bridges scalded right back, unmoved and unimpressed by Joseph Kennedy's power and wealth. Kennedy in turn apparently had great disdain for Bridges, saying "it's immaterial whether he's a Communist…he's a trouble-maker and a pest and does not deserve the tender consideration bestowed on him by Madame Perkins." Harold Ickes, *The Secret Diary of Harold L. Ickes* (1954), Vol.5, Pt.2 at 312.

38   Larrowe at 28.

39   Bernstein at 257.

40   Larrowe at 26-27.

41   Larrowe at 28.

42 Paul Eliel, *The Waterfront and General Strikes, San Francisco, 1934, A Brief History* (Leopold Classic Library 1934), at 7; Larrowe at 28-29; Bernstein at 262; Bridges Test. at 5242-43 (Feb. 7, 1950).

43 Larrowe at 28-29; Bernstein at 263.

44 Bridges Test. at 5244 (Feb. 7, 1950).

45 Larrowe at 38.

46 Schwartz at 20-21; Oral History of Harry Bridges at 11-12; Schwartz, "Harry Bridges: A Centennial Retrospective" at 13.

47 Bridges Test. at 5244-45 (Feb. 7, 1950). In Seattle, on the strike's second day, police attacked with riot clubs, but the longshoremen managed to disarm the police, sending several policemen to the hospital. Portland experienced similar violence, and the Portland Mayor demanded the Oregon Governor send in the Oregon National Guard. Larrowe at 46-50. In Los Angeles, on May 15, 1934, three hundred longshoremen stormed a stockade housing non-union workers, resulting in the deaths of two strikers, and on May 17, 1934, several hundred strikers broke a barricade around the piers in Oakland and boarded a ship. Eliel at 21-22; *see also* Cal Winslow, "The Strike that Shook San Francisco and Rocked the Pacific Coast," July 2, 2014, located at http://www.counterpunch.org/2014/07/02/the-strike-that-shook-san-francisco-and-rocked-the-pacific-coast/ (last accessed Feb. 29, 2016).

48 Eliel at 21; Larrowe at 46.

49 Paul Smith, *Personal File: An Autobiography* (Appleton-Century Co. 1964), at 152; Larrowe at 80.

50 Bridges Test. at 5288 (Feb. 8, 1950).

51 Bridges Test. at 5342-43 (Feb. 8, 1950).

52 Bridges Test. at 2502-03 (Aug. 2, 1939); Eliel at 37.

53 Larrowe at 59; Bridges Test. at 5244-46 (Feb. 7, 1950), Bridges Test. at 5390-92 (Feb. 9, 1950); Eliel at 31-34. In his oral memoirs, Bridges recounted that "Ryan was a conservative union leader who became a prisoner of the mob. In terms of money sell-outs, he got certain payoffs in one way or another." Schwartz, "Harry Bridges: A Centennial Retrospective," at 12.

54 Eliel at 35; Larrowe at 48-50, 57; Oral History of Harry Bridges at 12; Bridges Test. at 5392 (Feb. 9, 1950).

55 J.B. Flenner, Memo for Walsh, May 15, 1934, RG 85, Box 14, National Archives and Records Administration ("NARA"), San Bruno, CA; Larrowe at 45-46.

56 Daniel MacCormack Western Union Telegram to District Director, INS, May 22, 1934 (copy on file with author).

57 Confidential letter, Turner W. Battle to Marvin H. McIntyre, May 24, 1934, Franklin D. Roosevelt Papers, Official File 407b, Box 11, Folder 1934: Pacific Coast Longshoremen's Strike, Franklin D. Roosevelt Library.

58 Bridges Test. at 5323-27 (Feb. 8, 1950).

59 Perkins Oral History, Vol.6, Pt.2 at 330.

60 Larrowe at 62-63.

61 Oral History of Harry Bridges at 13.

62 Larrowe at 63-65.

63 Larrowe at 67-69.

64 Larrowe at 68-69.

65 Bridges Test. at 3085 (Aug. 3, 1939).

66 Larrowe at 69.

67 Larrowe at 68-72; Estolv E. Ward, *Harry Bridges on Trial* (Modern Age Books 1940) at 8; Bridges Test. at 5286 (Feb. 8, 1950); Eliel at 113.

68 Bridges Test. at 5285-92 (Feb. 8, 1950); Larrowe at 71; Eliel at 111-15; Kimeldorf at 105-06; Minton & Stewart at 186.

69 Larrowe at 68-72; Ward at 8; Bridges Test. at 5286 (Feb. 8, 1950); Eliel at 113. At the later-held inquests into the deaths, Sperry's death was ruled justifiable homicide by the police engaged in riot suppression and Counderakis was declared dead at the hands of unknown assailants. Eliel at 113. Meanwhile, violence also erupted at other ports on the West Coast during July 1934. Kimeldorf at 106-09.

70 Eliel at 127; Larrowe at 70.

71 Bridges Test. at 5291, 5302-05 (Feb. 8, 1950); Bridges Test. at 5408-11 (Feb. 9, 1950).

72 Ward at 8; Bridges Test. at 5295 (Feb. 8, 1950).

73 Bridges Test. at 5293 (Feb. 8, 1950).

74 Larrowe at 76-79; Ward at 9-10; Bridges Test. at 3084 (Aug. 3, 1939); Bridges Test. at 5296 (Feb. 8, 1950). At the inception of the general strike, the Mayor of San Francisco declared a state of emergency, thereby allowing him to address the strike without the typical legal formalities. Eliel at 146.

75 "'Frisco in Grip of Strike," *Pathe News*, 1934 Newsreel (with Mayor Rossi speaking), located at https://www.youtube.com/watch?v=GdM9GioUKw4 (last accessed June 12, 2016).

76 Schwartz at 37; Larrowe at 80-91; Bridges Test. at 5296-5300 (Feb. 8, 1950); Eliel at 166-67.

77 Bridges Test. at 5275-90, 5296-5300, 5351-55 (Feb. 8, 1950); Bridges Test. at 5976-78, 6012 (June 2, 1941).

78 Perkins Letter to American Legion Chairman Chadwick, as reprinted in "Replies to Legion on Bridges Delay," *New York Times*, Nov. 20, 1938; Minton & Stewart at 189.

79 Perkins Oral History at 325.

80 Wilbur Carr/Department of State Letter to Perkins/Department of Labor, October 6, 1934, referencing July 17, 1934, letter with information about Bridges, from National Archives, San Bruno, CA (copy on file with author); INS Witness Interviews of Charles Peed, July 3, 1934, RG 85, Bridges INS Inv. File 12020/25037, Box 4, NARA, San Bruno, CA (copy on file with author); Robert W. Cherny, "Harry Bridges, Labor Radicalism and the State," paper presented at "Harry Bridges and the Tradition of Dissent Among Waterfront Workers," University of Washington, Jan. 28, 1994, at 7 (hereafter "Cherny").

81 Statement of Charles Peed to Immigration Inspector Farrelly, July 3, 1934, RG-85 "Records of the Immigration & Naturalization Service," Box 1, NARA, San Bruno, CA (copy on file with author).

82 Perkins Oral History at 325.

83 Commissioner J. Mackay Letter to W. Quinn, Chief of Police San Francisco, Feb. 8, 1937, RG 85 "Bridges INS Inv. Files" Box 18, NARA, San Bruno, CA.

84 U.S. Dep't of Labor February 2, 1935 Letter form Thomas Donoghue to District Director, RG 85 Boxes 1-17 (compartment 2116A), NARA, San Bruno, CA.

85 Immigrant Inspector Thomas V. Donoghue Letter to INS Inspector, February 2, 1935, RG-85 "INS Inv. Files," Box 16, Folder 0606-36231[2], NARA, San Bruno, CA (copy on file with author).

86 *See generally* Smith at 190; Larrowe 1-125; Kimeldorf at 61-62.

87   Ronald Collins & David Skover, *On Dissent* (Columbia University Press 2013), at 129.

88   Jill Lepore, "The Sharpened Quill," *New Yorker Magazine* located at http://www.newyorker. com/archive/2006/10/16/061016crbo_books (last accessed June 3, 2016).

89   *On Dissent* at 130.

90   Gregory Claeys, *Thomas Paine, Social and Political Thought* (Routledge 1989); Victoria Bassetti, "In Search of the Right to Vote," *Harper's Magazine* (Oct. 2012).

91   *On Dissent* at 131.

92   Thomas Paine, *Common Sense* (1776).

Chapter 2

1   Perkins Oral History, Vol.6, Pt.2 at 341.

2   Larrowe at 95.

3   *Time Magazine*, "National Affairs," July 19, 1937, at 13 (quoting speech).

4   Schwartz, "Harry Bridges and the Scholars," at 70.

5   Larrowe at 98.

6   International Longshoremen's and Warehousemen's Union, *Harry Bridges: A Biography*, located at http://www.ilwu19.com/history/biography.htm (last accessed June 3, 2016).

7   Bruce Nelson, *Divided We Stand: American Workers and the Struggle for Black Equality* (Princeton University Press 2001), at 96.

8   Bridges Test. at 5343-54, *ibid.* for specific quotes at 5354, 5349 (Feb. 9, 1950).

9   Minton & Stuart at 202.

10   Larrowe at 112-17. Fearing Bridges' growing sway with union workers, the ship-owners also declared in 1936 that they were shutting the port until Harry Bridges was removed as head of the Pacific Coast District of the ILA. The maritime workers rallied behind Bridges, but after a week with the Port of San Francisco closed, even Bridges got nervous and questioned whether the union would be better off without him. "You can't do that. We can't let the employers tell a union who shall lead it," Mike Casey the head of the powerful Teamsters responded. Bridges held firm, and the ship-owners quickly abandoned that tack to oust Bridges. Larrowe at 108.

11   International Longshoremen's and Warehousemen's Union, *Harry Bridges: A Biography*, located at http://www.ilwu19.com/history/biography.htm (last accessed June 3, 2016); Ward at 15. In the 1950s the AFL and CIO merged to form the AFL-CIO, still in existence today. *See also* Bridges Test. at 5392-97 (Feb. 9, 1950). The vote was 80-90% to leave the AFL and affiliate with the CIO. *Ibid.* at 5397.

12   Larrowe at 124; *Time Magazine*, "National Affairs," July 19, 1937 at 13 ("a pronounced Australian accent (an exaggerated Cockney)…"); ILWU Local 10, "Harry Bridges," located at http://ilwulocal10.org/harry-bridges/ (last accessed June 3, 2016); Cherny at 3. As Professor Cherny demonstrates, in 1964 for example Harry Bridges received $17,000 in salary while Jimmy Hoffa received $91,000 in salary from the Teamsters and Joe Curran received $106,000 from the National Maritime Union. Cherny at 3.

13   Larrowe at 124-25. This occurred in the 1950s when Bridges had already been running the union for almost two decades. Even the passage of time did not alter his resolute stance.

14   Bridges Letter to Grossman, March 8, 1937, and Bridges 1937 Tax Return, Box 1, File 1, Southern California Library, Los Angeles, CA (copy on file with author); Larrowe at 124-25.

15 Kimeldorf at 6-7.

16 *Time Magazine*, "National Affairs," July 19, 1937, at 13-14; Perkins Oral History at 323-30 (originally badly dressed), 379, 529 (subsequently well-dressed).

17 Smith at 156-57; Larrowe at 99-100; Minton & Stuart at 202.

18 8 U.S.C. § 137(a)-(e), as codified by the Immigration Act of 1918, 40 Stat. 1012 (repealed 1952).

19 American Legion, *SAL Americanism Report* (Feb. 24, 2012), located at http://www.legion.org/sons/161913/sal-americanism-report (last accessed June 3, 2016).

20 Landis Decision at 49-50.

21 Landis Decision at 49-50.

22 Knowles Letter to INS Commissioner McCormack, Dec. 18, 1935, NARA, San Bruno CA (copy on file with author); Landis Decision at 51.

23 Perkins Oral History at 341.

24 Perkins Oral History at 445. Secretary Perkins also kept President Roosevelt abreast of the Bridges' investigations. "I told him all we knew about Bridges. He laughed heartily over the picture of this dangerous fellow playing his mandolin in his San Francisco boarding-house in the evenings." Frances Perkins, *The Roosevelt I Knew* (Viking Press 1946), at 318.

25 Landis Decision at 51.

26 Landis Decision at 50-51.

27 Landis Decision at 56-57; Bridges Test. at 5333-34 (Feb. 8, 1950).

28 Landis Decision at 56-57.

29 Doyle Affidavit to INS, August 20, 1937, from NARA, San Bruno, CA (copy on file with author). In the Affidavit, Doyle attests that he had spent the last two years investigating Bridges and that he had procured several witnesses and could procure more if needed, all of whom would say Harry Bridges was a Communist Party member. *See also* Cherny at 9.

30 Robert Cherny, "Anticommunist Networks and Labor: The Pacific Coast in the 1930's," at 21, a chapter from the book *Labor's Cold War* edited by Shelton Stromquist (University of Illinois 2008); "40&8, La Societe des Quarante Hommes et Huit Chevaux," located at www.fortyandeight.com/what-is-the-408/ (last accessed Feb. 20, 2016).

31 Landis Decision at 18; *State v. DeJonge*, 51 P.2d 674 (1935); Ward at 223.

32 Landis Decision at 12.

33 Landis Decision at 12.

34 DeJonge's conviction was affirmed by the Oregon Supreme Court, but a unanimous United States Supreme Court reversed the conviction. *DeJonge v. State of Oregon*, 299 U.S. 353 (1937).

35 Landis Decision at 18.

36 Landis Decision at 20-21; Ward at 65.

37 Landis Decision at 24-25.

38 Landis Decision at 25, 32.

39 Landis Decision at 27-28; Aug. 20, 1937 Leech Affidavit to Portland INS, NARA, San Bruno, CA archives (copy with author).

40 Sworn Statement of Stanley Doyle, Aug. 30, 1937, RG-85 "Bridges INS Inv. Files" Box 18, NARA, San Bruno, CA.

41 Cong. Rec. App'x (March 18, 1941) at A1221; Examination of Harry Bridges, INS, New York, NY (October 18, 1937), at 6; Cherny at 9.

42 Doyle to Boyd Letter, Oct. 21, 1949, Westbrook Pegler Papers, Herbert Hoover Presidential Library, Box 91, Longshoremen, at 2 (copy on file with author).

43 Ward at 21.

44 Raphael Bonham to INS District Director Letter, April 30, 1935, located at National Archives (San Francisco) RG-85 "Records of the Immigration & Naturalization Service," Box 1 (copy on file with author).

45 Stanley Doyle to Bonham Letter, Sep. 7, 1937, California Surveillance/Harper Knowles Papers, "Correspondence of Harper Knowles and Stanley Doyle" folder, J. Paul Leonard Library, San Francisco State University (copy of letter on file with author); Doyle to Bonham Letter, Sep. 20, 1937, California Surveillance/Harper Knowles Papers, "Correspondence of Harper Knowles and Stanley Doyle" folder, J. Paul Leonard Library, San Francisco State University (copy on file with author).

46 Stanley Doyle to Bonham Letter, Sep. 25, 1938, California Surveillance/Harper Knowles Papers, "Correspondence of Harper Knowles and Stanley Doyle" folder, J. Paul Leonard Library, San Francisco State University (copy on file with author); Doyle to Bonham Letter, Sep. 20, 1937, California Surveillance/Harper Knowles Papers, "Correspondence of Harper Knowles and Stanley Doyle" folder, Normal Leonard Library, San Francisco State University (copy of letter on file with author).

47 Ralph Bonham INS Seattle District Director, Nov. 24, 1937, Letter to Roy Norene INS Divisional Director, Box 10, File 1, Southern California Library, Los Angeles, CA (copy on file with author).

48 Stanley Doyle to Senator Arthur Vandenburg Letter, March 2, 1938, California Surveillance/Harper Knowles Papers, "Correspondence of Harper Knowles and Stanley Doyle" folder, J. Paul Leonard Library, San Francisco State University (copy on file with author).

49 Senator Arthur Vandenburg to Doyle Letter, Feb. 7, 1938, California Surveillance/Harper Knowles Papers, "Correspondence of Harper Knowles and Stanley Doyle" folder, J. Paul Leonard Library, San Francisco State University (copy on file with author).

50 Larrowe at 139; Charles P. Larrowe, "Did the Old Left Get Due Process? The Case of Harry Bridges," 60 Cal. L. Rev. 39, 45 (hereafter "Larrowe, 'Did the Old Left'"); Cherny at 10.

51 Perkins Oral History at 423; Cherny at 10.

52 Cherny at 10 and n.60 (citing press clippings).

53 Larrowe at 139-140.

54 Perkins Oral History at 437-38; Cherny at 10. As Professor Cherny explains, Secretary Perkins even dispatched one of her INS officials to the West Coast to personally review the evidence and meet the witnesses, because they all believed the evidence had been "manufactured." After the investigation, the conclusion remained the same: the evidence was dubious at best and not worthy of an arrest warrant standing alone. Cherny at 10; *see also* Reilly to Perkins Letter, Oct. 4, 1937, Perkins Papers, Box 38, folder "Reilly, G, Oct. 13, 1937" (Columbia University). Indeed, Secretary Perkins believed that the West Coast INS officials had been bedazzled by the anti-Bridges forces and so had lost their objectivity. Larrowe, "Did the Old Left," at 45.

55 Larrowe 141; Cherny at 10.

56 Perkins Oral History 423, 476-78.

57 Cherny at 11; "Bridges Demands a Hearing," *New York Times*, Feb. 10, 1938.

58 Larrowe at 139-42.

59   L.S. Tellier, "American Law Reports: Right of Accused to Bill of Particulars," 5 A.L.R.2d 444, at § 1 (ALR 2d 1949). Bills of particular were abolished in the federal and state systems starting in the 1940s and 50s in favor of a more open, and fair, discovery process that required furnishing of evidence that the prosecutor intended to use as well as exculpatory evidence.

60   Memorandum for the Solicitor, T.B. Shoemaker, April 14, 1938, RG 85 Bridges INS Inv. Files Box 18, NARA, San Bruno, CA (copy on file with author); Larrowe at 142.

61   *Strecker v. Kessler*, 95 F.2d 976, 977-78 (5th Cir. 1938).

62   Perkins Oral History at 465-67; Larrowe at 144-45.

63   Perkins Oral History at 469-481.

64   Bonham Western Union Telegraph, April 20, 1938, RG 85 Bridges INS Inv. Files Box 19, NARA, San Bruno, CA.

65   Immigration Commissioner Houghteling Letter, April 21, 1938, reprinted in Cong. Rec. App'x (March 18, 1941) at A1222.

66   Cong. Rec. App'x (March 18, 1941) at A1223 (May 8, 1938 entry); Larrowe at 144.

67   Larrowe at 145.

68   Perkins Oral History at 469; "The Bridges Case," *New York Times*, January 25, 1939.

69   Larrowe at 143-44; Perkins Oral History at 463-69.

70   *New Republic*, June 15, 1938, at 158; Cong. Rec. (May 26, 1938) at 7568, 7570.

71   Cong Rec. (May 26, 1938) at 7574.

72   Cong. Rec. App'x (March 18, 1941) at A1223.

73   Cong. Rec. App'x (March 18, 1941) at A1223.

74   Hearings before HUAC, 75th Cong. 3d Sess., Vol. 3 (Oct. 24-26, 1938) at 1715, 1746, 1912.

75   Cherny at 11.

76   Perkins Letter to Dies, August 30, 1938, reprinted in Hearings before HUAC, 75th Cong. 3d Sess., Vol. 3 (Oct. 24-26, 1938) at 1926.

77   Perkins Oral History at 478.

78   Cong. Rec. House, 76th Congress, 1st Session, at 702-703 (Jan. 24, 1939); Perkins Papers at 501-04.

79   H. Res. 67, 76th Congress, 1st Session (Jan. 24, 1939) at 19, 42-43, 46-47.

80   Cong. Rec. House at 711 (Jan. 24, 1939).

81   Perkins Oral History at 512, 470-75, 514.

82   House Rep. No. 311, 76th Congress 1st Session, Report to Accompany H. Res. 67 (March 24, 1939), at 10-11.

83   Perkins Oral History at 527.

84   *Kessler v. Strecker*, 307 U.S. 22, 30-33 (1939).

Chapter 3

1   Lai, Him Mark, Genny Lim, and Judy Yung, *Island Poetry and History of Chinese Immigrants on Angel Island*, 1910-1940, (University of Washington Press, 1991); Cary Nelson, *Anthology of Modern Poetry* (Oxford University Press 2000).

2   *Yamataya v. Fisher*, 189 U.S. 86, 101 (1903) ("[N]o person shall be deprived of his liberty without opportunity ... to be heard.... Therefore, it is not competent ... arbitrarily to cause an alien who has entered the country ... to be taken into custody and deported without giving

him all opportunity to be heard...."); *Yepes–Prado v. INS*, 10 F.3d 1363, 1369 n. 11 (9th Cir. 1993) ("Deportation is a drastic measure and at times the equivalent of banishment or exile."); *see also Padilla-Agustin v. INS*, 21 F.3d 970, 974 (9th Cir. 1994) ("We think it cannot be gainsaid that the private liberty interests involved in deportation proceedings are among the most substantial.").

3   *Marbury v. Madison*, 5 U.S. 137 (1803).

4   Larrowe, "Did the Old Left" at 48, quoting Perkins Internal Labor Memorandum (1939) in Perkins Oral History (Columbia University); Kirstin Downey, *The Woman Behind the New Deal: The Life and Legacy of Frances Perkins* (Anchor 2010), at 283.

5   Ritchie, Donald A., *James M. Landis: Dean of the Regulators* (Harvard University Press 1980); Larrowe, "Did the Old Left," at 48-49 n. 51; Downey at 283; "Bridges Hearing Will Open Today," *New York Times*, July 10, 1939.

6   Landis at 2-3; Ward at 20, 60.

7   Ward at 18-20.

8   Ward at 21.

9   Department of Justice Official Letter (Feb. 14, 1992), located at http://www.justice.gov/about/doj-seal-history-and-motto.htm (last accessed June 3, 2016).

10   Ward at 23.

11   Bridges Test. at 9-10 (July 10, 1939); Ward at 27.

12   Bridges Test. at 10-11 (July 10, 1939).

13   Ann Fagan-Ginger, *Carol Weiss King: Human Rights Lawyer, 1895-1952*, (Univ. Press of Colorado 1993), at 535, quoting *New York Times* obituary.

14   Bridges Test. at 12 (July 10, 1939).

15   Bridges Test. at 12-14 (July 10, 1939); Ward at 25.

16   Laurence Milner Test. at 18, 21, 26-37, 215-16 (July 10, 1939).

17   Milner Test. at 21-34; Ward at 27.

18   Milner Test. at 33-35.

19   Milner Test. at 21-59, 204-05; Landis Decision at 16.

20   Milner Test. at 194-259, 360.

21   Milner Test. at 252-69.

22   Milner Test. at 266-67.

23   Milner Test. at 207-08.

24   Milner Test. at 282-83.

25   Milner Test. at 283-93.

26   Milner Test. at 231-36.

27   Larrowe, "Did the Old Left," at 53.

28   Milner Test. at 404 (July 11, 1939).

29   *San Francisco News*, July 12, 1939, at 4, Col. 5; Larrowe, "Did the Old Left" at 53.

30   Landis Decision at 22-23.

31   Landis Decision at 23.

32   Cal. Penal Code § 11400 *et seq.* (now repealed); *100 Americans Making History*, Edited by Melvin I. Urofsky, "Charlotte Anita Whitney v. California: Free Speech for Radicals," (Sage Publications, www.library.cqpress.com, Supreme Court Collection), last accessed Nov. 23, 2014.

33   Cal. Edu. Code 44932(a)(2).

34   Bridges Test. at 2924-25 (Aug. 4, 1939).

35   Landis Decision at 27-28; Aug. 20, 1937, Leech Affidavit to Portland INS, NARA, San Bruno, CA (copy with author).

36   Landis Decision at 42-43. Notably, even the government's handwriting expert conceded the signature was Leech's.

37   Doyle to Boyd Letter, Oct. 21, 1949, Westbrook Pegler Papers, Herbert Hoover Presidential Library, Box 91, Longshoremen (copy on file with author).

38   Authentication is a condition precedent to admissibility and this condition is satisfied by evidence sufficient to support a finding that the matter in question is what its proponent claims. *See, e.g.*, Fed. R. Evid. 901(a).

39   Fed. R. Evid. 901(a); *Orr v. Bank of America*, 285 F.3d 764, 773-74 (9th Cir. 2002) (authentication established by laying foundation of personal knowledge).

40   James Landis, Trial Transcript at 987-88. Professor Cherny also details the evidence that shows that the card was in fact fabricated by Doyle or one of his associates. Cherny at 9 & n.52.

41   Phelan to Bonham Letter, July 9, 1938, RG 85, INS Inv. Files, NARA, San Bruno, CA (copy on file with author); J. Edgar Hoover Letter to E.J. Connelley, Sep. 7, 1940, FBI FOIA File 039-SF-30 Section 2 (copy on file with author).

42   United Press, "Police Captain Testifying at Bridges' Probe," *Pittsburgh Press*, Aug. 9, 1939, located at http://news.google.com/newspapers?nid=1144&dat=19390809&id=9ssaAAAAI-BAJ&sjid=PkwEAAAAIBAJ&pg=1476,4922896 (last accessed June 3, 2016).

43   Aaron Sapiro Testimony at 1048-52 (July 19, 1939).

44   Sapiro Test. at 1052-60 (July 19, 1939).

45   Sapiro Test. at 1099-1100, quoting March 31, 1938 Order of New York District Judge Knox.

46   Sapiro Test. at 1094-1100.

47   Sapiro Test. at 1123-25.

48   Sapiro Test. at 1187-99.

49   Sapiro Test. at 1217-1220.

50   Undercover Informant Report, Portland, Oregon, Oct. 17, 1937, "Correspondence of Harper Knowles and Stanley Doyle" folder, J. Paul Leonard Library, San Francisco State University (copy of letter on file with author).

51   Miriam Feingold Stein, *The Shipboard Murder Case: Labor, Radicalism and Earl Warren, 1936-1941*, Regional Oral History Office, University of California, Berkeley, 1972, at iii-v.

52   Earl King Testimony, Vol. 33 at 5853-60 (August 25, 1939).

53   Ernest Ramsay Testimony, Vol. 33 at 5786-5902 (Aug. 25, 1939).

54   Larrowe at 169; Ward at 102. Newspaperman Paul Smith remarked that, "Bridges stood up under the most extraordinary pressures with a remarkable, quiet personal strength. He moved around without bodyguards and seemed afraid of nothing, though for years physical violence lay just beneath the surface of events. And throughout the toughest years of his struggle he maintained a wry sense of humor that I always found engaging." Smith at 191.

55   Garfield King Testimony at 5365-66 (Aug. 23, 1939).

56   Garfield King Test. at 5371-74.

57   Landis Decision at 73-74.

58   Harper Knowles Testimony at 3162 (Aug. 7, 1939).

59   Knowles Test. at 3219.

60   Knowles Test. at 3156-3161.

61   Knowles Test. at 3182.
62   Knowles Test. at 3175-83.
63   Knowles Test. at 3185.
64   Knowles Test. at 3409 (Aug. 8, 1939).
65   Knowles Test. at 6068-70.
66   Knowles Test. at 3248-56.
67   Knowles Test. at 3248-56.
68   Knowles Test. at 3347-48.
69   Knowles Test. at 3423-25.
70   John Keegan Testimony at 3512-3534 (Aug. 9, 1939).
71   Keegan Test. at 3535-37, 3550-53.
72   Keegan Test. at 3548-3615.
73   Keegan Test. at 3680.
74   Keegan Test. at 4231 (Aug. 15, 1939).
75   Keegan Test. at 3704 (Aug. 9, 1939).
76   Fagan-Ginger at 302.
77   Bridges Test. at 2660 (Aug. 3, 1939).
78   Bridges Test. at 2481 (Aug. 2, 1939); Bridges Test. at 2821-22 (Aug. 3, 1939).
79   Bridges Test. at 2544 (Aug. 2, 1939).
80   Bridges Test. at 5288 (Feb. 8, 1950).
81   Landis at 124-25.
82   Landis at 125-26.
83   Bridges Test. at 2660 (Aug. 3, 1939); Landis at 127.
84   Bridges Test. at 2748-50 (Aug. 3, 1939); Landis at 130-31.
85   Landis at 128.
86   Landis at 129.
87   Other rebuttal witnesses were called, almost eighteen just in the last week of trial, mostly addressing the issue of Communism in America. Larrowe, "Did the Old Left," at 75.
88   Landis Decision at 140-41.
89   Stanley Doyle Hearing at 7622-49 (Sep. 13, 1939).
90   Doyle Hearing at 7649-66.
91   Doyle Hearing at 7666-73.
92   Doyle Hearing at 7677-95.
93   Doyle Hearing at 7695-7708.
94   Doyle Hearing at 7709-11.
95   Doyle Hearing at 7711-25; *see also* Landis Decision at 142.
96   Landis Decision at 2; Larrowe, "Did the Old Left," at 58-78.
97   The Reminiscences of James M. Landis, Oral History Research Office, Columbia University 1964, at 55.
98   *In the Matter of Harry Bridges*, Findings and Conclusions of the Trial Examiner (Dec. 28, 1939), at 87.
99   The Reminiscences of James M. Landis, Oral History Research Office, (Columbia University 1964), at 55-56.
100 Landis at 51.
101 Landis at 56.

102 Landis at 20 n.47.

103 Dean Landis also concluded the government's witness Miles Humphries had a "tendency towards prevarication [that] was almost pathological" and echoed similar comments about other witnesses. Landis at 110-16 (Witnesses James Engstrom and Ida Castor).

104 Landis at 132-34.

105 "Miss Perkins Drops Move to Deport Bridges in Accepting Landis Report on 'Red' Charge," *New York Times*, Jan. 9, 1940.

106 "Action on Bridges in Congress Likely," *New York Times*, Dec. 31, 1939 "Counsel Hails Finding"); "Landis Absolves Bridges of Being a Red,"" *New York Times*, Dec. 30, 1939.

107 Inspector in Charge, *September 13, 1939 Memorandum*, located at RG 85, INS investigative Files, Box 4, 12020/25037, File 11 Bridges Temporary File, NARA, San Bruno, CA (copy of document on file with author). Even Bridges' lawyers' in-laws, who apparently happened to attend the trial, were placed on the Communist Party list. *Ibid.*

108 Ward at 240; "Bridges Not a Communist," *Sydney Morning Herald*, Jan. 1, 1940, located at http://trove.nla.gov.au/ndp/del/article/17653947 (last accessed Dec. 1, 2014).

Chapter 4

1   "Action on Bridges in Congress Likely," *New York Times*, Dec. 31, 1939 (quoting Dec. 30 statements by Senator King of Utah).

2   H.R. 9766 (June 13, 1940).

3   Appendix to Cong. Rec., March 18, 1941, at A1223, "Legion Head Scores Bridges Case Report," *New York Times*, Jan. 4, 1940 (quoting the American Legion's National Commander on need for more legislation to deport Bridges).

4   Erwin Chemerinsky, *Constitutional Law* (Aspen 1997), at 363-67.

5   86 Cong. Rec. 8189 (June 13, 1940).

6   86 Cong. Rec. 8181-82 (June 13, 1940).

7   86 Cong. Rec. 8182 (June 13, 1940).

8   86 Cong. Rec. 8193 (June 13, 1940).

9   86 Cong. Rec. 8203 (June 13, 1940).

10   86 Cong. Rec. 8204 (June 13, 1940).

11   86 Cong. Rec. 8192 (June 13, 1940). This exact phraseology was repeated by others throughout the day. 86 Cong. Rec. 8206 (June 13, 1940).

12   86 Cong. Rec. 8183 (June 13, 1940).

13   86 Cong. Rec. 8188-89, 8204, 8210 (June 13, 1940).

14   86 Cong. Rec. 8189 (June 13, 1940).

15   86 Cong. Rec. 8189-91 (June 13, 1940).

16   Sen. Rep. No. 2031, 76th Cong., 3d Sess. at 8-10 (1940).

17   Stanley Kutler, *The American Inquisition* (Hill & Wang 1982), at 135.

18   *Kessler v. Strecker*, 307 U.S. 22, 30-33 (1939); 8 U.S.C. § 137(g) (1939).

19   Smith Act § 23, 8 U.S.C. § 137(g) (June 28, 1940).

20   Kutler at 136; Robert Jackson Oral History 1952, Columbia University, Vol. 7 at 1030-34.

21   86 Cong. Rec. 9031 (June 22, 1940).

22   Smith Act § 23, 8 U.S.C. § 137(g) (June 28, 1940).

23 Reorganization Plan V of 1940, 5 F.R. 2223, 54 Stat. 1238, effective June 15, 1940.

24 Reorganization Plan No. I of 1939, 4 F.R. 2727, 53 Stat. 1423, effective July 1, 1939. In fact, this plan not only did not propose to move the INS from the Department of Labor to the Department of Justice, but actively sought to keep the INS within the Department of Labor proposing some additional internal changes to the Department of Labor's immigration structure.

25 Kutler at 134.

26 86 Cong. Rec. 6608-09 (May 22, 1940).

27 86 Cong. Rec. 7290 (May 31, 1940, quoting May 27, 1940).

28 Reorganization Plan V of 1940, 5 F.R. 2223, 54 Stat. 1238, effective June 15, 1940.

29 *In re Harry Bridges*, 52 Yale L. J. 108, 109 (1942); *New York Times*, Nov. 29, 1940, p.16, col. 3.

30 Larrowe, "Did the Old Left," at 80.

31 J.K. Petersen, *Understanding Surveillance Technologies: Spy Devices, Privacy, History, and Applications* (Auerbach Publications 2d ed. 2001), at 136.

32 Francis Biddle, *In Brief Authority* at 297 (1962); *New York Times*, Dec. 17, 1940, p.1, Col.2; Fagan-Ginger at 328.

33 *In the Matter of Harry Renton Bridges*, Memorandum of Decision, Sep. 26, 1941, at 2 (hereafter "Sears Decision"). The FBI at the same time also delivered a report to the Attorney General detailing Bridges' lawyer, Carol King, and her alleged Communist Party activities. Fagan-Ginger at 325-28.

34 J. Edgar Hoover Letter to E.J. Connelley, Sep. 11, 1940, FBI FOIA File 039-SF-30 Section 2 (copy on file with author).

35 Suzanne Aiardo, "The Judges of the New York Court of Appeals - Charles Brown Sears," (Fordham University Press), at 522; Kutler at 136. Carol King's research indicated to her that Judge Sears was "seldom analytical, allows himself to be convinced by prima facie case," which conclusions troubled King. Fagan-Ginger at 329.

36 Sears Decision at 14.

37 Fagan-Ginger at 329.

38 Fagan-Ginger at 331.

39 Fagan-Ginger at 331.

40 Testimony of Harry Lundeberg at 7036-37, 6999-7002 (June 10, 1941).

41 Lundeberg Test. at 7007.

42 Lundeberg Test. at 7008.

43 Lundeberg Test. at 7009-10.

44 J. Edgar Hoover Letter to Special Agent in Charge NY, Aug. 30, 1940, FBI File SF-39-30-, Section 1, under FOIA Request 126423-000 (copy on file with author).

45 Sears Decision at 10-11.

46 Lundeberg Test. at 7042-46.

47 Lundeberg Test. at 7060-61.

48 Lundeberg Test. at 7036-37, 7007, 7009, 7062.

49 Lundeberg Test. at 7082.

50 Lundeberg Test. at 7087-88.

51 Lundeberg Test. at 7093-94.

52 Lundeberg Test. at 7089-92.

53 Lundeberg Test. at 7095-97.

54 Lundeberg Test. at 7100.

55 Lundeberg Test. at 7092.

56 Lundeberg Test. at 7122-24.

57 James O'Neil Test. at 2275-77, 2311 (April 28, 1941).

58 O'Neil Test. at 2278.

59 O'Neil Test. at 2307-09, 2341-42; Schofield Test. at 4810.

60 O'Neil Test. at 2335-36, 2364-68.

61 *In re Harry Bridges*, BIA Decision (January 3, 1942), Case No. 55973/217 (hereafter "BIA Decision"), at 62-70 (quoting then-existing INS regulations § 150.1(c) & (d) and § 150.6(i)).

62 Lemuel Schofield Test. at 4810-12 (May 21, 1941).

63 Gertrude Segerstrom Test. at 2399-2414 (April 28, 1941).

64 O'Neil Test. at 2352. Del Guercio repeatedly charged Bridges' lawyers with being communists, in what reads as a transparent effort to poison the proceedings before Judge Sears. In another instance, when Bridges' lawyer apparently told Del Guercio that his hand was shaking, Del Guercio bizarrely responded, "That's because I'm not a communist like you." Fagan-Ginger at 332 (quoting transcript).

65 O'Neil Test. at 2385-93.

66 Maurice Cannalonga Test. at 1125-38 (June 9, 1941).

67 Cannalonga Test. at 1043-44, 1070.

68 Cannalonga Test. at 1070-76.

69 Bridges Test. at 5781 (May 29, 1941).

70 Bridges Test. at 6111 (June 3, 1941).

71 Fagan-Ginger at 340 (quoting transcript).

72 Bridges Test. at 6120 (June 3, 1941).

73 Bridges Test. at 6148-49 (June 3, 1941).

74 Bridges Test. at 5979 (June 2, 1941).

75 Bridges Test. at 6104 (June 2, 1941).

76 Bridges Test. at 5788 (May 29, 1941). Judge Sears on another occasion admonished Del Guercio to cease "improper" conduct and to "keep within some bounds." Bridges Test. at 6005 (June 2, 1941).

77 Bridges Test. at 5961-62 (June 2, 1941).

78 Fagan-Ginger at 340-41.

79 Clair McKelway, "A Reporter at Large: Some Fun with the FBI," *New Yorker Magazine*, at 53-57 (Oct. 11, 1941); Bridges Test. at 5367-70 (Feb. 8, 1950).

80 *In re Bridges*, Case No. 55973.217, Harry Bridges Affidavit, Aug. 29, 1941 (on file with author); Sears Decision at 182-85; Richard Smith, *OSS: The Secret History of America's First Central Intelligence Agency* (Lyon's Press 2005), at 18.

81 Sears Decision at 183.

82 Sears Decision at 184-85.

83 J. Edgar Hoover Affidavit, 9/19/41 and E.J. Connelley Affidavit, 9/19/41 (copy on file with author), from FBI Declassified documents, FBI Series Box 12 Folder 40 File 14 (Marquette University).

84 Foxworth to Director Hoover Memorandum, Sep. 18, 1941 (copy on file with author), from FBI Declassified documents, FBI Series Box 12 Folder 40 File 14 (Marquette University).

85 J. Edgar Hoover to Miss Gandy Handwritten Memorandum (copy on file with author), from FBI Declassified documents, FBI Series Box 12 Folder 40 File 14 (Marquette University).

86 Sears Decision at 1-82.

87 Sears Decision at 177-82.

88 Sears Decision at 107-118.

89 Sears Decision at 106.

90 Sears Decision at 147, 151.

Chapter 5

1 BIA Decision at 3.

2 BIA Decision at 83-93.

3 BIA Decision at 73 n.96.

4 Fagan-Ginger at 356.

5 Annual Report of the Attorney General of the United States, Fiscal Year Ended June 30, 1941 (1941), at 225. *See also* Daniel Kanstroom, *Deportation Nation*, Harvard University Press 2007), at 198 (on rareness of Attorney General overruling BIA at that time).

6 8 C.F.R. § 90.12 (1940); *In re Harry Bridges*, 52 Yale L. J. 108, 123 n.88 (1942)

7 Harry Bridges Before the Attorney General Francis Biddle, U.S. Department of Justice, May 28, 1942, at 6 (hereafter "Biddle Decision").

8 Lemuel Schofield, *Memorandum for the AG, In re Harry Bridges*, (February 14, 1942); Kutler at 138-39. What is more, the General Counsel of the INS, Edward Ennis, read the BIA decision and told Biddle he should not reverse it because it was correct. Biddle instead ignored the INS's own chief legal counsel. Fagan-Ginger at 356.

9 Francis Biddle, *In Brief Authority*, at 302 (Doubleday & Co., 1962).

10 Biddle Decision at 302; Alien Registration Act of 1940, Title III, § 30, 8 U.S.C. § 452(a) (1940) (repealed); Fagan-Ginger at 334.

11 Biddle Decision at 26.

12 Fagan-Ginger at 361.

13 *Ex Parte Bridges*, 49 F. Supp. 292, 307 (N.D. Cal. 1943).

14 *Bridges v. Wixon*, 144 F.2d 927, 932-38 (9th Cir. 1944); *ibid.* at 937-38 (Stephens, J. concurring, joined by Wilbur and Mathews for the majority).

15 *Bridges v. Wixon*, 144 F.2d at 943-44; ibid. at 939.

16 *Bridges v. Wixon*, 144 F.2d at 943-44. Judge Healy was referencing the H.R. 9766 bill of attainder that had previously sought to simply deport Bridges without any hearing.

17 Erwin Chemerinsky, *Federal Jurisdiction* (3d ed. 1999), at 628-32.

18 Federal Judicial Center, Judicial Facts and Figures 2013, Tables 2.1, 3.1 & 6.1, located at http://www.uscourts.gov/statistics-reports/judicial-facts-and-figures-2013 (last accessed June 3, 2016); U.S. Department of Justice, Executive Office of Immigration Review, "FY 2013 Statistics Yearbook," April 2014, located at https://www.justice.gov/sites/default/files/eoir/legacy/2014/04/16/fy13syb.pdf (last accessed June 3, 2016).

19 Harvard Law Review, "The Supreme Court 2013 Term, Statistics," 128 Harv. L. Rev. 401 (Nov. 2014), at Table I; *Moncrieffe v. Holder*, 133 S. Ct. 1678 (2013). In 2014, the Supreme Court also decided one immigration appeal. *See Scialabba v. De Osorio*, 134 S. Ct. 2191 (2014).

20   *Costco Wholesale Corp. v. Omega*, 562 U.S. 40 (2010) (even split rule); Kutler at 141.

21   *Bridges v. Wixon*, Supreme Court Oral Argument Transcript, April 3, 1945, at 68 (copy on file with author).

22   Justice Murphy Papers, *Bridges v. Wixon*, No. 788, Roll 131, at 131, Bentley Historical Library, University of Michigan (copies on file with author). Chief Justice Stone quoted Justice Holmes as saying "a man has no constitutional right to be a policeman," a statement that comes from an opinion Justice Holmes authored while a Massachusetts Supreme Court Justice, *see McAuliffe v. City of New Bedford*, 155 Mass. 216, 220, 29 N.E. 517 (1892), which statement was addressed by Justice Douglas in the 1950s. *See, e.g., Barsky v. Board of Regents*, 347 U.S. 422, 472-73 (1954) ("The dictum of Holmes gives a distortion to the Bill of Rights. It is not an instrument of dispensation but one of deterrents. Certainly a man has no affirmative right to any particular job or skill or occupation. The Bill of Rights does not say who shall be doctors or lawyers or policemen. But it does say that certain rights are protected, that certain things shall not be done. And so the question here is not what government must give, but rather what it may not take away.") (Douglas, J., dissenting).

23   Justice Murphy Papers, *Bridges v. Wixon*, No. 788, Roll 131, at 131, Bentley Historical Library, University of Michigan (copies on file with author).

24   Justice Murphy Papers, *Bridges v. Wixon*, No. 788, Roll 131, at 132-33, Bentley Historical Library, University of Michigan (copies on file with author).

25   Justice Murphy Papers, *Bridges v. Wixon*, No. 788, Roll 131, at 135-36, Bentley Historical Library, University of Michigan (copies on file with author).

26   Justice Murphy Papers, *Bridges v. Wixon*, No. 788, Roll 131, at 136, Bentley Historical Library, University of Michigan (copies on file with author).

27   "Supreme Court Clears Docket in Final Day of Close Decisions," *New York Times*, June 19, 1945; Patricia McCabe Estrada, Deputy Public Information Officer, December 4, 2014 email to Afrasiabi (copy on file with author).

28   *Bridges v. Wixon*, 326 U.S. 135, 157 (1945). *See also* Lewis Wood, "High Court Blocks Bridges' Expulsion," *New York Times*, June 19, 1945.

29   *Bridges v. Wixon*, 326 U.S. at 157.

30   326 U.S. at 159 (internal quotations and citation omitted).

31   Biddle Decision at 306.

32   Sidney Roger, "A Liberal Journalist on the Air and on the Waterfront: Labor and Political Issues, 1932-1990," Oral History Interview by Julie Shearer 1989-90, at 290, Regents of the University of California (1990), located at http://content.cdlib.org/view?docId=kt1000013q&query=&brand=calisphere (last accessed June 3, 2016) (hereafter "Sidney Roger Oral History"); Vincent Hallinan, *A Lion in Court* (Putnam 1963), at 238.

33   Superior Court of California, Naturalization Proceedings of Harry Bridges, Judge Thomas Foley, Sep. 17, 1945 (copy on file with author); Hart to Garner Memorandum, In re Harry Bridges A-5-800-844, Sep. 17, 1945, RG 85 Bridges INS Inv. Files, 19030/1-1, Box 5, File 284-P-28152, Part II, NARA, San Bruno CA (copy on file with author).

34   Superior Court of California, *Naturalization Proceedings of Harry Bridges*, Judge Thomas Foley, Sep. 17, 1945 (copy on file with author); Hart to Garner Memorandum, *In re Harry Bridges A-5-800-844*, Sep. 17, 1945, RG 85 Bridges INS Inv. Files, 19030/1-1, Box 5, File 284-P-28152, Part II, located at NARA, San Bruno (copy on file with author).

35 Fagan-Ginger at 421.

36 Schwartz at 48.

Chapter 6

1 8 U.S.C. § 746(a) (1946).

2 Bruce Barber Confidential Memorandum, Sep. 1, 1948, RG 85, Bridges INS Inv. Files (copy on file with author).

3 Boyd to Wixon Memorandum, May 24, 1948, RG 85, Bridges INS Inv. Files Naturalization Div., 19030/1-1, Box 5, NARA, San Bruno, CA (copy on file with author).

4 Ralph Bonham INS Seattle District Director Nov. 24, 1937 Letter to Roy Norene INS Divisional Director, Box 10, File 1, Southern California Library, Los Angeles, CA (copy on file with author); Keegan Test. at 4231 (Aug. 15, 1939).

5 Special Agent Drayton Memorandum to Assistant FBI Director Connelley, Aug. 28, 1940, FBI File SF-39-30-, Section 1, under FOIA Request 126423-000 (copy on file with author).

6 Stanley Doyle to Boyd Letter, Oct. 21, 1949, Westbrook Pegler Papers, Herbert Hoover Presidential Library, Box 91, Longshoremen, at 4 (copy on file with author).

7 J. Edgar Hoover Testimony before HUAC, March 26, 1947, reprinted in Ellen Schrecker, *The Age of McCartrhyism* (Bedford/St. Martin's Press 2d ed. 2002), at 127.

8 Schwartz, "Harry Bridges and the Scholars," at 71; Oral History of Harry Bridges at § 3, located at http://www.ilwu.org/oral-history-of-harry-bridges/ (last accessed June 3, 2016).

9 *United States v. Bridges*, 133 F. Supp. 638, 639 (N.D. Cal. 1955). The specific charges were under the then-existing federal criminal statutes of 18 U.S.C. § 746 (knowingly making a false statement under oath in a citizenship hearing, and aiding and abetting the same) and 18 U.S.C. § 88 (conspiracy to secure citizenship by fraudulently representing membership in the Communist Party).

10 Department of Justice Form G-59 to FBI on Aubrey Grossman and Richard Gladstein, FBI RG 85, Misc. Inv. Records Civil Trial Box 2, NARA, San Bruno, CA (copies on file with author).

11 Grossman Memorandum of Conversation with Donohue, Nov. 7, 1949, Box 10, File 10, Southern California Library, Los Angeles, CA (copy on file with author) (quoting Donohue, "I would very much like to have Gladstein in this case... there are some things I would like to have Gladstein in this case for."); Department of Justice Form G-59 to FBI on Aubrey Grossman and Richard Gladstein, FBI RG 85, Misc. Inv. Records Civil Trial Box 2, NARA, San Bruno, CA (copies on file with author).

12 "Interview with Robbie Bridges," conducted by Peter Afrasiabi, March 9, 2016 (correspondence/notes on file with author); John Hutchison, "Julie in the Afternoon; Julie Bridges' Long Journey Home," October 28, 1991 located at http://www.well.com/user/sfflier/Bridges.html (last visited March 13, 2016).

13 Henry Schmidt, "Secondary Leadership in the ILWU, 1933-1966," an oral history conducted 1974-1981 by Miriam F. Stein and Estolv E. Ward, Regional Oral History Office, The Bancroft Library, University of California, Berkeley, 1983, at 303 (hereafter "Schmidt Oral History").

14 Larrowe at 304.

15   *United States v. Bridges*, 86 F. Supp. 931, 933 (N.D. Cal. 1949).

16   Bridges Affidavit in Support of Motion to Disqualify Judge Harris, Case No. 32117-H (Nov. 1949), at 11-12, RG 85, NARA, San Bruno, CA (copy on file with author).

17   Bridges Affidavit in Support of Motion to Disqualify Judge Harris, Case No. 32117-H (Nov. 1949), at 11-12, RG 85, NARA, San Bruno, CA (copy on file with author).

18   17 U.S.C. § 455(a) (1948).

19   *See, e.g., Potashnick v. Port City Constr. Co.*, 609 F.2d 1101, 1110-11 (5th Cir. 1980).

20   *United States of America v. Harry Renton Bridges, Henry Schmidt and J.R. Robertson*, Case No. 32117-H, Official Court Docket, Nov. 22, 1949 (copy of docket on file with author as retrieved from NARA, San Bruno, CA).

21   *United States of America v. Harry Renton Bridges, Henry Schmidt and J.R. Robertson*, Case No. 32117-H, Trial Transcript, Nov. 17, 1949, at 477-83 (hereafter "Trial Transcript, (date), at (page number).").

22   *United States of America v. Harry Renton Bridges, Henry Schmidt and J.R. Robertson*, United States District Court for the Northern District of California, No. 32117-H, Trial Transcript, at 485-88 (Nov. 17, 1949) (hereafter "Trial Transcript at __ (date)").

23   Trial Transcript at 491-92 (Nov. 17, 1949).

24   Trial Transcript at 494.

25   Trial Transcript at 497-99.

26   Trial Transcript at 511-12.

27   Trial Transcript at 511-518, 518.

28   Trial Transcript at 519.

29   Trial Transcript at 524, 533.

30   Trial Transcript at 533-34.

31   Trial Transcript at 534.

32   Trial Transcript at 511-40.

33   Trial Transcript at 551 (Nov. 18, 1949).

34   Trial Transcript at 541-555, 555.

35   Trial Transcript at 556.

36   Trial Transcript at 569.

37   Trial Transcript at 557.

38   Trial Transcript at 565.

39   Trial Transcript at 574.

40   Trial Transcript at 698-99 (Nov. 21, 1949).

41   Trial Transcript at 702.

42   Trial Transcript at 733.

43   Trial Transcript at 738, 740.

44   Trial Transcript 776, 806, 776, 811 (Nov. 22, 1949).

45   Trial Transcript at 811-18.

46   Trial Transcript at 813-14.

47   Trial Transcript at 845.

48   Trial Transcript at 842, 846-47.

49   Trial Transcript at 848.

50   Trial Transcript at 848-49.

51   Trial Transcript at 850.

52 Trial Transcript at 851-52.

53 Trial Transcript at 855.

54 Trial Transcript at 855.

55 Trial Transcript at 851-54, 857-66.

56 Trial Transcript at 856.

57 Trial Transcript at 857.

58 Trial Transcript at 868.

59 William Shakespeare, *Hamlet*, Act III, Sc. II (1602).

60 Trial Transcript, Nov. 22, 1949, at 869-71.

61 Manning Johnson Testimony at 2310-13, 2334-35 (Dec. 13, 1949); Johnson Test. at 2322-2332 (Dec. 13, 1949); Johnson Test. at 2502-08, 2549-2558 (Dec. 14, 1949).

62 "Normal Leonard, Life of a Leftist Lawyer," Interview Conducted by Estolv. E. Ward (University of California, Bancroft Library Oral History Office 1985), at 57 (copy on file with author).

63 Johnson Test. at 2343-2356 (Dec. 13, 1949); Johnson Test. at 2423 (Dec. 14, 1949); Johnson Test. at 2476-77 (Dec. 14, 1949); Johnson Test. at 2397 (Dec. 13, 1949).

64 Paul Crouch Testimony at 2577-82 (Dec. 16, 1949); Crouch Test. at 2746-2801 (Dec. 19, 1949).

65 Crouch Test. at 2609-20, 2649-54, 2678-85 (Dec. 16, 1949).

66 Crouch Test. at 2678-85 (Dec. 16, 1949).

67 Crouch Test. at 2931-54, 2954 ("bloodhounds") (Dec. 20, 1949).

68 Crouch Test. at 2955 (Dec. 20, 1949).

69 Crouch Test. at 2973-75 (Dec. 20, 1949).

70 Lawrence Ross Testimony at 3145-46 (Jan. 4, 1950).

71 Hallinan at 259; "Normal Leonard, Life of a Leftist Lawyer," (University of California, Bancroft Library Oral History Office 1985), at 55 (copy on file with author).

72 Ross Test. at 3200 (Jan. 4, 1950).

73 Ross Test. at 3167 (Jan. 4, 1950).

74 Ross Test. at 3471 (Jan. 6, 1950).

75 Ross Test. at 3419-25, 3458-59 (Jan. 6, 1950).

76 Ross Test. at 3459-61 (Jan. 6, 1950).

77 Ross Test. at 3467-83 (Jan. 6, 1950).

78 Ross Test. at 3517 (Jan. 9, 1950).

79 Ross Test. at 3453, 3569 (Jan. 9, 1950).

80 Ross Test. at 3466-67 (Jan. 9, 1950).

81 Ross Test. at 3657, 3660 (Jan. 10, 1950).

82 Ross Test. at 3667 (Jan. 10, 1950).

83 Schmidt Oral History at 309.

84 Larrowe at 310, quoting *San Francisco Chronicle*.

85 Schmidt Oral History at 311.

86 George Wilson Testimony at 3998-4014 (Jan. 13, 1950).

87 Wilson Test. at 4014-17 (Jan. 13, 1950).

88 Larrowe at 310; Schmidt Oral History at 309-10.

89 Father Paul Meinecke Testimony at 4902-03 (Feb. 1, 1950).

90 Meinecke Test. at 4765-4771 (Feb 1, 1950).

91   Meinecke Test. at 4772 (Feb 1, 1950).
92   Meinecke Test. at 4787 (Feb 1, 1950).
93   Meinecke Test. at 4778-4783, 4787-4792 (Feb 1, 1950).
94   Meinecke Test. at 4793-95 (Feb 1, 1950).
95   Meinecke Test. at 4795-97 (Feb 1, 1950).
96   Meinecke Test. at 4798-99 (Feb 1, 1950).
97   Meinecke Test. at 4873-97 (Feb 2, 1950).
98   Bridges Test. at 5343-54 (Feb. 8, 1950), *ibid.* at 5354, 5349 (for specific quotes); Bridges Test. at 5402 (Feb. 9, 1950).
99   Bridges Test. at 5427-5449 (Feb. 9, 1950).
100 Bridges Test. at 5413-14 (Feb. 9, 1950), 5493-97 (Feb. 14, 1950).
101 Bridges Test. at 5512-14 (Feb. 14, 1950).
102 Bridges Test. at 5602 (Feb. 14, 1950).
103 Bridges Test. at 5604 (Feb. 14, 1950). "Anybody in the union, no matter who they are, can stand up and speak their piece…if anyone wants to get up and extol the real or perceived advantages of communism, they have the right to do it in the union…" *Ibid.*
104 Bridges Test. at 5607 (Feb. 14, 1950).
105 Larrowe at 318; Sidney Roger Oral History at 326; Bob Robertson Interview with Harvey Schwartz (early 1970s) as reported by Harvey Schwartz (Feb. 2016).
106 Trial Transcript, Mar. 16, 1950, at 7497.
107 Trial Transcript, Mar. 16, 1950, at 7505.
108 Katherine Pinkham, "Harry Bridges Federal Court Perjury Trial Longest in San Francisco Federal Court History," *Lewiston Evening Journal*, April 5, 1950, located at http://news.google.com/newspapers?nid=1913&dat=19500405&id=RbU0AAAAIBAJ&sjid=_WYFAAAAIBA-J&pg=3245,399833 (last accessed June 3, 2016).
109 Hallinan at 275.
110 Sidney Roger Oral History at 334.
111 Hallinan at 277.
112 Sidney Roger Oral History at 334-35.
113 Trial Transcript, April 4, 1950, at 8654.
114 *United States v. Harry Bridges*, 90 F. Supp. 973, 974 (N.D. Cal. 1950).
115 Sidney Roger Oral History at 334-35.
116 "Jury Instructions in Bridges Perjury Trial," 10 F.R.D. 81 (N.D. Cal. 1950); Hallinan at 277.

Chapter 7

1   *Mills v. State of Alabama*, 384 U.S. 214, 218-19 (1966); *see also New York Times v. Sullivan*, 376 U.S. 254, 273 (1964) ("central meaning of the First Amendment").
2   Motion for Order to Revoke Order Granting Bail to Harry Bridges (July 30, 1950), Case No. 32117-H, at 1-15, located at RG-85, Revocation of Bail Proceedings, Box 1, NARA, San Bruno, CA.
3   *United States of America v. Harry Renton Bridges*, Case No. 32117-H, Bail Revocation Hearing, Harry Bridges Testimony, Aug. 4, 1940, at 199, 203.

4 Motion for Order to Revoke Order Granting Bail to Harry Bridges (July 30, 1950), Case No. 32117-H, at 1-15, located at RG 85, Revocation of Bail Proceedings, Box 1, NARA, San Bruno, CA.

5 *United States of America v. Harry Renton Bridges*, Case No. 32117-H, Bail Revocation Hearing, Aug. 3, 1950, at 85, 93 (hereafter "Bail Revocation Hearing").

6 Bail Revocation Hearing at 69-70.

7 Bail Revocation Hearing at 205, 208, 353.

8 Bail Revocation Hearing at 69-70.

9 *United States v. Harry Bridges*, 90 F. Supp. 973 (N.D. Cal. 1950).

10 *In re Harry Bridges*, 184 F.2d 881, 884-45 (9th Cir. 1950).

11 184 F.2d at 887.

12 184 F.2d at 888.

13 Talbot, David, *Season of the Witch*, (Free Press 2013), at 12.

14 John M. Vance & Associates, Juror Interviews, April 19, 1950 and May 17, 1950, Box 10, Folder 4, Southern California Library, Harry Bridges Collection (copy on file with author).

15 Larrowe at 305.

16 Trial Transcript, Nov. 21, 1949, at 698-702.

17 Hallinan at 276-77.

18 Commissioner John Boyd, "Confidential Memorandum United States Government" Sep. 1, 1948, RG85, NARA, San Bruno, CA, at 24 (copy on file with author).

19 *Harry Bridges v. United States*, 199 F.2d 811 (9th Cir. 1952). The Ninth Circuit noted that Judge Harris' questions "might be subject to misunderstanding," but held that any impropriety was not significant given the full scope of the case.

20 Schmidt Oral History at 408.

21 Schrecker at 237 (quoting Senator McCarthy's famed 1950 speech claiming "I have in my hand fifty-seven cases of individuals who would appear to be either card carrying members or certainly loyal to the Communist Party..."), at 155-70 (detailing Ronsenberg death penalty in 1953) and at 242 (detailing Hollywood's blacklisting of Communists that began in December 1947).

22 *Harry Bridges v. United States*, Supreme Court Oral Argument Transcript, Case No. 1952-548, at 64, 75.

23 *Harry Bridges v. United States*, 346 U.S. 209 (1953).

24 Hallinan at 238; Schmidt Oral History at 409-10.

25 Even decades later in his oral memoirs, Judge Harris seems noticeably uncomfortable talking about the trial, his reversal, and his conflict with Hallinan. When asked why the civil case was transferred to a different judge, he refused to offer detail, instead answering with non-responsive statements, ending with a curt "That's enough." When asked about the tension with Hallinan, Judge Harris offered that he felt Hallinan's trial comments were unfair, but again refused to discuss in detail the issue, offering "I think this is on a tangent." Gabrielle Morris, "George B. Harris – Memories of San Francisco Legal Practice and State and Federal Courts, 1920's-1960's," (University of California, Bancroft Library Oral History Office 1980), at 187, 75, respectively (hereafter "Harris Oral History").

Chapter 8

1   *See, e.g., Hudson v. United States*, 522 U.S. 93, 98-99 (1997) ("The Double Jeopardy Clause provides that no 'person [shall] be subject for the same offence to be twice put in jeopardy of life or limb.' We have long recognized that the Double Jeopardy Clause does not prohibit the imposition of all additional sanctions that could, " 'in common parlance,' " be described as punishment...The Clause protects only against the imposition of multiple *criminal* punishments for the same offense...").

2   Maurice Robert, *The Harry Bridges Cases*, Interpreter Releases (Sept. 20, 1999), at 1388.

3   Oshinsky, David M., *A Conspiracy So Immense: The World of Joe McCarthy* (Oxford University Press 2005), at 464.

4   Edward Murrow, *See it Now: A Report on Senator Joseph R. McCarthy*, CBS-TV, March 9, 1954.

5   Harris Oral History at 187, 75, respectively. When asked why the civil case was transferred to a different judge, he refused to offer detail, instead answering with non-responsive statements, ending with a curt, "That's enough."

6   "McCarthy Says West Point Critic Has 'Unresolved' Loyalty Record," *New York Times*, Dec. 1, 1953; "Taylor Predicts Ruin of McCarthy," *New York Times*, Jan. 20, 1954.

7   David Rudenstine, "Telford Taylor 1908-1998," Benjamin N. Cardozo School of Law – Yeshiva University (Fall 1998), located at http://www.cardozo.yu.edu/life/fall1998/taylor/ (last accessed June, 2016).

8   "Taylor Predicts Ruin of McCarthy," *New York Times*, Jan. 20, 1954.

9   Tina Rosenberg, "The Lives They Lived: Telford Taylor; Atrocities Answered," *New York Times*, Jan 3, 1999, located at http://www.nytimes.com/1999/01/03/magazine/the-lives-they-lived-telford-taylor-atrocities-answered.html (last accessed June 3, 2016).

10 Telford Taylor, *Grand Inquest: The Story of Congressional Investigations*, (Simon & Schuster 1955), at 283.

11 Larrowe, "Did the Old Left," at 41.

12 Robert Cherny, "Telford Taylor and the Everlasting Case of Harry Bridges," *Telford Taylor Papers Conference*, Columbia University, April 8, 2005.

13 *United States of America v. Harry Renton Bridges*, Case No. 28876, Trial Transcript, at 25 (June 20, 1955).

14 Trial Transcript at 28-29 (June 20, 1955).

15 John Schomaker Testimony at 376-80, 392-410 (June 22, 1955).

16 Schomaker Test. at 1955, at 435-464, 470-72, 496-503.

17 Schomaker Test. at 1955, at 499-502.

18 Schomaker Test. at 503.

19 David Saunders Testimony at 245 (June 21, 1955).

20 Saunders Test. at 276-79.

21 Saunders Test. at 284.

22 Saunders Test. at 307.

23 Saunders Test. at 303.

24 Trial Transcript at 1801-02, 1807-08 (July 21, 1955).

25 Trial Transcript at 1811.

26 Trial Transcript at 1811-1811A.

27 Trial Transcript at 1813-14.

28 Trial Transcript at 1856-57.

29 Trial Transcript at 1879.

30 Trial Transcript at 1879-80.

31 *United States v. Bridges*, 133 F. Supp. 638, 641 (N.D. Cal. 1955).

32 Schmidt Oral History at 420.

33 133 F. Supp. at 641.

34 133 F. Supp. at 642-43.

35 133 F. Supp. at 645-46.

36 133 F. Supp. at 643, 646-47.

37 Schmidt Oral History at 420.

Epilogue

1   Phillip Earl, *Nevada's Miscegenation Laws*, 37 Nevada Historical Society Quarterly 1, 8-16 (1994); Noriko (Nikki) Bridges, "Brush With the Law," *California Lawyer* (Dec. 1993).

2   *Loving v. Virginia*, 388 U.S. 1 (1967).

3   Passport Security Hearings Before the Committee on Un-American Activities, House of Representatives, 86th Cong., 1st Sess., April 21, 1959, at 666-67 (hereafter "HUAC Passport Security Hearings").

4   HUAC Passport Security Hearings at 667, 723.

5   United States Constitution, Fifth Amendment.

6   *Miranda v. Arizona*, 384 U.S. 436 (1966).

7   HUAC Passport Security Hearings at 671.

8   HUAC Passport Security Hearings at 688.

9   HUAC Passport Security Hearings at 733.

10 David Frum, *How We Got Here: The '70s* (Basic Books 2000), at 265.

11 Miriam Feingold Stein, *The Shipboard Murder Case: Labor, Radicalism and Earl Warren, 1936-1941*, Regional Oral History Office (University of California, Berkeley, 1972), at iii-v.

12 Seth Rosenfeld, *Subversives: The FBI's War on Student Radicals* (Picador 2013), at 312, 395.

13 JD Chandler, *Portland on the Take: Mid-Century Crime Bosses, Civic Corruption & Forgotten* (History Press 2014); "Action on Bridges in Congress Likely," *New York Times*, Dec. 31, 1939.

14 Department of Justice, "United States Government Manual 1945," (1st ed.), located at http://www.ibiblio.org/hyperwar/ATO/USGM/Justice.html; *Delgadillo v. Del Guercio*, 68 S. Ct. 105 (1947); Minerva Baumann, "Retiring NMSU Astronomy Professor Wins Prestigious Science Writing Award," New Mexico State University (May 11, 2015, located at https://newscenter.nmsu.edu/Articles/view/11132/retiring-nmsu-astronomy-professor-wins-prestigious-science-writing-award (last accessed June 3, 2016); Reineck's Lawyer in Perjury Case, *SF Chronicle*, April 5, 1974.

15 Fagan-Ginger at 534, 536, 542-43.

16 Hallinan at 286-87; "Hallinan Free Today," *New York Times*, Aug. 17, 1952.

17 Colin Wark and John R. Galliher, *Progressive Lawyers Under Siege: Moral Panic During the McCarthy Years* (Lexington Books 2015), at 69-100.

18   David Rudenstine, "Telford Taylor 1908-1998," Benjamin N. Cardozo School of Law – Ye-
      shiva University (Fall 1998), located at http://www.cardozo.yu.edu/life/fall1998/taylor/ (last
      accessed June 3, 2016).

19   Del Dickson, *The Supreme Court in Conference 1940-85* (Oxford University Press 2001), at
      200.

20   New York State Unified Court System, "Charles Brown Sears (1870-1950)," located at http://
      www.nycourts.gov/history/legal-history-new-york/luminaries-appellate/sears-charles.html
      (last accessed Dec. 2, 2013).

21   *Korematsu v. United States*, 323 U.S. 214 (1944); Katyal Neal, Acting Solicitor General of
      the United States, "Confession of Error: The Solicitor General's Mistakes During the Japa-
      nese-American Internment Cases," (May 20, 2011), located at http://www.justice.gov/opa/
      blog/confession-error-solicitor-generals-mistakes-during-japanese-american-internment-cases
      (last accessed June 3, 2016).

22   "Interview with Robbie Bridges," conducted by Peter Afrasiabi, March 24, 2016 (correspon-
      dence on file with author); John Balzar, "Ex-Atty. Gen. Evelle Younger Is Dead at 70," *Los
      Angeles Times*, May 5, 1989.

23   "The ILWU Story: End of An Era," located at http://www.ilwu19.com/history/the_ilwu_sto-
      ry/end_of_an_era.htm (last accessed June 3, 2016); Sadik to Bridges Letter, Nov. 9, 1977 and
      Bridges to Sadik Letter, Feb. 14, 1978, ILWU History Files, Harry Bridges Collection, Box 24
      (copies of file with author).

Policy

1   Abraham Lincoln, "Address Before the Young Men's Lyceum of Springfield, Illinois," Jan. 27,
     1838, printed in *The Collected Works of Abraham Lincoln* at 108 (1953).

2   J. Edgar Hoover, The J. Edgar Hoover Foundation: Keeping the Legacy Alive, located at
     http://www.jedgarhooverfoundation.org/ (last accessed June 3, 2016).

3   Department of Justice Official Letter (Feb. 14, 1992), located at http://www.justice.gov/
     about/doj-seal-history-and-motto.htm (last accessed June 3, 2016).

4   "McCarthy Says West Point Critic Has 'Unresolved' Loyalty Record," *New York Times*, Dec. 1,
     1953.

5   199 F.2d at 828.

INDEX

Made in the USA
Middletown, DE
19 September 2023

38819039R00179